LAND WARS

Brian DeMare

LAND WARS

The Story of China's Agrarian Revolution

Stanford University Press
Stanford, California

Stanford University Press
Stanford, California

Printed in the United States of America on acid-free, archival-quality paper

Library of Congress Cataloging-in-Publication Data

Names: DeMare, Brian James, author.
Title: Land wars : the story of China's agrarian revolution / Brian DeMare.
Description: Stanford, California : Stanford University Press, 2019. | Includes bibliographical
    references and index.
Identifiers: LCCN 2018052952 (print) | LCCN 2019003609 (ebook) | ISBN 9781503609525
    | ISBN 9781503608498 (cloth : alk. paper) | ISBN 9781503609518 (pbk. : alk. paper)
Subjects: LCSH: Land reform—China—History—20th century. | Social conflict—China—
    History—20th century. | Collectivization of agriculture—China—History—20th
    century. | Communism and agriculture—China—History—20th century. | Propaganda,
    Communist—China—History—20th century. | Mao, Zedong, 1893–1976—Political and
    social views. | China—Rural conditions—20th century. | China—History—Civil War,
    1945–1949.
Classification: LCC HD1333.C6 (ebook) | LCC HD1333.C6 D45 2019 (print) | DDC
    338.10951/09045—dc23
LC record available at https://lccn.loc.gov/2018052952

Cover design: John Barnett | 4 Eyes

For Nina. For Miles.

CONTENTS

PREFACE

Throughout decades of tumultuous revolutionary fervor, China remained a deeply rural nation, home to hundreds of millions of villagers dispersed within a staggeringly diverse countryside. Between 1945 and 1952, these villagers underwent agrarian revolution: Mao Zedong's attempt to bring his vision of rural China, at once egalitarian and confrontational, to life. Mao and his comrades in the Communist Party, declaring the countryside to be under feudal control, dispatched work teams to the countryside to totally transform village China. First came campaigns targeting feared strongmen, the cruelest of China's rural exploiters, and those who had collaborated with Japanese invaders. Only then came land reform (*tudi gaige*), a confrontational program of land redistribution that promised economic prosperity and socialist liberation.

During land reform, impoverished farmers were molded into peasant activists through rigorous ideological training, a process that Communist Party work teams carefully managed. These teams, largely composed of urban intellectuals, helped give every villager a new Maoist class label, the most feared being the "landlord" classification. Unlucky landlords were "struggled," a violent and humiliating form of public class conflict that resulted in countless deaths. According to Mao's grand tale of rural revolution, passage through land reform's fierce crucible of class struggle awakened villagers to their power as the great peasant masses who would create a new China. The importance of this story of agrarian revolution to the course of modern Chinese history cannot be overstated. Early years of campaigning helped bring the Chinese Communist Party to power. After the founding of the People's Republic of China (PRC) in 1949, massive rounds of land reform cemented the party's rule over its vast but young state. And even today, the party's claim to have liberated China's peasant masses remains a bedrock of its political legitimacy.

Due to its scope and complexity, Mao Zedong's agrarian revolution has proved an uneasy topic for historical inquiry. Over the course of over a half-dozen years, the Communist Party launched systematic and thorough campaigns in the hopes of completely transforming the Chinese countryside. Mao's attempt to remake village China was not a single event in one place and time, but a long series of interrelated campaigns with differing terrains, land laws, and political contexts. During these years, moreover, the Communists went from revolutionary upstarts to rulers of the world's most populous nation. Transcribing the history of these campaigns has been further complicated by the powerful stories that the Communists told about their revolution. These stories, fully fleshed out in novels claiming to realistically represent the entire process of local transformation, have done much to confuse the lines between the literal and the literary. Even nonfiction accounts of land reform owe much to Mao's narrative of rural revolution.

This study investigates the entire process of agrarian revolution in order to explore the discrepancies and disjunctions within the campaigns. It also recognizes the power of the Maoist narrative of exploited peasants who found liberation through class struggle. During the years of land reform, this story was inescapable. Chinese citizens need not read the lengthy novels penned by party authors on rural revolution or attend the operatic performances that brought rural class struggle onstage. Even the illiterate could attend huge exhibits that meticulously showed the transition from the feudal past to the liberated future. I wrote this book because of my belief that historians must engage Mao's narrative of revolution in order to understand what truly occurred in rural China as the Communists came to power. The party indoctrinated a vast army of would-be revolutionaries with this story before dispatching them to the countryside in work teams to make fiction become reality. In writing this book, I drew heavily on the sources historians have traditionally employed to understand rural China: archival documents, internal party reports, newspaper articles, and firsthand accounts of village life. But I also sought inspiration from the powerful stories that have been told about this revolution. Having studied land reform for almost two decades, I have found the lines between fact and fiction blurred and permeable. This book is my attempt to make sense of how the stories told about the revolution became the revolution itself.

The Introduction to this book traces the development of Mao's revolutionary narrative within the context of the party's long engagement with village China. Subsequent chapters begin with narrative treatments of land reform as an entry point into the various steps of rural revolution. In chapter 1, work teams arrive in newly liberated villages to announce the onset of revolutionary change. In chapter 2, team members search out poor peasant activists and train them to speak out against their wealthy neighbors. During later chapters, class statuses are determined and counterrevolutionary plots discovered. In this book, just as in Mao's story of agrarian revolution, everything builds up to class struggle, the ferocious ritual that allowed peasants to obtain their true liberation by publicly attacking landlords and other class enemies. But while this book uses the land reform plotline and draws on stories of revolution, it simultaneously deconstructs and questions Mao's narrative to show how it was manufactured, deployed, and received in a diverse countryside, all too often with unexpected, even deadly, results.

Investigation into the relationship between revolution and narrative reveals that stories have shaped not only our understanding of the past, but the contours of history itself. Despite the diversity of China's vast and populous countryside, the party demanded that work teams overseeing agrarian revolution follow its established plotline, which assumed the need for fierce class struggle against evil landlords. The stories the party told about land reform and other mass campaigns in the countryside made agrarian revolution understandable and desirable. But this tale was never intended to be confined to the page and would prove to have massive implications for China. Even today, the dissonance between Mao's grand story and the realities of these years of campaigning reverberate across the countryside.

This project originated many years ago when I was a graduate student at UCLA, studying with Kathryn Bernhart, Philip Huang, and Lynn Hunt. Since then I have accumulated a tremendous debt to many scholars. Foremost among them are the colleagues who found the time to provide invaluable feedback on various chapters of this book: Jeremy Brown, Christian Hess, Jeffery Javed, Matthew Johnson, Fabio Lanza, Fangchun Li, and Aminda Smith. Of course, the remaining mistakes are mine alone. I also thank Andrew Endrey and Felix Wemheuer for helping me access new historical materials. I commend their generosity and commitment to academic exchange. Many others helped me think through the challenges of writing this book, including Deng Hongqin, Edward Friedman, Carma Hinton, Huaiyin Li, Ma Weiqiang, Zhao Ma, Ralph Thaxton, and Yiching Wu.

A deep thanks to everyone at Stanford University Press, starting with Marcela Maxfield. Her strong editorial voice and belief in this project were essential in getting this book into print. Tim Roberts skillfully managed the production of the book. And a special thanks to Bev Miller, who painstakingly oversaw the copyediting of the manuscript. The Stanford University Press design team astounded me with their work for the book. I also owe a tremendous debt to the two anonymous reviewers whose perceptive critiques made me rethink many aspects of this book.

Researching China from New Orleans, the city that care forgot, presents a unique challenge. Working at Tulane University, however, has been a blessing. A Young Mellon Professorship, awarded by the School of Liberal Arts, provided critical research funding. My colleagues in the history department have given me camaraderie and a true academic home. As this book came to completion, my fellow historians Emily Clark, Kris Lane, Jana Lipman, Liz McMahon, Linda Pollock, and Randy Sparks shared much needed advice on writing and publishing. I also thank the department administrators, whose hard work allowed me to finish this book: Donna Denneen, Susan McCann, and Ericka Sanchez. And I cannot forget my students, some of whom have put up with my rants about narratives and grassroots China for years. Three talented students volunteered to comment on this book: John Berner, Colin Boyd, and Drew Pearson. My research assistant, Xiaoyu Yu, helped me navigate through a collection of particularly challenging handwritten documents. Off campus, these friends helped make New Orleans home: Amy Arthur, Ryan Farishian, James Gentry, Nowell Raff, and John and Sarah Wachter.

My parents, Maggie and Paul, chose to raise their 'ohana in Hawaii. I grew up there, spending years in the sunshine with my siblings Pam, Jeff, and Tracey. I often thought about those blissful days as I worked on this project. As readers will discover, the story of China's rural revolution is not always a happy one. I suspect that I never would have finished this book without Nina and Miles DeMare. Thanks to them, my life has been filled with aloha, which has sustained me during the most depressing moments of archival discovery. Nina, from our days living in a hutong not far from Tiananmen, always believed that I would finish graduate school, find a job, and get tenure. She never once suspected that this book might not see publication. Her love and unrelenting faith in me pushed me to be a better scholar, husband, and father. Miles, my young son just entering kindergarten, rejuvenated my soul with his good humor and joy for life. His essential kindness has proven that Mencius was right all along. There is nothing I could ever say to properly express how wonderfully happy they have made my life. All I can do is dedicate this book to them.

LAND WARS

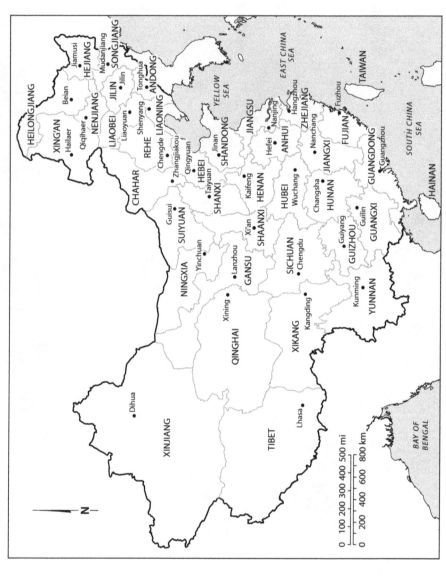

IMAGE 1. China, Administrative Divisions, 1948. Source: Adapted from CIA map ("China, administrative areas 1948").

INTRODUCTION

The Story of Mao's Revolution

In early 1927, Mao Zedong returned home in search of evidence. He found a story. At the age of thirty-four, Mao was an increasingly visible figure in the Chinese Communist Party, well known for his early advocacy of peasants as a revolutionary force.[1] It was for this reason that he now found himself out of step with party leaders. Like many other concerned citizens, Mao understood that rural distress was one of the greatest challenges facing reformers and revolutionaries alike.[2] Land, an existential commodity for the vast majority of the Chinese people, was distributed unevenly. Some farmers prospered. Most got by. Many others suffered bitterly with little or no land at all. The leaders of the Communist Party, founded in 1921, knew this all too well. But eager to emulate the example of the Soviet Union, they envisioned their revolution as a proper Marxist affair, led by the urban proletariat in pursuit of collective ownership. The party's first leader, Chen Duxiu, emphatically argued that the Communists must rely on industrial workers: "In a country such as China, over half the farmers are petit bourgeois landed farmers who adhere firmly to notions of private property."[3] How, Chen wondered, could such farmers ever embrace the Communists? Mao had experimented with rural activism, only to run into conflict with his party leaders and their Soviet advisors. And so Mao returned home to Hunan, determined to arm himself with data that might force Communist leaders, perhaps even the great Joseph Stalin himself, to recognize the centrality of the peasantry to China's revolution.

Mao's journey home occurred during a critical moment in the course of modern Chinese history. In 1923, the Communists had established a United Front with the Nationalists, a rival party that was also committed to saving the Chinese nation through revolution, albeit a revolution that promised to serve all social classes, not just the laboring masses. The Nationalists, by a wide margin the more powerful of the two parties, was then headed by Sun Yat-sen, China's most respected revolutionary. Educated in Hong Kong and Hawaii, Sun had long pursued help from foreign powers, only to find frustration. Comintern agents, dispatched by Stalin to foment worldwide revolution, brokered the alliance between the two parties. Offering financial and military aid in exchange for the United Front, they found in Sun a willing partner. Despite their mutual suspicion, both parties experienced spectacular growth during their United Front. The Communists, primarily urban intellectuals, focused their organizational efforts on workers in China's largest cities. Most party members viewed peasants with disdain, but Mao Zedong and a handful of activists started the process of reform in villages scattered across several provinces, helping the Communists make their first inroads into the countryside.[4]

Their success, coupled with policy trends within the United Front, encouraged the Communists to recognize the peasantry as an important ally in their proletarian revolution. This rural turn developed rapidly, thriving on the synergy between the gains Mao and like-minded comrades were making in the countryside and Sun Yat-sen's growing belief in the need for agrarian reform. Influenced by his new Russian advisors, Sun had radicalized his approach to the land question, calling for a policy of "land to the tiller" (*gengzhe you qi tian*). Sun's vision, centered on the idea of transferring property to land-hungry farmers, posed a direct threat to wealthy landlords who relied on rental income.[5] Meanwhile, the alliance with the much larger Nationalist Party provided new opportunities for Mao and the Communists to deepen their experiments in rural reform. The founding of the Peasant Movement Institute in 1924 allowed the training of hundreds of agitators and organizers, fueling the growth of what was now called a peasant movement. Observing the movement firsthand, Mao began to insist that the party's path forward lay not in China's urban factories but in the vast and impoverished countryside.

The untimely death in of Sun Yat-sen, today still revered as a revolutionary hero on both sides of the Taiwan Strait, threw the alliance between the two parties into turmoil in 1925. Chiang Kai-shek, a military officer whose intense nationalism easily matched his hatred of the Communists, quickly established himself as Sun's successor. Emboldened by the growth of his military forces, Chiang launched the Northern Expedition in summer 1926, rapidly expanding the territory under Nationalist rule. Rural organizers, many of them Communists, moved in advance of Northern Expedition troops to organize revolts in support of Chiang's forces. They also made sure to establish peasant associations, village organizations that promoted the interests of poor farmers. Some peasant association activists seized land and attacked rural elites, disturbing Nationalist Party members with ties to rural landholders. With the peasant movement showing no sign of abating, internal debates over rural policy assumed ever greater importance. Factional divisions within the Communist Party came into full relief during a December 1926 meeting in Wuhan: Mao Zedong pushed for further radicalism in the countryside, while party leader Chen Duxiu, under Comintern orders to save the tenuous United Front, attempted to appease potential allies within the Nationalist Party. As the Comintern spoke for Stalin, Chen's call to dampen class struggle and ignore the land problem won the day.[6]

This brings us to Mao in Hunan in early 1927, with the future of the revolution torn between city and countryside. Mao intended to investigate the peasant movement that had thrown the United Front into doubt. Evidence of farmers becoming political activists and transforming their village communities might convince Communist leaders that peasants, long derided as backward and self-interested, were in fact potential revolutionaries. Such a revolution had no historical precedent. Had not Karl Marx himself blamed the failure of France's 1848 revolution on the passivity of the peasant class?[7] Mao would have to draft a blueprint to explain not only how this grand experiment could possibly succeed, but why it must succeed. Investigating the peasant movement in five counties over the course of a month, Mao seized on a metaphor to capture his bold vision of rural revolution: the hurricane. This metaphor would become inexorably linked with what the party called land reform (*tudi gaige*), thanks in part to the talented author Zhou Libo, who decades later penned *The Hurricane*, a novel documenting the arrival of Communist power in a Northeast village. Zhou, however, was simply paying belated homage to

Mao. According to Mao's famous forecast, which Zhou would later use to preface his novel,

> In a very short time, in China's central, southern and northern provinces, several hundred million peasants will rise like a mighty storm, like a hurricane, a force so swift and violent that no power, however great, will be able to hold it back. They will smash all the trammels that bind them and rush forward along the road to liberation. They will sweep all the imperialists, warlords, corrupt officials, local tyrants and evil gentry into their graves.[8]

Formulated by Mao and enshrined by Zhou, the hurricane metaphor took flight, framing rural revolution as a destructive tempest: violent, unstoppable, and utterly transformative. If Mao's comrades did not flock to the countryside to lead the peasantry, he warned, they would find themselves smashed underfoot.

Mao's blueprint, immortalized in his "Report on an Investigation of the Peasant Movement in Hunan," would eventually became the story of land reform: a tale that made sense of peasant revolution by casting landlords as evil men running roughshod over moral peasants in oppressive feudal strongholds.[9] The arrival of the revolution, Mao's vision promised, would unleash the vast powers of the peasantry, liberating and revitalizing the realm. As Mao forcefully argued in 1927, village revolution was not a dinner party but a violent act of class struggle. He detailed how farmers could be remade into political activists, providing a revolutionary road map that the party would follow for decades. As Mao outlined, peasants gained power by settling accounts (*qingsuan*) and leveling fines (*fakuan*) on landlords, punishments that would cause class enemies to completely lose face (*timian saodi*) as news of their crimes spread. The most powerful attacks on rural elites were violent public rituals designed to destroy feudal power. This included major demonstrations (*da shiwei*), during which peasants would rally together and march to the houses of class enemies, slaughtering pigs and feasting on grain. In another highly ritualistic political attack, activists forced a landlord to don a dunce cap (*gao maozi*) for a humiliating parade through the village. Mao, noting that "this sort of thing is very common" during the peasant movement, outlined the proper method of ritualized class struggle and its expected results:

> A tall paper-hat is stuck on the head of one of the local tyrants or evil gentry, bearing the words "Local tyrant so-and-so" or "So-and-so of the evil gentry." He is led by a rope and escorted with big crowds in front and behind. Sometimes brass gongs are beaten and flags waved to attract people's

attention. This form of punishment more than any other makes the local tyrants and evil gentry tremble. Anyone who has once been crowned with a tall paper-hat loses face altogether and can never again hold up his head."[10]

As Mao emphasized in early 1927, violent and ritualistic struggle coupled with economic expropriation was the most effective method of striking against class enemies. Only the worst local tyrants and evil gentry, who "literally slaughtered peasants without batting an eyelid," needed to be executed.[11]

In Mao's "Hunan Report," the Chinese village, insular and cleaved by class hatred, was controlled by landlords who ruthlessly oppressed moral peasants. Those with land were bullies, ruffians unafraid to use force to get what they wanted from the poor. And all gentry were by nature evil. In reality, rural China was an expansive and endlessly diverse place, and it stubbornly resisted any simple characterization. Village communities were typically not isolated but deeply engaged with larger market systems, especially when located in the orbit of towns or urban centers.[12] Large landholders certainly existed, but the villains that Mao used to justify agrarian revolution were far from universal. Many villages lacked true examples of economic exploitation.[13] Partible inheritance, the time-honored tradition of equally dividing property among male heirs, promoted social mobility both up and down the village hierarchy. As one activist in Heilongjiang later recalled, landlord wealth in his village was due to hard work and never lasted even three generations. There was no reason to care too much about a landlord: "His grandson would be poor."[14]

Ideology, however, now trumped reality. Mao vilified the very idea of owning a surplus of land that could be rented out for additional income.[15] To be sure, many Communists, including Chen Duxiu, were repulsed by Mao's violent vision of rural revolution, which to them seemed to go too far and too fast.[16] Li Weihan, then in party central, was particularly concerned with Mao's insistence on relying on the poorest members of rural society. These men had revolutionary potential, he noted, but were also quite "destructive": they gambled, took liberties with women, and tended toward violence.[17] More important, Mao's "Hunan Report" was an ill fit with the Comintern line. Stalin, then locked in an ideological battle with Leon Trotsky, had doubled down on the United Front. With the Nationalists reliant on landlord supporters, the Communists backed away from rural revolution in hopes of appeasing their allies.

Prelude: The Land Revolution

The Comintern's ability to push the Chinese Communists away from rural radicalism did little to placate Chiang Kai-shek. While Northern Expedition troops under Chiang dallied outside Shanghai in April 1927, right-wing Nationalist Party leaders engineered the Shanghai Massacre, a brutal crackdown that left hundreds of Communists and workers murdered in the streets.[18] After the Shanghai Massacre, Stalin backed away from his embrace of Chiang Kai-shek while still insisting on a United Front with leftist elements within the Nationalist Party. His thinking on the peasant movement, however, evolved: class struggle in the Chinese countryside was not to be feared after all.[19] During the August 7 Conference of 1927, with Chen Duxiu no longer in control, the new Communist leader, Qu Qiubai, embraced the call to deepen rural radicalism while also preparing for military uprisings. Political power, Mao had explained, was obtained from the barrel of the gun. The Chinese revolution had now reached a new stage, that of the land revolution (*tudi geming*). A prelude to the story of agrarian revolution told in this book, the land revolution era cemented the role of violence in transforming village China.

This first attempt at property redistribution, designed to fund the newly formed Red Army and win over poor farmers, was carried out in the isolated base areas that had emerged in the aftermath of the collapse of the United Front. Most famously, Mao Zedong fled to the Jinggang Mountains, lying between Jiangxi and Hunan provinces, in October 1927. Zhu De, the talented general who would eventually help lead Mao and the Communists to military victory, joined him there in April of the following year. Within this and other rural base areas, the Communists carried out their land revolution, a chaotic attempt at transforming village societies. During the opening salvo of the land revolution, party central issued vague guidelines, calling for the confiscation of the property of large and medium landlords for distribution to land-hungry peasants, while reducing rent paid to small landlords.[20] Finally free to formulate his ideal land policies, Mao instead called for the confiscation and redistribution of all land, hurting wealthy farmers as well as landlords. Lineage organizations resisted redistribution, as did many farmers. At times, redistribution did not start until the Red Army opened fire on villagers.[21] Tensions flared with the party's allies among the local elite, leading to open attacks on military units carrying out the land revolution.[22] Many farmers fled, sending the local economy into a spiral. Only after land had been redistributed and just weeks before the Red Army abandoned the base area were these policies formalized in law.[23] This dynamic interplay between revolutionary experiments and legal frameworks established a precedent: action on the ground typically outpaced official party policies.

Despite the strategic location of his first base area, Mao abandoned the Jinggang Mountains in January 1929, moving to southern Jiangxi. The land revolution, which had done much to destabilize the Jinggang Mountains base, continued as the Red Army roamed the countryside. Mao's next land law called only for the confiscation of landlord and public land; wealthy farmers were to be politically isolated but would keep their land.[24] This proved a brief moment of leniency to wealthy farmers. Less than a year later, a third land policy once again targeted wealthy farmers. According to this law, largely opposed by local Jiangxi Communists, farmers would lose anything more than "what is needed for self-support."[25] In practice, confiscations were widespread, leading many farmers to flee in fear.[26]

Shortly before the declaration of his third land law, Mao had written that the revolution, which seemed in mortal danger, was in fact ready to explode. Using the old Chinese adage that "a single spark can start a prairie fire," Mao predicted rapid growth for the Communists. The continued inability of the Red Army to take and hold cities, however, demonstrated that the party still needed to follow its rural path by forming new base areas in the countryside. Mao selected a strategically placed base in northwestern Jiangxi, from which the Red Army could strike at nearby wealthy settlements. Officially established in November 1931, the Jiangxi Provincial Soviet Government provided Mao with his largest and most secure base yet. A testament to the military strength Mao found in the countryside, in Jiangxi the Red Army would successfully repulse four attempts by Chiang Kai-shek to encircle and destroy the base area. It was an ideal place to experiment further with rural revolution.[27] Mao, meanwhile, insisted more than ever before that the countryside offered the party its best chance for military and political success, especially after another round of rural investigation in 1930 had confirmed what Mao had learned on his trip home in 1927: villages were rife with class conflict. This time, Mao explained that wealthy peasants, who farmed their own land, had to be attacked because their prosperity had earned them the hatred of the rural poor. According to Mao, if the Communists attempted to shield rich peasants from activists, "those poor peasants could not but hate" the party.

Attacking wealthy farmers was thus "the paramount policy of the rural struggle."[28]

Communist leaders continued to view Mao's successes in the countryside as a sideshow to the main event: urban revolution. But things were not going well in the cities, especially after the April 1931 arrest of Gu Shunzhang, who had overseen the Communists' assassination squads. Information provided by Gu, who had been recognized while passing himself off as a juggler in a Hankou park, allowed the Nationalists to arrest thousands of underground party members.[29] Communist leaders, mainly either escaping from Shanghai or returning from study in Moscow, streamed to the Jiangxi Soviet throughout 1931. Their attempts to discredit and push Mao aside had an immediate influence on the land revolution; one of the main charges levied at Mao was his supposed leniency to wealthy farmers.[30] Under prodding from Wang Ming and other newly arrived leaders, the Jiangxi Soviet passed what would prove to be the party's most radical land law.[31] With the Comintern mindful of Stalin's own war against the kulaks, the December 1931 land law demanded the confiscation and distribution of all land owned by wealthy peasants and landlords. Rich peasants were to be given the poorest-quality land available. Even more extreme, the law denied landlords a share of land, leaving them utterly destitute. As was to be the case throughout the party's decades of agrarian revolution, the fates of individuals targeted as class enemies were to be shared by their families.

In 1933 Mao Zedong penned two articles that provided his first analysis of rural classes. Declaring the landlord class the "principal enemy of the land revolution," Mao announced the party's intention to "annihilate the landlord class" by confiscating all their lands and properties.[32] The subsequent "land investigation" (*tiancha*) campaigns proved particularly effective in realizing the party's most radical vision of agrarian reform. Gong Chu, then a Communist military leader in the Guangdong-Jiangxi region, would later recall that "settling accounts led to more settling accounts, killings led to more killings." Even locals serving in the Red Army saw their family members attacked and left with nothing. According to Gong, activists used extreme torture to extort cash from landlords. Under the slogan of "cutting the weeds to eliminate the roots," they put entire families to death.[33] As one PRC study of the land revolution admitted, while "land investigation" campaigns did mobilize the masses and attack some forms of feudal power, they also "severely encroached on the interests of the middle peasants, excessively attacked landlords and rich peasants, injured a good number of cadres, and ruined agriculture production."[34]

Military defeat, not faulty land policies, brought down the Jiangxi Soviet: Chiang Kai-shek's fifth encirclement campaign finally forced the Communist Party to abandon Jiangxi. By the time the ensuing Long March ended in the remote Shaan-Gan-Ning base area in Northwest China in 1935, Mao Zedong's stature in the party had grown considerably. Aware of the growing threat of Japanese imperialism, Mao called for a change in agrarian policies in order to facilitate a new alliance with the Nationalist Party. Over the following two years, ever mindful of establishing a new United Front, the Communists moved to protect the lands of landlords and rich peasants.[35]

In January 1937, the land revolution era quietly came to a close. The formal Second United Front soon followed.[36] During the war against Japan, the Communists initially did little to transform social or political relations at the village level.[37] While mass implementation of double reduction, which sought to reduce the amount of rent and interest paid by famers living in the base areas, was one of Mao's "Ten Great Policies" announced in August 1937, in practice little was actually done. The land revolution had typically damaged local economies; the party now focused on reclaiming wasteland and mobilizing farmers for production.[38]

But when tensions between the two parties inevitably began rising in the Second United Front, the Communist Party let it be known that village society was not to be left to its own devices. In 1940, the party's Shaan-Gan-Ning base area finally implemented double reduction, lowering rents and interest paid to village elites.[39] The double reduction campaign spread to other base areas, and with further experience, Mao Zedong refined the party's rural policies in January 1942. Most notable, with Mao deciding that the majority of landlords were patriotic, the party insisted on limited, private, and nonviolent class struggle. Only the most obstinate landlords were subject to public rebuke. Although the January 1942 directive is now seen as moderate in comparison to the later move to all-out agrarian revolution, the double reduction campaigns explicitly challenged landlord supremacy.[40] These campaigns remade rural societies by creating villages largely populated by farmers who owned their own fields.[41] Double reduction, while primarily an economic program, also contained clear political

and social components: the party encouraged tenants to personally negoti-
ate with their landlords in order to gain a sense of their political power.[42]
Over 70 percent of base area villages carried out double reduction campaigns, resulting in an overall drop in landlord power, as well as an increase
in agricultural production.[43]

Civil War: From "Land to the Tiller" to "Land Equalization"

Despite the successes of double reduction, Mao remained committed to his
own vision of rural revolution: the inevitable and violent hurricane. When
party propaganda chief Zhang Wentian, sent to investigate rural revolts
against the Communists, suggested that Mao's class scheme was unrealistic
and unfair to hard-working wealthy farmers, he was effectively silenced.[44]
As the shift from radical land revolution to double reduction had already
demonstrated, land policies were always subordinate to the military and
political realities facing the party. So just as the war with Japan had demanded a softening of rural policy, the start of another civil war with the
Nationalists required the opposite.[45] With a fragile peace still holding in
late 1945, rent and interest reduction remained the public centerpiece of the
party's land policy.[46] But new campaigns against traitors and rural tyrants
began the process of agrarian revolution, the topic of this book. These campaigns saw the return of the types of struggle Mao had first advocated in
his 1927 "Hunan Report." This was especially true in the Northeast, where
the forces of Lin Biao, a talented Communist general, rapidly expanded
the extent of party control after the collapse of Japanese power. Owning
land, coupled with cooperation with the Nationalists or the Japanese, was
enough to be branded as a "traitor to the nation." These traitors and tyrants
were often also denounced as landlords, foreshadowing a larger campaign
against landholders.[47] With a renewed double reduction campaign and these
increasingly confrontational and violent movements, many villagers began
to go beyond party policies by confiscating landlord property, often settling
accounts by demanding payment for past exploitation. Mao, having long
advocated settling accounts and now desperately in need of funding for the
looming Civil War, was eager to use confrontational class struggle to open
new revenue sources.[48] By 1946, Communist leaders sensed the impending
collapse of the party's uneasy cease-fire with the Nationalists, leaving few
political reasons to dampen peasant activism. Radical land reform, Mao
further believed, represented one of the keys to military victory. Through

fierce class struggle, peasants would gain land, political consciousness, and unbreakable ties to the party that would now protect them from landlord reprisals.[49] It was time for the Communists to make Mao's tale of rural revolution a reality.

With villagers throughout the party's base areas already confiscating and redistributing the property of landlords, traitors, and collaborators, the Communist Party sought to bring land policies in line with local realities. Leading cadres traveled to the Communists' capital in Yan'an to discuss the land question in a "report-back meeting" chaired by Liu Shaoqi, already one of the most powerful voices in the party. Liu's conference resulted in the May Fourth Directive, which explicitly endorsed the desire of land-hungry villagers to confiscate fields, officially launching the first of many rounds of land reform. This initial campaign rallied villagers using Sun Yat-sen's popular slogan, "land to the tiller."[50] In line with local demands, the party called for poor farmers to confiscate property from traitors, local tyrants, and bandits. Village cadres were instructed to use rent reduction and other peaceful methods to weaken the landlord class.[51] The cautious return to agrarian revolution promised limited violence, with execution and beatings reserved for "extremely wicked traitors and public enemies."[52] The purposefully vague land-to-the-tiller campaign proved a good fit in North China, where many impoverished villages lacked wealthy landlords.[53] But when local cadres moved to remake village political and social structures, all too often the result was widespread verbal and physical attacks on local elites, including wealthy farmers. Following the release of the May Fourth Directive, work teams organized by the party traversed the countryside with the explicit aim of helping the poorest of China's villagers turn the world upside down.

Over the course of the following six years of rural revolution, the party's work teams carried out land reform by following the Maoist script for the total transformation of the village. After arriving in a given village, teams began by disseminating propaganda and organizing poor farmers to "speak bitterness" against their wealthier neighbors. Team members then led these activists in determining the village's class structure, dividing the vast majority of the community into Maoist classes: landlords, rich peasants, middle peasants, poor peasants, and hired hands. This class structure identified enemies and provided the framework for the transfer of economic and political power from established elites to a new and party-sanctioned core of impoverished activists. The public struggling of landlords served as the dramatic denouement of the campaign. Afterward, peasants, now considered enlightened, would take possession of the "fruits of struggle" (*douzheng guoshi*): the property of defeated class enemies. The novelist Ma Jia, recalling his own observation of land reform, aptly summarized the process of events necessary for the completion of a village's revolutionary transformation:

> The old village society was proclaimed to be over, for a new life was starting. The meeting place beckoned, and workers and poor peasants mobilized to determine class statuses, form a poor peasants and hired hands association, research the situation, arrest and try the landlords, collect movable property, hold struggle sessions, divide movable property, organize small production teams, measure the land, establish the party branch, and support the front line.[54]

Ma Jia was just one of the gifted writers to use the experience of taking part in the first rounds of land reform as the basis for a novel documenting the campaign. Ding Ling and Zhou Libo penned far more famous fictionalized accounts of their time in the countryside that would serve as handbooks for rural revolution.[55]

That intellectuals would transcribe their time on work teams into narratives is far from surprising. Stories are essential to human lives, helping construct both personal and social identities.[56] Future work team members drew on these land reform novels as they prepared to carry out rural revolution. As one later noted, reading these novels was like "following Ding Ling and Zhou Libo as their work teams traveled to the countryside, experiencing the entire process of land reform."[57] These riveting accounts reduced the messy and diverse realties of agrarian revolution into a neat and tidy Maoist narrative, helping to inform operas, songs, and even exhibits that informed the expectations of future work team members. This shared narrative would have profound implications for the course of Chinese history.

These initial land-to-the-tiller land reform campaigns were marked by a diversity of methods. Different base areas experimented with a multitude of techniques of wealth transfer; broad policies for the confiscation and division of land emerged during land to the tiller, but with cadres reacting to local conditions and shifting fortunes of war, land reform remained unique in each base area.[58] Outside North China, the Northeast was the most important base area for the first rounds of land reform.[59] Following the arrival of the Soviet army in August 1945, Chinese Communist soldiers and cadres from "inside the pass" (*guannei*) had rushed to the northern side of the Great Wall. First focusing on establishing order by redistributing land owned by the Japanese or leading collaborators, work teams oversaw a moderate land reform campaign that lasted until the following year.[60]

Communist leaders encouraged work teams throughout the scattered base areas to employ a trial-and-error approach, with successful methods popularized through glowing reports in the party-run media. Some early experiments, including the purchase of landlord land for redistribution to the poor and allowing "enlightened" landlords to donate land, were briefly implemented but then discarded.[61] These policies had failed to mobilize the peasantry in accordance with Mao's vision of rural revolution, which demanded ritualized struggle. Other work teams, following the precedents of speak bitterness meetings and settling accounts from the recent campaigns against traitors and local tyrants, found a formula for land reform that dovetailed with Mao's violent and confrontational approach to remaking village China. These cadres met with poor villagers and encouraged them to speak of the bitterness they had endured due to exploitative and evil landlords. Mobilized peasants would then settle accounts, confronting newly labeled class enemies by detailing every instance of economic exploitation, political oppression, and even personal humiliation. These landlords were considered "struggle targets" (*douzheng duixiang*), to be subjected to "struggle" (*douzheng*), the party's ritualized enactment of rural class struggle. Not until they admitted their guilt and agreed to give up their lands were accounts considered to be truly settled.[62]

After a long summer of land to the tiller brought land reform to some 20 million villagers, the Communists moved to ramp up their rural revolution. The September announcement for a "fill the gaps" (*tian ping bu qi*) campaign echoed Mao's "Hunan Report," declaring that the question of the moment was not if the party was going too far (*guo huo*) but instead how to release the energies of the masses even more. Noting that some villages, perhaps fearing the period of chaos (*luan yi dun*) that was needed to build the new revolutionary order, had settled accounts with traitors but not solved the land problem, the call to fill the gaps promised to ensure that the poor received sufficient land, taking property from rich peasants as needed.[63] Base areas moved to fill the gaps by rectifying the primary mistake of land to the tiller: the failure to fully mobilize the masses. Recognizing a common problem in land to the tiller, village cadres, activists, and militiamen who had taken an unfair share of property were asked to return fields and goods for another round of redistribution. The primary means of filling gaps, however, was through once again settling accounts with landlords, now seen as a potentially inexhaustible source of wealth.[64] In the Northeast, meanwhile, the moderate rural program that had previously targeted only traitors and the worst local despots was similarly moving to a new phase. There, party leaders began describing the results of initial attempts at land reform as "half-cooked" (*ban sheng bu shou*); despite the division of land and the appearance of successful rural revolution, in reality peasants had not been mobilized to topple landlord power. Work teams were once again dispatched to the countryside, this time to reexamine and restart the process of land reform.[65]

As 1946 came to a close, party leaders increasingly viewed agrarian revolution through the lens of the ongoing Civil War. With Chiang Kai-shek's armies on the move and threatening the Communists' Yan'an capital, the party announced a new drive to complete land reform before farmers returned to their fields for spring planting. One report, published in *Liberation Daily*, claimed that after land reform, peasants were joining the Communists' military force, now renamed the People's Liberation Army (PLA), in record numbers; in one region, nearly one in every five poor peasant and hired hand households sent a son to join the fight against Chiang Kai-shek and the Nationalists. This *Liberation Daily* report made a direct connection between land reform and military victory, and even noted how the two campaigns intertwined. Some peasants conducted guerrilla warfare during the day, returning home to settle accounts with class enemies at night. In other places, men left to fight while women took the lead in class struggle.[66] Party leaders would eventually realize that mobilizing for war through land reform was in fact extremely difficult. In the first years of the Civil War, however, the desire to use agrarian revolution to fight the Nationalists would bring much chaos to the countryside. This was especially true after Liu Shaoqi and Zhu De, overseeing land reform in Hebei's Pingshan County, allowed the use of violence during struggle, leading to two deaths. As news of party central's lax attitude toward violent struggle spread, so did beatings and killings.[67]

In summer 1947, with a year of experience in all-out land reform, the Communist Party called for a conference on agrarian policy to unify ongoing and future campaigns. Originally scheduled to start on the one-year anniversary of the report-back meeting that had produced the May Fourth Directive, the meeting had to be postponed and relocated after Chiang Kai-shek's troops occupied Yan'an. During the conference, held in Hebei's unassuming Xibaipo village, Liu Shaoqi took the lead by noting that land reform was hampered by problems with local leadership. In some cases, cadres forced land reform on reluctant villagers, yet at other times, cadres protected potential struggle targets. Liu may have been the conference chair and in charge of land reform, but Moscow-trained Kang Sheng, a leading radical and head of party intelligence, spoke on Mao's behalf.[68] Kang's tales of extracting hidden landlord wealth in Shanxi's Linxian County made Mao's support for fierce class struggle in the countryside clear.[69] Kang and Liu called for a "moving stones" (*ban shitou*) campaign: peasants would throw off the leadership of their local cadres, seen as heavy weights holding back a revolutionary upsurge. One slogan that emerged that summer declared, "Do everything as the masses want it done."[70] Months of meetings resulted in the 1947 China Outline Land Law. Passed on September 23 and promulgated on October 10, the law's sixteen articles promised the end of feudal exploitation by eliminating land rents and the landlord class. The Communists proudly announced that Sun Yat-sen's dream of giving land to the tiller was finally coming true. But perhaps the party should have used Sun's earlier slogan, "equalization of land holdings": the most important aspect of the law was its sixth article, which called for even land distribution.[71]

The release of the land law was followed by "land equalization" (*pingfen tudi*), an intense round of campaigning that lasted well into the following year. These campaigns were paired with cadre rectification (*zhengdang*) campaigns to combat corruption, which party leaders had seen as one of the major reasons for previous problems in agrarian reform. In the party's established base areas where land had already been redistributed, often more than once, the call to equalize landholdings was unpopular. Attempts to force land equalization at times even resulted in violent attacks on peasants.[72] But a steady stream of military victories starting in the latter half of 1947 brought new lands under Communist rule, allowing the further spread of land equalization campaigns. In its attempts to establish base areas, it was only natural that the party turned to their established method of creating local support: rituralistically attacking local bullies and carrying out land reform. Following the spirit of his "Hunan Report," Mao continued to insist that cadres not interfere with violence against class enemies.[73] Work teams fanned out to "key point" (*zhongdian*) villages to implement the land law, but new conditions gave land reform violence a new set of problems. Because newly won areas were not militarily secure, peasants had to deal with the constant fear of landlord and Nationalist reprisals.

A lack of established activists, meanwhile, meant that work teams often had to rely on self-interested peasants whose bravery in standing up to village leaders was often coupled with impure motivations. This included preying on village women, an aspect of rural revolution that has so far escaped systematic examination. Mao, well aware of the plight of rural women, had noted as early as 1930 that these women, typically sold into marriage, essentially belonged to men and lacked personal freedom, to say nothing of political rights: "No one suffers more than women."[74] But in his "Hunan Report," Mao had praised poor activists for barging into the houses of class enemies to seize grain and "even loll for a minute or two on the ivory-inlaid beds belonging to the young ladies in the households of the local tyrants and evil gentry."[75] The party never explicitly endorsed attacks on landlord women, but for some newly empowered men, many previously unable to afford a wife, these women were little more than another form of property to take from class enemies. This dynamic is clearly present in *Fanshen*, an account of land reform penned by William Hinton that brought Mao's narrative of rural revolution to a global audience. Hinton was an American radical and highly sympathetic to Mao's rural revolution, but he did not shy away from reporting on the abuses that local cadres and activists carried out. According to Hinton, one poor peasant rapist made the connections between sexual assault and rural revolution clear, proclaiming, "Bastard landlords, they took our women, why shouldn't we take theirs?"[76] This was one of seventeen instances of sexual assault committed by cadres and activists in a single village. Because the victims were wives and daughters from landlord or rich peasant households, the rapists were never punished.[77] This was not an isolated problem. One work team cadre reported that activists were killing class enemies and dividing not just their fields but their wives and daughters as well. When the cadre attempted to rein in this violence, he was himself struggled and disarmed.[78] Even a poor peasant wife might be stripped and beaten when her husband came under attack.[79]

While the Communists were seemingly unconcerned with what seems to have been widespread sexual assault, they did note with alarm other forms of violence during land equalization land reform. During a "swept-out-of-the-house" campaign, peasant activists left landlords with nothing, often using violence and torture to extract wealth.[80] A round of land reform in Shandong killed over 150, including peasants and cadres deemed ideologically suspect.[81] Violence spiraled out of control. Deng Xiaoping later chillingly summarized his experience leading the campaign in western Anhui:

> The masses would hate a few landlords and want them killed, so according to the wishes of the masses we would have these landlords killed. Afterwards, the masses would fear reprisals from those who had ties to those we had just killed, and would draw up an even bigger list of names, saying if these people were also killed, everything would be alright. So once again, according to the wishes of the masses, we would have these people killed as well. After we killed these people, the masses felt that even more people wanted revenge for these deaths, and would draw up an even bigger list of names. So once again, according to the wishes of the masses, we killed these people. We kept on killing, and the masses felt more and more insecure. The masses were frightened, scared, and took flight. The result was that over two hundred people were killed, and work in twelve administrative villages was ruined.[82]

Rumors of rural violence spread widely. In Beijing, citizens heard tales of landlords being "swept" out of their houses. They also heard stories of activists "lighting sky lamps" (*dian tiandeng*), turning the heads of victims into torches.[83] According to an angry land reform veteran, other torture methods included "standing on the tiger's stool" and "spreading phoenix wings."[84] With violence threatening the Civil War effort, Communist Party leaders eventually realized that their hurricane had to be postponed: land reform in newly won territories would have to wait.[85]

Xi Zhongxun, father of current Chinese president Xi Jinping, now emerged as a voice of reason. Xi, then overseeing the Northwest Bureau, wrote directly to Mao in early 1948 and explicitly detailed the horrors the peasant masses had suffered during the chaotic push to equalize landholdings.[86] Xi's ideas were in line with the thinking of Ren Bishi, a party leader well trained in Marxist theory. Ren had been calling for a relaxation of class struggle since late 1947, and his January 1948 speech calling on cadres to correct past errors signaled a coming shift in land policy just as violent struggle reached its peak in the countryside.[87] But change was slow. Not until April were work teams made aware that land reform policy had shifted to curb violent tendencies and attacks on farmers.[88] Now land reform was made contingent on three conditions: villages must be militarily secure, peasants must want land reform, and local cadres must be well trained and ready to lead the campaign. As only a few new areas under Communist control qualified, land reform was essentially halted in summer 1948 in favor of double reduction. Work teams, meanwhile, revisited villages to undo some of the damage done to wrongly expropriated owner-cultivators.[89] For many villages in the old base areas, this represented a third round of land reform.[90] The importance of adequately preparing a village for land reform was a costly lesson, learned only after many areas where land reform had been carried out were subject to heavy reprisals when the Nationalists temporarily returned to power.[91]

Rural Revolution in the Early PRC

The accomplishments of Civil War–era campaigns were impressive. By the eve of military victory, of the over 270 million living under Communist control, over 150 million had taken part in land reform, and another 80 million had participated in double reduction; over 25 million hectares of land had been confiscated, largely from landlords and rich peasants.[92] Agrarian revolution had proved a critical factor in military victory by tying the peasants of North and Northeast China to the fates of the Communist Party, which was now firmly ensconced in the countryside.[93] Land reform would continue in peacetime, and in fact it moved to a much larger scale following the total breakdown of Chiang Kai-shek's military forces and the subsequent establishment of the People's Republic of China. The campaign resumed, with parts of North China, including the countryside surrounding Beijing, carrying out land reform in the winter of 1949 to 1950. This round of land reform, however, differed from Civil War campaigns. Treatment of landlords was considerably improved, with most avoiding public struggle.

In early spring 1950, party central moved to finally replace the Outline Land Law that had encouraged so much violence during the years of the Civil War. Requesting opinions from various regional leaders, party central floated the idea of dividing land reform into two stages separated by months, if not years. During the first stage, work teams would move only against landlords, leaving rich peasants for the second stage of land reform. Party central also raised the idea of confiscating only the lands that rich peasants rented out and wondered what would happen in places without much landlord wealth.[94] The party's rural policies thus remained very much in flux, even as Communist leaders prepared to release the land law that would guide agrarian revolution for the hundreds of millions living in the "new liberated areas." But a trend toward moderation was clear. In a letter to Deng Zihui, a leading voice in land reform policy, Mao Zedong finally reversed course on the confiscation of rich peasant land. Noting that these lands would not have a significant impact on distributions to the poor, Mao declared the policy of not touching these lands "appropriate."[95]

More lenient treatment of landlords and rich peasants became official with the promulgation of the Land Reform Law of the People's Republic of China in summer 1950. Landlords would still lose their "five big properties": land, draft animals, agricultural tools, excess grain, and any extra housing located within the village. Unlike earlier campaigns, however, landlords would be allowed to keep their other belongings, including commercial enterprises. This new law also lacked the references to land equalization found in the 1947 Outline Land Law. The property of middle peasants, the seventh clause clearly stated, was not to be touched.[96]

With this law, the party now promoted a more nuanced approach to class division, reducing the number of struggle targets in an effort to unite the broad peasant masses in opposition to a limited number of landlords. Civil War–era work teams had often started with the organization of "poor peasant leagues." Now teams were to only form more inclusive "peasant associations." Of central importance was the return of what was once dismissively referred to as the "rich peasant line": the law's sixth article, stipulating that the rich peasant economy must be preserved. Those unlucky rich peasants who had lost property during earlier campaigns would not be compensated, but this was the first time the Communist Party actively protected the rich peasant economy during land reform. Unlike the Jiangxi Soviet era, when the Comintern pushed the Chinese Communists to attack wealthy farmers, Stalin now gave his full support to the "rich peasant line." Many peasants and cadres had difficulty accepting this new policy, however, believing the poor would not benefit from land reform without access to rich peasant property. In response, party leaders argued that the rich peasant class did not possess enough wealth to make a real difference in raising the standard of living for the poor. Furthermore, with the war over, the Communists sought to boost production by reducing the percentage of the population labeled as class enemies.[97]

A constant stream of information and propaganda concerning land reform, coupled with the active recruitment of city dwellers to participate in the campaigns, made rural revolution an inescapable part of urban life during the first months and years of the PRC. The party had found in land reform a powerful tool in the remaking of China's national political culture. As Liu Shaoqi posited in his 1950 report on land reform:

> During land reform, besides conducting widespread propaganda in the countryside, there should also be propaganda for all city residents and army units. The land reform policies and laws of the People's Government should be explained to workers, students, office workers, merchants, officers, as well as soldiers, so that they understand, and even sympathize with and help the peasantry, while refusing to sympathize with or help landlords, and certainly not protect landlords, even those family members or friends who are landlords.[98]

Or as one of the 90,000 urbanites to see a Suzhou land reform exhibition proclaimed, "Before I did not know what land reform was, but now I understand."[99]

This Suzhou exhibition was a minor affair. One of the grandest exhibits, sponsored by the South Central China Bureau, opened in 1952 at the height of a huge campaign that would affect some 130 million villagers. Visitors to the exhibition saw images of suffering peasants who gained liberation through taking part in class struggle. Cutting the ribbon to open the exhibit in Wuhan, senior party leader Deng Zihui made the party's purpose explicit:

> From these materials and artifacts we can see how landlords cruelly exploited the peasantry, and how politically landlords bloodily controlled and oppressed the peasants; we can see the fiendish, brutal, and totally uncaring nature of the landlord class; we can see how the landlord class squeezed and then extravagantly squandered the blood and sweat of the peasantry; we can see how imperialism ganged up with feudalism to squeeze the peasantry; we can see the brave and heroic record of how the great laboring and brave peasantry, under the leadership of the Chinese Communist Party, implemented an unyielding resistance and struggle against the landlords.[100]

Some 636,464 Chinese citizens attended the Wuhan exhibit, which was said to be only one of "countless" exhibits held throughout the region.[101] For visitors this was no simple day at the museum, but another chance to absorb Mao's narrative of exploited peasants finding emancipation and liberation through fierce struggle with evil landlords. For villagers and work team members alike, these stories helped make rural revolution both

IMAGE 2. Chinese citizens flock to the South Central Land Reform Exhibit in Wuhan, 1952. Source: *Zhongnan tudi gaige de weida shengli*, 13

meaningful and understandable. During the years of the campaigns, the land reform narrative was inescapable. Tales of village transformation were found in novels, operas, news accounts, and even the couplets Chinese families hung on their doorways.

The arrival of land reform propaganda in Chinese cities was not only about education. Hundreds of thousands of urban residents would soon join work teams to personally take part in the campaigns to remake the countryside. One reluctant land reform work team member, the talented writer Zhang Ailing, would later use her time in the countryside to help inform her own novel on the Chinese revolution.[102] Zhang, better known in the West as Eileen Chang, worked with American agents to structure her novel *Love in Redland*. Unlike the accounts of Ding Ling and William Hinton, which followed and praised Mao's narrative of revolution, Zhang provided her readers a counternarrative of agrarian reform, attacking the Communists in an attempt to delegitimize the party's promise of peasant liberation. Her deeply cynical account of rural revolution suggests how the implementation of Mao's vision was a traumatic experience, one that could deeply scar villagers and work team members alike.

With victory over the Nationalists and a new land law in place, the party seemed primed to bring agrarian revolution to its vast new territories. One observer noted that in Chengdu, citizens in the midst of regime change feared not the arrival of the Communists but what havoc the Nationalist troops and bandits might wreak before the establishment of the new order. As was often the case in the first years of the PRC, however, the arrival of the PLA brought a tax bill: a request for a massive amount of grain, deliverable immediately. One of the first messages given to Sichuan villagers was the need to turn over grain to support the new government. Party propagandists emphasized that this grain requisition was different from those demanded by the Nationalist government.[103] But the fierce push for grain caused many locals to turn against the newly arrived Communists, who were unprepared for the challenges they faced far from Beijing. In some places, local resistance succeeded in delaying the party's takeover, even forcing a temporary retreat.[104] Land reform would have to wait.

The Communists, now calling for a slow and orderly implementation of agrarian revolution, deemed most villages unready for the arrival of work teams. Long after the founding of the PRC, Nationalist soldiers still roamed the countryside, and their presence gave pause to peasants still fearful of landlord retaliation.[105] Having learned a painful lesson in the Civil War, the Communists insisted on establishing military dominance before bringing rural revolution to newly liberated villages. Peasants, meanwhile, unorganized and without trained local cadres, were ill prepared for public political activism. The party now demanded highly structured campaigns, emphasizing the gradual preparation of the countryside for land reform. Most notable, land reform was aided by two 1950 campaigns promising to "purge bandits" (*qing fei*) and "oppose tyrants" (*fan ba*). The first was a military operation carried out by the PLA as its soldiers hunted down "bandits": rogue Nationalist army units, which in emulation of the Communists had turned to guerrilla warfare. These soldiers had been joined by secret societies, augmented by farmers angry over the party's harsh requisition of grain.[106] This was no minor uprising. Over seventy thousand bandits were caught in a single year in Hunan alone.[107] Deng Xiaoping counted nearly half a million in the Southwest.[108] During the "oppose tyrants" campaign, meanwhile, the party directed activists to publicly struggle "evil tyrants" (*eba*), estimated to compose 10 percent of the landlord population.[109] This campaign typically represented the arrival of rural revolution, although unlike land reform, struggle was not brought to every village. Instead, the party singled out a small number of particularly exploitative landlords and power holders for massive struggle meetings that drew spectators from miles around.[110]

The campaign against evil tyrants revealed much about the unruly and seemingly lawless countryside that the Communists would attempt to tame through mass campaigns. In Beibei, a region on the outskirts of Chongqing, the men attacked as evil tyrants were accused of a wide range of crimes. Chen Xiangji, a landlord in his seventies, hailed from Liangtan village. According to charges leveled against him by the new government, in 1943 he forcibly evicted his tenant Yan Binglin, leaving the farmer without housing and fields and wrenching Yan's family apart. In a 1950 feud with another tenant, he poisoned three of the tenant's pigs. Chen, like many of the other accused evil tyrants, was initially unimpressed with the new regime, refusing to pay the grain tax demanded by the new government. But with land reform looming, he hid his belongings, concealed landholdings, and prayed for the return of Chiang Kai-shek. Condemned as an evil tyrant, he was executed by firing squad.[111] Liu Guoqing, a second evil tyrant, was a well-known landlord in Dengzi village, where he often held leadership positions before the arrival of the Communists. Regime change did little to change Liu, who was accused of bribing cadres, spreading rumors, and threatening activists.[112] According to a transcription of his struggle meeting, a dozen accusers came forward to levy charges against Liu for a host of crimes, including embezzling public property and causing the death of a famer. Liu meekly admitted his guilt, but he was executed after villagers demanded that his blood debt be paid with blood.[113]

After neutralizing such men, the most hated power holders in the countryside, the party launched further campaigns to mobilize peasants and begin the process of agrarian revolution. Most common were the familiar campaigns to reduce rent and interest, but the party also organized peasants to "retrieve deposits" (*tui ya*) to help renters get back the hefty fees they sometimes paid for the right to plant crops.[114] Like land reform, cadres used peasant associations during these campaigns to determine classes and transfer wealth. And while these were intended to be generally peaceful campaigns, their links to land reform often led to outbreaks of extreme violence. Once these campaigns to secure the social order and organize the peasantry in opposition to landlords were completed, land reform could begin.

This final stage of land reform in size, scope, and complexity would go well beyond what the Communist Party had accomplished during the Civil War. Facing a widely divergent countryside as well as an acute lack of cadres, the party continually emphasized the need for controlled campaigns that would not begin until villages were declared ready for the campaign. While brutality against class enemies continued throughout land reform, these final campaigns called for fewer struggle targets and stressed legality over spontaneous violence.[115] All of this would have been impossible without the massive recruitment of intellectuals and professionals to join work teams; in the city of Changsha alone, the party mobilized five thousand citizens to join work teams.[116] A push by the fledgling government in 1951, meanwhile, drew over six thousand prominent figures from Beijing and Tianjin into work teams. Educators, artists, scientists, and physicians all took part.[117] Many would discover that their recruitment was predicated on the belief that taking part in rural revolution would serve as a crash course in Maoist ideology.

The first wave of PRC land reform kicked off in autumn 1950 throughout the East, South Central, Southwest, and Northwest regions. During these campaigns, work teams perfected their methods in select villages before spreading throughout the countryside. East China's land reform progressed the fastest, with most areas there finished by spring 1951. Other regions, especially where party rule came relatively late, such as the Southwest, did not finish until the following year. Land reform in what the Communists called the "new liberated areas" followed the model established in the earliest years of the campaign, now increasingly formulaic. As one work team summed up its time in working in Southwest China, land reform was essentially a step-by-step process. The team first mobilized the peasantry by announcing land reform and disseminating land reform propaganda. Far more important, work teams and local cadres brought villagers into the process of agrarian revolution by "visiting the poor and asking of their bitterness" (*fangpin wenku*). Next came the most dramatic stages of rural revolution: work teams helped villagers determine classes and struggle newly labeled landlords. Passage through the furnace of class struggle, the Communists promised, led to the liberation of the peasant masses. After overseeing the fair distribution of confiscated landlord property, finally, work teams would compile reports while mobilizing peasants to celebrate their liberation and increase agricultural production.[118]

This step-by-step process followed the plotline of the land reform narrative: a heroic tale of the victory of peasant revolution over evil feudal exploitation. Novels penned by party authors during the first days of land reform were heralded as literary field guides for fomenting class struggle in the countryside. Visitors to land reform exhibits saw this narrative visualized through photographs, paintings, and rural artifacts. In recognition of the centrality of this story for the course of land reform, the chapters of this book follow the narrative's arc, analyzing the party's attempt to transform the Chinese countryside through revolution, step by step. Each chapter begins with narrative treatments drawn from the work of the most talented authors to detail land reform: Ding Ling, Zhang Ailing, and William Hinton. The book also presents images from the massive Wuhan land reform exhibit, which visualized the story of agrarian revolution from start to finish. The first chapter of this story is, naturally, the arrival of the work team.

ARRIVING

Work Teams

The rumors? Well, Old Gu had heard all of them. Rumors, after all, had become just about the only sure thing left in Nuanshui, the North China village that Old Gu called home. It was true, he knew, that the Communists had already found ways to mobilize villagers, giving many of his Nuanshui neighbors hope for even greater changes. But with the Civil War raging on without end, might not the armies of the Nationalists return? If they did, anyone who had aided the Communists would be in mortal danger. And what to make of the Communists' promise to liberate the masses from the feudal forces that exploited the poor peasant brothers of Nuanshui? Old Gu had heard through the village grapevine that the party was sending a work team to bring revolution to the village. Who exactly would they target? Old Gu was what the Communists called a middle peasant. He was by no means wealthy, but he at least owned the farmlands that he tilled year after year. The work team was expected to organize an attack on Nuanshui's land-lords, redistributing their fields and belongings to the poor. Would they stop there? Old Gu and his fellow peasants supported the Communists, but the fear of what their revolution meant in practice created a sense of trepidation that permeated the village. Of the many rumors that quietly wormed their way through Nuanshui, the one that troubled Old Gu the most was the possibility that the land reform work team might not be satisfied with expropriating the village's landlords. Might they not simply communize (*nao gongchan*) all property and make everyone poor (*naocheng qiongren*)?[1]

Old Gu, the stereotypical wavering character penned by party author Ding Ling, exemplified how the Communists viewed Chinese villages: insular and fearful of outsiders. Ding Ling, however, relied on more than her imagination when she wrote *The Sun Shines over the Sanggan River*, the novel that told the fictional account of rural revolution in Nuanshui. Unsurprising given Mao Zedong's insistence that party intellectuals accumulate revolutionary practice, Ding Ling had spent months supervising land reform before writing the novel. Working in the party's Jin-Cha-Ji base area over the course of about five months from 1946 to 1947, she found inspiration in actual events: observing a poorly treated middle peasant directly spurred the creation of Old Gu.[2] Ding Ling later defended the authenticity of her novel, noting that having lived with her village friends, she felt obligated to "record their actual situation."[3] As a land reform work team veteran, she also made sure to describe the intellectuals such as herself who traveled to village China to upend the rural order. Work teams, just as much as villagers, were essential to the campaigns. Not long after its publication, *China Youth*, a journal that counted many future team members as readers, advocated reading Ding Ling for "great inspiration."[4] Ding Ling's novel was said to reveal much about land reform, including the actual process of carrying out these campaigns in the countryside.[5]

And so in *Sanggan River*, the team that Old Gu feared, led by Wen Cai, arrived in due course. Blessed and cursed with the airs of China's old literati elites, the intellectual was an unlikely patron of rural revolution. Hampered by his bookish tendencies and lacking practical revolutionary experience, the insecure Wen Cai exaggerated his education, claimed connections with high-ranking party artists, and made widely inaccurate theories about books he had never read, all to impress others. These transgressions were in his past, which is to say they occurred before he arrived in Yan'an, then the Communists' capital. Wen Cai, like the many others who had traveled to base areas to join the revolution, had engaged in round after round of self-examination. This soul searching had encouraged him to follow Mao Zedong's call to learn directly from the wise peasant masses.[6]

His impressive learning convinced the cadres running the district government to promote him to leader of his work team. Wen Cai, however, was not ready for the task. In Nuanshui, he struggled to cast off his intellectual airs and fully integrate himself into this new world that stressed revolutionary practice over textual learning. He rightly feared that the other work team members did not respect him, and his lack of revolutionary practice led to problem after problem during his time in Nuanshui. Wen Cai found his lack of authority, firmly rooted in his inexperience in the countryside, increasingly frustrating. After one particularly painful clash with his work team, he fumed silently. He knew that he was a newcomer to rural revolution but refused to believe that their opinions were any more valid than his own. Their meager revolutionary experience, what monumental value did it have? Their experience had not been summarized or elevated into theory. It was simply one-sided and not at all reliable. He could accept that his underlings were closer to the masses. They were, after all, out all day among the people. This was not the same as admitting that they were correct![7]

Liberation found Beijing. When the new government put out the call for students to take part in agrarian revolution, Liu Quan, of famed Peking University, rushed to sign up. He was not alone. Looking around the back of the lumbering pickup truck, he could see that all of his fellow work team cadres were also students from Beijing-area colleges. Together they were traveling down to the feudal countryside to bring revolution and emancipation to the peasant masses of Hanjiatuo village. Even Liu recognized the cliché of young revolutionaries singing songs as they traversed the vast plain, the young women of the team dressed in the Russian-style jackets favored by China's new leaders. It was a scene, Liu privately mused, seemingly taken straight out of one of the Soviet films now popular back in Beijing.[8]

This scene would also be at home in Ding Ling's narrative of rural revolution, but Zhang Ailing, the novelist who created Liu Quan, was no party loyalist. Having fled to Hong Kong shortly after the Communists came to power, Zhang found employment with the US Information Service, which promoted American interests overseas. During her three years working for the agency, Zhang, better known in the West as Eileen Chang, mostly translated English literature into Chinese. One of China's most talented writers, she also found time to use narratives to bitterly attack the new order she had left behind. *Love in Redland*, the tragic tale of Liu Quan, was written at the bequest of the US Information Service. Zhang even used a plot outline from American agents to help structure her text.[9] As a result, the novel is clearly informed by Cold War anti-Communist paranoia and lacks the poetry and nuance of Zhang's other works. And while Ding Ling's narration of rural revolution was immensely influential, *Love in Redland* had little impact. Today the book has largely been forgotten despite the immense fame of its author. Zhang's tale of land reform, however, cannot be dismissed as an imperialist fantasy. She forcefully insisted that her account of Liu Quan was based on "real people and real events" and would allow readers to "smell some of the authentic fragrance of life."[10] According to recent scholarship, this was not an empty claim: shortly before fleeing to Hong Kong, Zhang herself seems to have spent three to four months in the countryside on a work team. *Love in Redland* may have been conceived by cold warriors, but it was penned by a deeply perceptive woman who had joined other Shanghai intellectuals in observing and carrying out land reform in northern Jiangsu from late 1950 to early 1951.[11]

And so while *Love in Redland* begins in a stereotypical manner, the narrative quickly subverts the work team's mission. Surveying his comrades as they rambled through the countryside, Liu Quan allowed his eyes to linger on an attractive young woman before reminding himself that he was on an important mission. He would not be distracted. As a low-level cadre, he dared not make a bad impression on China's new leadership, which frowned on romantic entanglements among its young revolutionaries. The team's ride to Hanjiatuo was a long one, and as the trip dragged on, songs and laughter were replaced by restless sleep as the truck sped down ramshackle country roads. Excitement returned late that night when the work team finally arrived in Hanjiatuo amid a heavy rainfall, drums sounding as they approached the old village walls. Red lanterns appeared, lighting the way as peasant women and children emerged to greet the team with the *yangge* folk dances the Communists now promoted in the countryside. Not to be outdone, the young men of the village militia raised spears adorned with white handkerchiefs. As the rain continued to fall, there was no shortage of waving flags or shouted slogans to welcome the team. The time for agrarian revolution had come. Liu had brought with him a set of expectations about rural life, but mere minutes after he arrived in Hanjiatuo, doubts began to emerge. He listened in on a group of villagers expressing their disdain for class struggle. Why, one asked, could they not simply divide the land without struggle?[12] Moments later, Liu overheard the chair of the local peasant association confess that the village did not possess even a single large landlord. A neighboring village had a true large landlord, the peasant association chair continued, but local cadres there had simply kept all of his property for themselves.[13]

A dutiful revolutionary, Liu Quan quickly reported this information to his team leader, Zhang Li. Zhang, a Communist attached to the new government's Ministry of Culture, would surely know what to do. In response to Liu's thoughtful concerns, team leader Zhang first explained that a bit of corruption among local cadres was no big deal, and in any case, the work team had to remain focused on the task at hand. And as for those peasants who seemed to be opposed to class struggle, well they were simply backward. "Just how confused their minds are, you have no idea," Zhang explained. "They only see the profit that is right in front of their eyes and they usually cannot tell good from bad, thinking that enemies of the people are good people. They often vacillate, are often unreliable, and their minds are filled with the belief that things will eventually return to as they were in the old days. They are so timid, that a falling leaf scares them out of their wits."[14] If agrarian revolution was to succeed, the work team would have to take the lead.

The young American radical found himself in the midst of China's rural revolution, an adventure that would define his life. William Hinton was only in his late twenties when he first arrived in China as a tractor technician for an idealistic United Nations program. Working in Communist-held territory when the program shut down in 1947, he had decided to stay in the base area and accepted a position teaching English at a party-run university. Just as he arrived to take up his post, about half of the faculty and staff abruptly left to join land reform work teams. Decades later, when Hinton finally had the chance to transcribe his experiences into *Fanshen*, his epic account of rural revolution, he described the excitement of joining a work team: "Young men and women in blue ran back and forth tying up belongings, rolling their quilts into tight bundles, fastening shoulder straps to improvised bedrolls," singing songs and talking of revolution.[15] After watching the soft-spoken historian Fan Wenlan send off the young intellectuals with an appropriately scholarly talk, Hinton felt compelled to join them on their journey to remake the countryside.[16] How could teaching English compare with changing the world? Accompanied by Qi Yun, a young woman who served as his guide and interpreter, he made his way to a village within walking distance to the university: Zhang Zhuang, these days much better known by the name he gave the place, Long Bow. Long Bow may in fact be the most famous Chinese village, at least outside China. Because the massive scale of land reform eludes easy textualization, Hinton's "documentary" of revolution in this single Chinese village has become entrenched as the primary source to consult for a global understanding of Maoist rural revolution. A few years after its publication, *Fanshen* was already declared a classic, listed as one of the essential fifteen books on China in an essay by a noted China expert in *Harvard Magazine*.[17]

The American was an outsider, but with his affable nature and belief in the party's call to bring Mao's revolution to rural China, Hinton quickly integrated himself with the work team, which was roughly divided between rural cadres and urban intellectuals. Among these students and teachers, he singled out Professor Xu as being the stereotypical academic, making endless mistakes due to his inability to translate Marxist theory into revolutionary practice. But other intellectuals on the team were adept at their work, especially Cai Jin, whose passage through an arduous 1945 rectification campaign gave him "a new class outlook, a new code of loyalty."[18] Team leader Cai oversaw the creation of a village-wide peasant association and brought the village's land reform campaign to a successful end. In Hinton's mind, intellectuals such as Cai Jin were better equipped than peasant cadres for overseeing peasant revolution. These enthusiastic young men and women were the perfect agents of rural revolution:

> They plunged into the heart of village affairs with eagerness and enthusiasm, made discovery after discovery about the life of their own country-men, developed new and interesting friendships with people whom they never would have met in a lifetime of academic pursuits, and looked on the hardships involved partly as adventure and partly as steeling for future revolutionary activity, a test they hoped to pass without flinching.[19]

Peasant cadres, in contrast, were prone to depression and even distraction. One simply decided to ignore land reform after finally affording a wife.[20] But not every intellectual was up for the task at hand. Hinton had once met a crazed student, a graduate of Beijing's Qinghua University, who had been arrested for striking a peasant during land reform. After a failed attempt to flee the base areas, he had been confined to his room and gone insane. As Hinton would later remark, "Here was one young cadre whom the land reform movement had failed to remold. Temporarily, at least, it had crushed him."[21]

Hinton and his team had arrived in Long Bow intent on remaking rural life in accordance with Mao's vision of the revolutionary village. In his estimation, the village had not changed for centuries, seemingly frozen in time.[22] True, Long Bow peasants had taken part in violent struggle when they took revenge on local traitors in the immediate aftermath of the war against Japan. Later they had settled accounts with their most hated village landlords. And following the release of the May Fourth Directive, Long Bow's activists had carried out a brutal land reform campaign with the hopes of fundamentally transforming local society. But the work team, assigned to investigate land reform in Long Bow, assumed that nothing of real significance had been accomplished: peasants had yet to find true liberation, and the forces of counterrevolution lurked behind every corner. And so it was that William Hinton, wearing a bulky wool-lined coat, arrived in Long Bow on a shivering cold March day in 1948.

The work team (*gongzuodui*) was the primary instrument of agrarian revolution. PLA soldiers armed with Maoist ideology and American weapons won the war against Chiang Kai-shek's armed forces, but civilians in work teams remade the Chinese countryside according to Mao's grand vision. The party's first mass campaigns in the aftermath of Japan's unexpected surrender focused on mobilizing peasants to take revenge on hated traitors. This initial foray into rural revolution was typically led by county and district cadres; one county leader not far from Long Bow traveled from village to village on horseback to jump-start the campaign.[23] Most of these lower-level cadres were of peasant origin, but when the scope of the rural revolution expanded with the release of the May Fourth Directive, the party increasingly staffed rural work teams with intellectuals (*zhishifenzi*). [24] According to Mao, these bookish types were "subjective and individualistic, impractical in their thinking, and irresolute in action."[25] But the party had a long history of relying on China's educated elite, and many came to the Communists' capital in Yan'an to join the revolution.[26]

Despite the fact that Mao Zedong and most other leading Communists were well educated, the party largely disdained its growing numbers of intellectuals. The Communists had inherited a critical view of China's educated elite from the May Fourth era, and traditional forms of learning were increasingly falling out of fashion in Yan'an.[27] In his 1937 "On Practice" lecture, Mao argued, "The truth of any knowledge or theory is determined not by subjective feelings, but by objective results in social practice. Only social practice can be the criterion of truth."[28] Theoretical knowledge was subordinate to and dependent on engaging the social world through practice. Mao's insistence that the attainment of knowledge was impossible without social practice deprived most educated Chinese of any claim to legitimate knowledge.

Even more troubling for future work team members was the question of political allegiance and the demonstration of loyalty to the new regime. In the parlance of the time, Chinese citizens would have to cultivate a proper class stance. As Liu Shaoqi stressed in his 1939 lecture "How to Be a Good Communist," class stance could be acquired only through revolutionary practice, not study.[29] One could memorize the Marxist canon, but one could not truly side with the masses without personally taking part in revolution. Liu Shaoqi heavily criticized those who believed that the theory and method of Marxist-Leninism could be learned solely through book study, warning that "without a firm proletarian stand and pure proletarian ideals it is impossible for anyone thoroughly to understand or master the science of Marxism-Leninism."[30] In early 1942, a mass study campaign forcefully demanded that intellectuals living in the party's base areas adopt the political standpoint of the proletariat.[31] By the start of the party's campaigns to implement agrarian revolution, Chinese intellectuals understood that there were few better ways to express their loyalty to the party than by actively siding with the peasantry in class struggle, adding practice to theory.

With the start of the Civil War in 1946, the Communists reaffirmed that intellectuals had a place within their political coalition, even as the party continued to highlight Mao's dismissive views of the group. In practice, the party's policies on the educated elite were largely shaped by their ongoing military conflict with the Nationalists: the Communists applauded agitation against Generalissimo Chiang Kai-shek throughout China while also welcoming the thousands who fled to the base areas.[32] Despite huge challenges, China's educated elite who joined work teams played a pivotal role in bringing Mao's vision of agrarian revolution to life. Furthermore, through participation in land reform and other mass rural campaigns, these work team members were to be reborn through the fire of revolutionary practice. Just as land reform promised to transform farmers into class-conscious revolutionary peasants, so too were team members to be reborn as they helped implement rural revolution.

Intellectuals joined rural work teams in droves. Of the thirteen team members in David and Isabel Crook's account of a 1947 campaign in Ten

Mile Inn, a small village in North China, for example, ten were intellectuals. And while team leader Lou Lin was a peasant cadre, his southern accent and shy demeanor limited his ability to run the campaign: the team leader worked behind the scenes while intellectuals ran the show. Although all the team members, mostly journalists, took part in visiting and organizing the poor, the Crooks singled out two intellectuals as being particularly skilled campaigners. The first, Geng Xi, was best at communicating difficult ideas to villagers. Using a "simple question-and-answer technique," Geng expertly explained new concepts and subtly influenced peasant opinion. As a result, the work team selected him to chair the village peasant association.[33] Even more impressive was Leng Bing, by trade a reporter but now expertly implementing rural revolution. This included the delicate task of educating local cadres in thirteen days of closed-door meetings, rehabilitating dozens of villagers who had been falsely accused of various political crimes, and eventually reorganizing the party branch.[34] Leng's grasp on the campaign even exceeded that of the team leader; in a significant disagreement over the nature of local cadres, the party judged Leng's more conciliatory views correct.[35]

The Communists mobilized educated party members in force following the release of the May Fourth Directive. In the Taihang Mountain base area, the directive led to the July Handan Conference, where the call went out for the mass mobilization of cadres to carry out land to the tiller.[36] The PLA's rapid push into the Northeast created an even greater demand for work team cadres, with the Northeast Bureau calling for a surge (*rechao*) of cadres to descend on villages.[37] Over twelve thousand responded to the call, and for the vast majority, as much as 80 percent, this was their baptism in the fires of rural revolution.[38] The Northeast Bureau initially found these urban revolutionaries harboring "ideological errors" and therefore deficient. Work team members, infatuated (*milian*) with the pleasures of city life, were instructed to discard their leather shoes, don peasant clothes, and go to the countryside.[39] With few experienced cadres in the field, work team members were given crash course training sessions with limited reading material, mainly consisting of Mao Zedong's two 1933 articles on rural class structures. Despite later reports of these cadres collecting a "great harvest" in land reform, their quick training hampered work team efforts. Some teams, largely composed of office workers and young students, made the mistake of moving in with village landlords, and as a result they were blamed for taking pity on their hosts and giving them both newly opened lands and the fruits of struggle. New cadres were also accused of abusing their positions for private gain through corruption and embezzlement.[40] Work team members in the Northeast eventually totaled some twenty thousand, but with 40 million living in the region, teams had to rush from village to village, hurrying through land reform in as quickly as a week.[41]

At the other end of the spectrum was the work team organized by the Central China Bureau under Li Jianzhen and Wang Wen. The bureau work team, active during the first summer of land to the tiller, carried out a "proper" (*zhengque*) land reform that was popularized as an example for future work team members. Deng Zihui praised Li and Wang, declaring that their experiences perfectly demonstrated the need for land reform and proving that anyone who failed to support the campaigns blocked China's march to independence, peace, and democracy. Deng lambasted such doubters as the "sinners of the revolution" (*geming de zuiren*). While he heaped accolades on the team, he also made sure to note how these "outside cadres" relied on respected village cadres who understood local realities.[42] With growing land-to-the-tiller experience, base areas continued to organize training conferences for work team members, with thousands of cadres meeting for weeks, or even months, as they prepared for land equalization campaigns. The Yetao training meeting, held in in the heart of the Taihang region, for example, lasted eighty-six days and involved over seventeen hundred cadres.[43] During these meetings, party leaders, stressing the importance of class division, again distributed copies of Mao's two 1933 articles on rural classes. These articles, edited by party central to eliminate references to "leftist" mistakes of giving no land to landlords and low-quality land to rich peasants, would serve as guides for the division of rural classes.[44]

During training for land equalization campaigns, work teams members were instructed that because previous land-to-the-tiller campaigns had failed, agrarian revolution would have to begin anew. Just as the new land law was released, Nie Rongzhen, a leading commander in North China, told about one thousand cadres that land reform carried out in the aftermath of the May Fourth Directive had been botched by "rightist" errors, leaving class enemies in power and damaging the war effort.[45] By the following year, investigations into the results of land reform had resulted in widespread "leftist" deviations, requiring "reexamination" campaigns.[46] On February 22, 1948, party central again announced that the results of early attempts at land reform had largely failed and called for new campaigns to correct past mistakes. In some places, land reform had been successful, but in many villages, landlords and rich peasants still had more than average landholdings. Elsewhere, land reform had failed, leaving the forces of feudalism dominant.[47] As a result, another army of work teams fanned out through the countryside to repeat the process of land reform anew. With each new round of land reform, the rural experiences of work team members accumulated, ironically creating new problems. In the Northwest, Xi Zhongxun noted that cadres sent down to the countryside were often dogmatic, forcing methods learned in established base areas in newly won territories, too proud to admit that they did not understand shifting local realities.[48]

Land reform was temporarily sidelined during the height of the Civil War in summer 1948, but as victory neared the following year, party leaders prepared their largest mobilization of work teams. This started with the training of rural cadres and activists. In Hebei, for example, the provincial party oversaw a series of land reform conferences, training thousands of rural cadres and tens of thousands of village activists in 1949. But the massive scale of land reform demanded the active participation of the educated elite living in newly liberated cities. This was partly due to problems with rural cadres; "not a small number" of the cadres educated at party schools in Hebei, for example, refused to take part in land reform outside their home villages. Some of these reluctant cadres had children or elderly parents at home to take care of, but many simply feared that they would be permanently transferred far from home. One such party school cadre noted, "I have three roads, one leads to the hospital, one leads home, the other leads to land reform, and if I do land reform I will most likely end up dead."[49]

As the Communists formally came to power in 1949, the new government called students and teachers to join the revolution by taking part in short-course schools, where they were to be inculcated in party ideology, including the need for land reform. In Beijing, China's educational capital, roughly twelve thousand participated in these programs.[50] According to Chen Tiqiang, who held an Oxford PhD and was teaching in the Qinghua Politics Department, a revolutionary study fever broke out following the arrival of Communist power in Beijing. During that year, Chen was one of many who learned to speak about "Marxism-Leninism's stance, viewpoint, and method."[51] Because study was not enough to prove loyalty to the masses, he and thousands of others would supplement traditional learning with revolutionary practice in the countryside. And it was not just Beijing-area students and teachers who were to be mobilized. The party's planned offensive on rural society demanded a massive recruitment of work team members for the final and largest rounds of land reform: during summer 1950, some 180,000 were in training to join work teams.[52] The following year, Du Runsheng, the Communist leader perhaps most identified with PRC-era land reform, oversaw the mobilization of another 100,000 work team members. These team members, mostly newcomers to rural revolution, would undertake land reform in the massive six-province South Central region, home to 130 million villagers. Beijing, Tianjin, Hankou, provincial assemblies, and democratic parties also sent work teams to take part in Du's land reform.[53] When land reform was finally complete, the leaders of the South Central China region boasted of having mobilized 545,742 work team members.[54]

During these PRC-era campaigns, only about 10 percent of work team members had experience in established base areas. Students, teachers, and other educated members of society formed the bulk of the work teams.[55] Many, especially students, had strong ties to families now considered class enemies. The pages of *China Youth* were filled with articles addressing the problem of family ties to newly labeled class enemies. The Youth League instructed members to "take a firm stand" and side with the laboring masses in the countryside by "thoroughly and completely implementing land reform."[56]

To be sure, PRC-era land reform work teams enjoyed several advantages when compared to the teams that had roamed the countryside dividing the land during the Civil War. The party's grip over rural China was growing stronger by the day, and preparatory campaigns had identified powerful landlords, redistributed some wealth, and established peasant associations. Despite these advantages, teams typically assumed that feudal power was strong and suspected that peasant organizations were in need of reorganization. Cheng Houzhi, a recent graduate of Qinghua's Politics Department, thus argued that before land reform, peasants were bereft of political awareness and "lack organization, lack strength, and do not dare to consider landlords as enemies." While this belief was in line with the land reform narrative's depiction of Chinese villages as feudal strongholds, teams discovered real challenges. Some local cadres conspired to protect their landlords from outsiders.[57] And work teams might encounter danger

IMAGE 3. Map visualizing the number of Chinese citizens mobilized for land reform work teams in the six provinces of the South Central region. Source: *Zhongnan tudi gaige de weida shengli*, 99.

while in the field: the team sent to Five Mile Bridge in late 1949 had to help organize a militia to fend off two bandit attacks on the village.[58]

Increased mobilization of urban intellectuals for land reform dovetailed perfectly with the party's effort at thought reform (*sixiang gaizao*). This ideological campaign, launched in late September 1951, focused on the educated elite and attacked pro-Western views in a renewed attempt to enforce ideological purity. In January of the following year, the Ministry of Education required all Chinese universities and high schools to carry out thought

IMAGE 4. Students at Zhonghua University in Wuchang prepare to bring Mao's revolution to the countryside. Source: *Zhongnan tudi gaige de weida shengli*, 98.

reform among teachers and staff through textual study, confessions, and criticism.[59] As a supplement to this study, many educated Chinese, including thousands of teachers and students from China's top universities, joined land reform work teams. Ma Xulun, minister of education, went as far as to compare land reform to the old imperial exam system that had once served as the pathway to officialdom for the literati elite. He told students and teachers, "The test for the 'number one scholar' happened once every three years, but land reform is difficult to meet in one thousand years."[60] Yang Rengeng, a Peking University professor, used his experience on a land reform work team to push his students to follow in his footsteps: "When I give my classes a report on my impression of land reform, I emphasize that peasants are waiting for their help."[61] Preparing urban citizens to carry out land reform, the party published a flood of materials on the campaigns, ensuring that the final and largest rounds of land reform were carried out by teams well versed in the narrative of peasant emancipation through fierce class struggle. Future team members were explicitly instructed to read the land reform novels of Ding Ling and Zhou Libo as part of their training. Potential work team members also flocked to land reform exhibits where they saw visual narratives of the campaigns: images of evil landlords, revolutionary struggle, and liberated peasants. But once drafted into work teams, would they be able to make Mao's vision of the countryside a reality?

What work teams found when they arrived in the countryside was widespread suspicion. Rumors swirled, casting doubt on the very nature of land reform. In the Northeast, one rumor went, work teams had massacred landlords and tenants alike so that there would be enough land for the survivors. Another rumor held that the Communists, having racked up a huge debt to the Soviet Union during their many years of fighting the Nationalists, would confiscate the grain that peasants harvested from their newly obtained fields. The most spectacular threat must have been the possibility of a renewed world war, but much more menacing was the idea that class struggle would inevitably engulf the entire village community.[62] With rumors still questioning the party's true intentions, inexperienced urban work team members faced a daunting task, especially when the expanding scope of land reform stretched experienced revolutionaries too thin. In Changshou County on the outskirts of Chongqing, for example, one district had only two experienced cadres overseeing work teams staffed by recently recruited students. With only ten days of study before being sent to the countryside, these students had difficulty establishing peasant associations and educating local leaders. As a result, landlords sent their underlings, colloquially known as running dogs (*zou gou*) and adopted sons (*gan erzi*), to turn villagers against the work team. According to one running dog, "Those government folk are all outsiders, relying on them and doing things for them is no good, and after all we are all neighbors."[63]

The situation in nearby Hechuan was even worse. There, urban work team members were deemed in need of "education, help, and control" if they had any hope of working with villagers. Team leaders were advised to keep a close eye on their charges and "not allow them to make irresponsible remarks." The advice was wise, given the shocking things visiting team members had said to Hechuan locals. One told a rich peasant that "not touching the land you farm yourselves is too kind, if you don't speak truthfully with us you will be struggled right alongside the landlords." One work team, misunderstanding the party's policy of relying on poor peasants and hired hands while uniting with middle peasants so that all could obtain liberation, instead created this slogan: "Poor peasants and hired hands find liberation (*fanshen*), while the middle peasants help." And as expected, some work team members were said to have an improper class stance, which led to confusion during the campaigns. One team, for example, held a meeting for landlords and announced that in the past, peasants had been "too left" and that the team now believed that "landlords are willing to be enlightened." Emboldened, village landlords praised the work team and claimed hardships that rightfully belonged to the poor. Or as it was framed in the new rhetoric of land reform, these crafty landlords "spoke the peasants' bitter water (*kushui*)."[64] The task of mobilizing the poor overwhelmed some work teams. One team in Guangdong had to rely on an enlightened member of the gentry to help them reach the poor. This team was heavily criticized, as was a team that used a gun to force Hunan peasants to speak bitterness.[65]

Dispatched throughout a vast and diverse countryside, work teams formed the army that implemented Mao's vision of rural revolution. Yet intellectuals writing about their experiences would typically downplay their own importance in carrying out these campaigns, choosing instead to emphasize how they had been transformed by engaging in revolutionary practice. Working within the limited discursive space available under party rule, intellectuals maintained that this transformation was necessary because "intellectuals" were a problematic social group with suspect class origins and a legacy of book learning. For these educated elites, real change could be accomplished only by securing a proper class stance through revolutionary practice. By becoming one with the peasantry, working with rural cadres, and engaging in class struggle against landlords, intellectuals declared themselves changed. Yet by insisting on the transformative power of observing and participating in agrarian revolution, these reports would ironically help essentialize "intellectuals" along the lines suggested by the party: as suspect members of society who, left to their own devices, would be a reactionary force.

Feng Youlan, China's preeminent expert on philosophy, had a typical approach to the problem of class loyalty, clearly identifying himself as not of the landlord class but still admitting that "the emotion that I felt for the landlord class in my youth still lurked in my heart."[66] Education was no cure for these emotions. Qinghua's Chen Zhenzhou, a specialist in composition and rhetoric, had imbibed the revolutionary education that swept through Chinese universities during the early days of the PRC, but wrote of still harboring uncertain class loyalties. Chen understood the lessons of his revolutionary courses, which taught the critical importance of standing on the side of the masses, but emotions were impervious to theory. He admitted "always considering things from the perspective of my family" and not from the perspective of the masses.[67] Feng Kexi, an academic involved in the Democratic League, a political party that had once seemed to offer an alternative to the Communists and the Nationalists, noted just how contaminating the culture of the class enemy had been for those hoping to transform themselves through rural revolution: "Regardless of being a landlord or not, by living in a feudal traditional culture, our ideology, emotions, and consciousness were all jumbled up. Because of this, we thought: most landlords are bad, but some are good."[68] Or as professor of sociology Yuan Fang wrote, during their initial visit to the countryside to help carry out land reform, he and other intellectuals still had "their original class characteristics, such as pitying landlords and viewing problems abstractly."[69]

As Yuan Fang's assessment suggests, suspect class loyalties were only half of the problem. First, just as Mao had postulated, intellectuals admitted to thinking of issues and approaching problems in an abstract and not sufficiently practical manner. Sun Zhizhong, then finishing his graduate work at Qinghua, noted how he and other "bookish intellectuals" at first had difficulty in implementing land reform, while Dang Qiaoxin, who took part in land reform in the Chongqing area, only hated landlords in an abstract manner.[70] Chen Tiqiang, who held an Oxford PhD and was then teaching in the Qinghua Politics Department, argued that the study of Confucian philosophy encouraged intellectuals to feel sympathy for the landlord class, which intellectuals mistakenly saw as worthy of pity.[71]

Besides their humanistic, idealistic, and reformist tendencies, intellectuals also held themselves accountable for hubris and denying the authority of those who now seemed destined to lead society. Wang Xuan, who held a Cornell PhD and was teaching international law at Peking University, noted that he had to "cast off the stinky airs of an intellectual" before he could engage in land reform work.[72] Dang Qiaoxin started his land reform report with much stronger language, admitting that he had trouble accepting a new social position below rural area cadres, whom he playfully derided as country bumpkins (*tubaozi*): "Why does the Communist Party always say that urban petty bourgeois intellectuals are like this or like that, always discussing our shortcomings? Perhaps it is because they fear that 'country bumpkins' cannot lead us, so they first want to beat out our bluster?"[73]

Suffering from suspect class loyalties and the problematic ways of thinking, intellectuals such as Dang Qiaoxin were in need of change, a process that started with study. But intellectuals on party work teams would follow Mao's understanding of knowledge and insist that while theoretical study was important, traditional learning was no substitute for revolutionary practice. Critically, in his report on land reform, Feng Youlan argued that by uniting with the peasant masses in land reform, his theoretical understanding of Marxist theory became a true understanding of class exploitation. Feng thus stressed the transformative effects of engaging in revolutionary practice during land reform. While studying Marxist theory had not been enough to change him, Feng argued that participating in land reform led him to identify with the peasantry rather than his landlord family.[74] According to Feng, class stance could only be obtained through revolutionary practice and thus could not be "faked." Or as Chen Tiqiang argued, only through revolutionary practice could an "intellectual" be complete. Noting that "Chairman Mao has said that those intellectuals who do not have the knowledge of struggle can only be called 'half intellectuals,'" he argued that only through the fierce struggle of land reform would intellectuals complete their mastery of stance, viewpoint, and method.[75]

The idea that petit bourgeois intellectuals were suspect due to ties with the landlord class was widely accepted. As college student Meng Gang argued, intellectuals such as himself were in the process of climbing out of the "mud" of old China, and "having some contamination from landlord class mud is expected and not at all out of the ordinary." Meng also stressed that students were not landlords because they relied on their mental labor, and because they were not members of the landlord class, land reform could change them. Again, revolutionary practice was essential for true transformation, for while he took part in revolutionary activities at school, little had changed. Only by spending six months in the countryside was Meng able to overcome his "petite bourgeoisie and intellectual airs."[76]

The difficulties that students from landlord families faced during land reform are perhaps best encapsulated in a letter written in 1951 by Zheng Huiren, a university student and Youth League member.[77] Zheng wrote to the editors of *China Youth* asking for advice concerning his relationship with his landlord father, who had fled his village as land reform approached. According to his letter, Zheng initially supported land reform but had believed that the campaign could be carried out without harming his father, an elderly and caring man. After being exposed to land reform propaganda, however, he had second thoughts: "I realized I had to use a class perspective when looking at these questions. Looking at problems from the perspective of the peasant class is very different than looking at problems from the perspective of the landlord class."[78]

Zheng Huiren recalled instances when his father had done "evil things" and wrote a letter to the peasant association reporting his father's whereabouts and alias, but his choice of political correctness over family loyalties left him conflicted. He confided to the editors:

> I was thinking, my father is quite elderly, and he has always been so good to me and my brothers, working day and night just to earn a bit more money to make our lives better, providing for us so we could go to school. And now to make my father return so that he can be struggled and suffer, while I am here, so fortunate to be in school, is this right? What if I am with my father and he asks me: "I raised you, spilled blood and tears for you, always thinking of you, and now you do this, now you treat me like this?" How can I respond to this?

Zheng turned to the editors for advice, for, as he admitted, "I know that many of my ideas are incorrect, but I just cannot understand where the errors lie, and there are so many questions I cannot figure out."[79]

The editors of *China Youth*, in publishing this letter, called for readers to send in their responses to Zheng Huiren's probing questions. The editors prefaced the letter with four sets of discussion questions, which served to suggest appropriate responses. The first set of questions implied that all landlord wealth was derived from exploitation; the second set stressed the importance of struggle in the division of the land; the third set, which ran the longest, focused on the proper relationship between landlord parents and their children. The final set, in comparison, was composed of one question, asking for the basis of Zheng's erroneous thinking. Over the next few issues, the journal published 46 letters from a total of 1,315 they received from their readers, all of which duly criticized Zheng Huiren for empathizing with a class enemy.[80]

Many of these letters also served as a forum for students to emphasize how they had learned to stand with the peasantry and see their parents as class enemies. A Qinghua student from a landlord family claimed that all landlords were evil, and as a result he "resolutely supports land reform and forsakes my landlord family."[81] A classmate noted that the Zheng Huiren case was a popular topic discussion on campus; he argued that his parents may have helped his education, but only because they wanted him to become a rich official. Therefore, his father's emotions could not be considered "real" and Zheng should forsake his own parents.[82] A People's University student referenced his time on a land reform work team, when he helped organize peasants in speak bitterness meetings, an experience that caused him to "mentally and emotionally feel the righteousness of land reform" as he stood firmly with the peasant masses.[83] The *China Youth* editors concluded in their final remarks on the case that young intellectuals from landlord backgrounds could be considered part of the people, but only if they "willingly turned their backs on their landlord families."[84]

In late 1949, Dong Shijin, China's leading agronomist, penned a letter to Mao Zedong, urging him to halt land reform. Boldly challenging Mao's sacrosanct views of rural society, he used his expertise in agriculture to argue that land reform would hurt production and demoralize landowners. Recognizing that poor peasants strived to become landlords, Dong denied the moral superiority of poor peasants and called on Mao to protect landlords and other village elites. Ignored, Dong eventually fled to the United States.[85] His was a rare voice. Most educated Chinese, well aware of the problem of rural poverty, welcomed land reform. Shao Yanxiang was one such figure. A poet and longtime supporter of the Communists and Sun Yat-sen's call to give land to the tiller, Shao eagerly joined a work team in 1951, eventually journeying to the far Northwest. He was assigned to Gansu, a poor province where nearly 8 million villagers awaited land reform work teams. Before departing, Shao and his fellow revolutionaries gathered in Beijing's Zhongshan Park on October 10, the second anniversary of the founding of the PRC. There, not far from Tiananmen, they heard An Ziwen, party central's organization chief, reminded his audience that while work teams had to rely on the poorest villagers to lead land reform, as outsiders they would have the utmost difficulty in organizing them. Any poor peasants who approached the team, An claimed, were most likely self-interested ruffians or operating at the behest of class enemies. The honest working poor would never seek out work teams. Two weeks later, Shao boarded a train for the countryside, nervous and feeling as if he was "overlooking an abyss or walking on thin ice."[86] Shao's trepidation was unsurprising. Party leaders had admonished Shao and other work team cadres that they had to guard against "the erroneous tendency of going too far" while at the same time "never pouring water on the masses."[87]

Shao, dismissing tales of rural violence as Nationalist rumors, had good reason to join his work team. Familiar with the party's various land laws and an avid fan of land reform novels, he fully supported the campaign to liberate the rural masses. Taking part in agrarian revolution offered an opportunity for Chinese citizens like him to quickly find accommodation with the Communist Party, which desperately needed the active participation of intellectuals and other urbanites if the campaigns were to be successfully completed. As work team members, they played a crucial role in organizing and mobilizing peasants for the complex task of agrarian revolution. And by joining a work team, intellectuals were able to engage in revolutionary practice and distance themselves from their past and their families while drawing closer to the party. Siding with peasants in rural revolution, team members believed, proved their political loyalty. After arriving in village China, however, work team members would discover that the next step in agrarian revolution, organizing poor peasants, was no easy task.

ORGANIZING

The Search for Bitterness

Not long after arriving in Nuanshui, Wen Cai's work team called for a meeting of the village's poor peasant league. The time had come to announce the start of land reform. Villagers gathered in a spacious courtyard, the entire crowd abuzz with excitement. But there was also tension in the air, and confusion over just who should be in attendance. The meeting was intended for Nuanshui's poorest, but many of the village's more successful farmers freely roamed the courtyard, curious to learn the work team's intentions. The villagers' intense interest in the formal start of land reform proved to be woefully misguided. The ever-bookish team leader Wen began his speech on the need for land reform in Nuanshui by discussing the history of humankind. Restlessness grew as he waxed poetic on Mao's class system and international politics, leaving villagers utterly bewildered. One militiaman complained that the speech was simply "too cultured." As the speech dragged on, another attendee quipped that before villagers could find liberation, they would have to "sit until our butts are sore."[1] Many fell asleep.

The entire work team knew the meeting had been a total failure and so they made a decision: team members would fan out and engage peasants in private conversations, encouraging the poorest Nuanshui farmers to "speak bitterness." Yang Liang, another intellectual on the work team, paid a visit to Liu Man, a lazy and disaffected poor peasant. As Liu spoke of the relentless bitterness in his life, Yang learned the man had once been a village cadre until he was pushed out of the local party branch by hooligans seeking to protect the scheming landlord Qian Wengui.[2] The team then brought Liu and their other newly cultivated activists together, calling a meeting for nine tenants of the landlord Jiang Shirong. When the assembled peasants' will to confront Jiang wavered, team leader Wen Cai imitated the landlord in a mock run-through of a confrontation. The peasants heatedly argued with their "landlord," but Wen was unmoved until the activists threated him with violence. One screamed: "If you do not hand over the land deeds today, we will beat you to death!"[3] The head of the work team then worried that the activists might be intimidated by the landlord's wife, known locally as a "broken shoe" due to her questionable sexual past. When the poor peasants vowed to curse and beat her as well, the team knew their pupils were ready. Fully enraged, the peasants ran off to confront Jiang and take possession of their land deeds.

Zhang Li had no love for the backward and timid peasantry, and yet as leader of Hanjiatuo's land reform work team, he was required to rely on the villagers he so casually disdained. But as team leader, Zhang noted that in land reform, relying on the masses was balanced by remolding the masses. As he pontificated to his underlings on the work team, they must "enlighten the masses, help the masses, and carry out ideological mobilization."[4] Shortly after arriving in Hanjiatuo, the team quickly called a mass meeting in a large ancestral hall in order to explain the need to carry out land reform. Liu Quan and other team members droned on with round after round of speeches over six long hours. Many peasants, listening to lectures that attempted to explain the historical development of societies, fell asleep.[5] The team did much better after the comrades started the process of visiting the village poor to discuss their bitter and sad lives. Meeting individually with potential activists, team members used casual conversation to "entice" (*youdao*) them to spit out their "bitter water."[6]

In these small group meetings, however, something entirely unexpected happened. The work team was confronted with Hanjiatuo farmers who had no interest in discussing local landlords. They instead spoke of the true source of their bitter water: village cadres who were already corrupted by their newly won power. The most common accusation concerned the recent harvest, when cadres competed to be the first to collect tax payments. As the work team members discovered, Hanjiatuo village cadres cared only about contending for the party's prized "red banner" and went all out pressing villagers for payment. When villagers pushed back, local cadres threatened to punish critics by drafting them to repair public roads. They later simply beat and arrested people at will. The work team, however, ignored complaints about cadre abuses and insisted that villagers refocus their anger on potential landlord targets. As for the peasants' seeming lack of hostility toward landlords, team leader Zhang explained, this was simply a matter of a lack of political awareness. Any member of the work team who was fooled into thinking the peasants did not have animosity toward the landlord class, meanwhile, was "deficient in their understanding of policy."[7] Sufficiently cowed, the comrades on the work team, including Peking University's Liu Quan, dared not question Zhang by believing the peasants of Hanjiatuo.

William Hinton had not yet arrived in Long Bow when village cadres first attempted to organize their neighbors, but his rich account of these first days of rural revolution remains one of the most gripping accounts of that revolution. According to Hinton, the first ever village-wide meeting, called by local activists to struggle a traitorous village head, started with high hopes. This was a rare opportunity for villagers to congregate in a public setting, and the result was nothing less than a festival-like atmosphere, complete with peddlers hawking snacks. Despite widespread excitement and an impassioned speech courtesy of the new village chair, no one dared to speak up and denounce the traitor, even after the village vice chair began thrashing him without mercy. Instead, the assembled peasants "waited fascinated, as if watching a play. They did not realize that in order for the plot to unfold they themselves had to mount the stage and speak out what was on their minds."[8] The Long Bow cadres eventually admitted defeat and called off the struggle, switching their focus to small group meetings where they could properly prepare activists. Peasants who had been unwilling to speak up against a well-known traitor in a mass meeting later met with cadres in small groups. Here they discussed what the hated traitor had done to them in the past and vowed to accuse their tormentor in public.

During the following settling accounts campaign, cadres established Long Bow's first peasant association to oversee attacks on landlords and rich peasants. Having learned their lesson, cadres once again called activists together in small groups in order to gather opinions, assembling a host of peasant accusations concerning future struggle targets.[9] But Hinton's own work team, which arrived months later, was not impressed with any of the organizing work that the local cadres had done. In fact, when Hinton first arrived in Long Bow, he found his new work team armed and agitated. The previous night, Zhang Qu'er, a peasant cadre serving on the team, had been targeted for assassination. Zhang, an experienced guerrilla fighter in his early twenties, had been walking alone after dark when an unknown assailant attacked him from behind, choked him unconscious, and nearly succeeded in throwing him down a nearby well. The team was never able to ascertain who the mysterious assassin might be. Many Long Bow peasants declared that Yulai, a corrupt cadre, was behind the plot against the work team. Yulai and his son were locked up, but the team suspected that the forces of counterrevolution ran deep in Long Bow.

Under the direction of team leader Hou the team shut down all mass organizations, leaving Long Bow without a working government or even a party branch. These actions were in line with the dictates of the county government, which had declared that previous attempts at organizing the poor had failed: landlords and rich peasants still ruled the countryside. The work team agreed, and did not even bother to investigate local conditions in Long Bow. Had not Mao declared the countryside a hotbed of feudal reaction? Had not Zhang Qu'er nearly been murdered in cold blood? The process of rural revolution would have to begin anew. Calling a mass meeting for the poorest Long Bow peasants, the team promised that all would now find economic prosperity: the land was to be divided equally among all villagers.[10] These poor farmers were the "basic elements" needed to start a new peasant organization, where a new round of class determination would take place. Only then could the team attempt to redo land reform in Long Bow.

Many years later, long after the publication of his opus *Fanshen*, William Hinton returned to Long Bow to catch up with old friends and see what had become of the village that he had made famous. The attempted assassination of Zhang Qu'er had never been solved. His work team had repeatedly investigated the assault, but could muster only circumstantial evidence against Yulai and his son as they sat in county lockup. Many who spoke up against the two men had an axe to grind. Long Bow cadres, meanwhile, were positive that the village's Catholic minority, chafing under party rule, lay behind the assassination attempt.[11] County leadership later criticized the team for arresting the two men and had them released, angering the still wounded Zhang Qu'er.[12] Returning to the village during the Cultural

Revolution, Hinton discovered that not everything in Long Bow was as it seemed: Zhang Qu'er, fearing the party would transfer him, had staged the entire event to ensure he remained home in Shanxi.[13] The work team, predisposed to believe the worst about rural society, had fallen for the charade without a second thought.

The army of work teams dispatched by the Chinese Communist Party during the years of agrarian revolution aimed not just to redistribute land but to utterly transform village societies. Local elites, vilified as representatives of the old feudal realm, were to be forcibly brought down and replaced by a new order led by formerly impoverished peasants. But work teams, following in the footsteps of victorious PLA armies, did not arrive in an untouched feudal countryside. Even before the arrival of the Communists' armed forces, underground party activists visited their neighbors in the secrecy of night, attempting to win them over to the cause.[14] Villages in the base areas established during the war against Japan had witnessed years of mass campaigns. When the territory under Communist control expanded with the PLA's military successes, cadres fanned out and helped bring much-needed order to the countryside. During the war with Japan, most rural violence had been committed by Chinese collaborators, leaving the party many targets.[15] In the Northeast, the party spent months targeting tyrants, bullies, and traitors.[16] In the party's Jin-Cha-Ji base area, the Communists implemented successive campaigns to settle accounts with traitors and reduce rents, beginning the process of remaking the countryside.[17] In Shandong, the party first launched a mass campaign targeting traitors and other local enemies, leading to hundreds of mass meetings and wholesale expropriations. In the aftermath of this campaign, the party lowered rents, distributed grain, and carried out multiple executions in preparation for land reform.[18] In North China's Wugong village, by the time land reform began, rural life had already been profoundly altered by a decade of Communist programs, a "silent revolution" that had eliminated extremes of inequality. Most Wugong men could afford wives, creating a prosperous community of owner-cultivators.[19]

As the lands under party control grew with Civil War victories in early 1948, the party targeted spies, collaborators, Nationalist Party agents, and the largest landlords before allowing work teams to target landlords and rich peasants broadly.[20] Work teams, in fact, were advised to not raise the issue of land reform until villages were free from bandits and order was firmly established.[21] Despite any previous work done locally, however, the Communists trained work teams to assume that feudal power remained strong. Work teams carrying out a second round of land reform in the old base areas, for example, were instructed that up to 80 percent of land was still controlled by class enemies. Because this meant that previous attempts at land reform had failed, local political organizations were assumed to be suspect and required work teams to begin the process of peasant mobilization anew.[22] Party directives spoke of "blank slate villages" (*kongbai cun*) where the masses had yet to be mobilized; tellingly, even some villages in established base areas were declared blank slates where land reform work had to start from scratch.[23] Because these villages were imagined to be insular feudal communities in need of party penetration, land reform reports spoke glowingly of work teams "breaking through" (*tupo*) villages to begin their revolutionary work.[24]

Arriving in what was assumed to be a feudal countryside, the work teams entrusted with bringing agrarian revolution to life sought out "bitterness" (*ku*). According to the Communists, the feudal forces controlling the countryside ensured that a peasant's life was one of "eating bitterness" (*chiku*): the poorer a peasant, the more bitter the life. And because the party declared social advancement impossible under the old regime, peasant bitterness was passed from one generation to the next. As a land reform report penned by two professors from Qinghua University explained, "In the exploitative feudal land holding system, it was impossible to prosper through labor; relying on labor to accumulate wealth and purchase a large quantity of land was even more of a dream."[25] The eternal bitterness of peasants, however, was bottled up and had to be released through the land reform process. This was done through "visiting the poor and asking them about their bitterness" (*fangpin wenku*) and encouraging them to "speak bitterness" (*suku*) in private conversations or in more formal "speak bitterness meetings" (*suku hui*).[26]

Peasant activists would again speak bitterness during struggle meetings, when landlords and other class enemies were confronted with these tales of woe. Under Communist rule, understanding bitterness and being able to speak bitterness became important skills for navigating the rapid changes that agrarian revolution brought to the countryside. As land reform unfolded, the ability to speak bitterness during struggle meetings often resulted in direct economic benefit. Peasants who claimed to have suffered the most feudal exploitation stood to receive a greater share of the fruits of struggle. Speaking bitterness was by no means limited to agrarian revolution. Political campaigns organized for PLA soldiers, for example, made ample use of speaking bitterness to encourage hatred for the Nationalists.[27] But the perceived effectiveness of speaking bitterness for awakening class awareness among Chinese farmers has made the practice synonymous with land reform.

The Communists made no secret that carrying out agrarian revolution was a monumental task. The *People's Daily*, the party's official newspaper, described the difficulty of finishing land reform by resorting to the old idiom: "ninety *li* is merely a half of a hundred *li* journey." In other words, the closer teams came to finishing land reform, the more difficult it became to bring the campaign to a successful completion.[28] But for many work teams, getting land reform started was a frightful challenge. The earliest work teams arrived in village China well versed in Maoist texts, but their training for rural revolution was generally limited to party-scripted outlines that instructed teams to win over poor peasants with broad moral arguments that could be later be directed against class enemies.[29] Many work teams discovered peasants unwilling to meet, to say nothing of truly opening up to outsiders. During the first land-to-the-tiller campaigns following the May Fourth Directive, work teams would also have to reach an accommodation with enlightened gentry and other village elites who had become allies during the long war against Japan. Some village cadres were themselves of landlord origin.[30]

According to the Central China Bureau, party organization was in fact a serious problem in the first round of land reform. Many established party branches were controlled by rich and middle peasants. As the result of impure membership, party branches were hotbeds of corruption and cowardice; many district and village cadres had in fact fled from a Nationalist offensive.[31] Complicating matters were reports of middle peasants who faked their activism in the hopes of material gain.[32] Other work teams were faulted for overlooking local activists. In an example from an early attempt at land reform in the Northwest, villagers had supported Ma Shoucai, a highly respected poor peasant and party member, to head their local poor peasant league. But the work team sent to the village wrongly classified Ma as a middle peasant, making him ineligible even to join the league.[33]

Work teams discovered that at times, even poor peasants proved difficult to mobilize. Party leaders, for example, had to accept that the slogan for the first land reform campaigns, land to the tiller, did not appeal to poor peasants, who could not even afford to rent much land. Others, believing that the protection of the interests of middle peasants meant that little would be distributed, similarly shunned work teams.[34] In established base areas, meanwhile, years of Communist rule had made the need for land reform questionable. Xi Zhongxun noted that work teams arriving in villages in the Northwest in early summer 1948 were surprised to find that villagers were relatively prosperous. These villagers, above all, wanted not land reform but peace and order.[35] In other locales, only the explicit promise of material benefits could persuade villagers to take part in political activism.[36] Even during later rounds of land reform, the mobilization of poor villagers remained a stubborn problem. According to An Ziwen, party central's organization chief, unlike the hooligans and running dog lackeys who sought out work teams, the honest poor would resist organization. This problem was compounded by the ideological backgrounds of most work team members; from petite bourgeoisie backgrounds, they did not fit in with the poor and preferred to seek out more prosperous farmers to serve as local leaders.[37]

Mobilization was further hampered by the threat of retaliation. During the Civil War, villagers carrying out agrarian revolution were risking their lives and had every reason to fear the many rumors of the return of Nationalist forces, especially the "homecoming regiments" (*huanxiangtuan*) attached to the Nationalist army. These units, led by vengeful dispossessed landlords, specialized in recovering villages under Communist control and had a well-earned reputation for carrying out horrific acts of brutality. Some poor activists declared their indifference. One brave peasant brother proclaimed, "The traitors will not return. If they do return, they won't kill me, I will kill them first."[38] But as another peasant later admitted, had the Nationalists and the old order returned, "I think they would have sent us to prison or killed us and returned all the land to the landlords."[39] Villagers were not afraid simply of the Communists; they in fact feared all outsiders and their military forces. Under the threat of forced conscription, they found it best to avoid any entanglement with strangers, even if they came with the promise of free land.[40] Well after the founding of the PRC, when the party's land reform campaigns concluded in the far Southwest, villagers were still fearful of the return of the Nationalists, in no small part because of the soldiers and bandits holed up in mountain hideouts.[41] For the party, however, peasant resistance to land reform served as proof of the feudal nature of the countryside and served only to validate agrarian revolution.[42]

After arriving in target villages, work team members during the first land reform campaigns preached a message of unity and order, seeking to tamp down fear and draw distinctions between the Communists and the representatives of the old order, be they Nationalist officials or imperialist collaborators. This message found broad appeal among middle and even rich peasants. These village mainstays had long been part of the Communists' broad class coalition during the fight against Japan, and many local cadres prized their agricultural production and economic contributions to the Communist cause.[43] Many villages in North China lacked a truly dominant elite, and the long war against Japan had served to unify villagers from different lineages and social strata in patriotic resistance. As land reform progressed, however, teams quickly focused on the mobilization of the bottom rungs of rural society. Solidarity would have to give way to class struggle. When land reform came to villages in established base areas, families that had supported the resistance against Japan and enlisted sons in the Communists' primary military force, the famed Eighth Route Army, might find themselves labeled as class enemies.[44] But as one directive in the first summer of land to the tiller emphasized, mobilizing the poor was the key to fierce struggle, which would calm middle peasants, neutralize rich peasants, and isolate landlords. To divide the land without fully mobilizing the poor was land reform "only in name, not reality."[45] And because these first land reform campaigns coincided with a Nationalist offensive into the base areas, party leaders such as Deng Zihui increasingly turned to the poorest villagers for support. Unlike middle peasant cadres who feared the return of landlord power and dared not engage in struggle, the poor had "nothing to lose" (*bu pa sunshi*) and were resolute activists. Praising the Central China Bureau work team for understanding that "finding and winning over activists" was the essential first step in starting land reform, Deng noted how the team had bypassed village leaders, mostly middle peasants, and instead relied on a core of poor activists in the party branch and peasant association.[46]

The party's first attempts at agrarian revolution proved how difficult it would be to organize China's rural poor. In the Northeast, thousands of cadres fanned out through the countryside during the first summer of land to the tiller. Outwardly, their efforts appeared an unqualified success. According to the Northeast Bureau's assessment that autumn, everything appeared to be in order, with land divided and peasant associations and militias founded throughout the region. Closer investigation, however, revealed "huge" problems and "very little" in terms of accomplishments. Land reform, the bureau concluded, was "half-cooked" due to a failure to properly mobilize the masses. Peasants, no fans of the activists trained by work teams, may have appeared fierce during struggle, but afterward they turned "cold and cheerless." The bureau, noting that it was impossible to carry out land reform quickly, demanded that work teams slow down and take the time to "ferment and ripen" the masses.[47] As the war progressed toward victory, meanwhile, work teams faced a new challenge, as cadres from North China were unfamiliar with rural realties in newly won territories. The East China Bureau, advising work team members in spring 1949, suggested organizers take a slow approach to rural revolution, perhaps finding young rural intellectuals and enlightened gentry to serve as local cadres.[48]

One of the first steps for any newly arrived land reform team was to hold a village meeting to announce the start of land reform. Ideally this would be done using simple language so that villagers might comprehend the need for land reform, how the campaign would be carried out, as well as what might be expected from them during this tumultuous time. But the party found such large gatherings of limited use. The Crooks, observing land reform in Ten Mile Inn, attended a mass meeting to announce the Outline Land Law of 1947. The main purpose of this meeting, which was open to all but those already deemed struggle targets, was to introduce the work team and underground local cadres to the village. The work team also discussed policy, but admitted afterward that many of the villagers had probably not understood their manifesto.[49] Members of the team were not too concerned because they already understood the importance of mobilizing peasants in small group meetings. The party trained work teams to first "visit the poor and ask about their bitterness" before carrying out class struggle. Understanding local conditions, these outsiders could then take root (*zhagen*) among the peasant masses, ideally by carrying out the three togethers: living, eating, and working together. Taking root in the countryside, work team members decoded the complex web of village relationships that they were to reframe in terms of Maoist classes.[50] Just

IMAGE 5. Establishing ties (*chuanlian*) with potential activists. Source: *Zhongnan tudi gaige de weida shengli*, 109.

as important, team members forged personal relationships, linking new class statuses with personal emotional bonds with the poor peasants they would need to lead through the crucible of ritualistic struggle.[51] This was not a simple process. Work teams, staffed with intellectuals believed to be hampered by obstructions (*zu'ai*) that made working with poor peasants and hired hands difficult, were easy to take advantage of. Corrupt village leaders could even direct work teams to "their people" to ensure that their secrets would remain confined to the village.[52]

The production and mass publication of land reform novels enshrined the importance of establishing connections with the rural downtrodden in the party's narrative for agrarian revolution, providing organizational models for work team members. In Zhou Libo's *The Hurricane*, a fictionalized account of his time in land reform in the Northeast, one of the work team's first allies was Zhao Yulin, known locally as "Bare-Assed Zhao" due to the fact that he was so poor that his family of three owned only a single pair of pants.[53] This pitiful condition deeply embarrassed Zhao, but his extreme poverty made him the ideal peasant activist. The party thus heaped praise on poor activists such as Li Aiji, whose politicization was due to a land

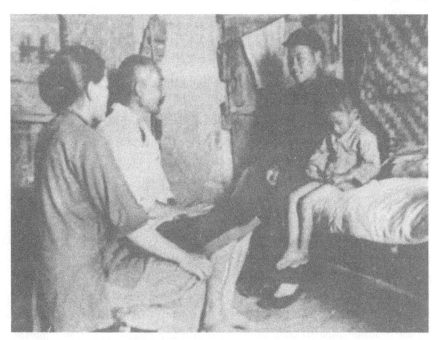

IMAGE 6. A work team member takes root (*zhagen*) among the peasant masses.
Source: *Zhongnan tudi gaige de weida shengli*, 108.

reform work team that had ignored rich peasants and the machinations of
landlord running dogs, and insisted on taking root among villagers such
as Li: "peasants who were missing teeth, had dirty homes, and talked as if
they were totally ignorant."[54] Small group meetings were also important for
educating village cadres, typically new to land reform themselves. The hope
was that reading articles concerning land reform, including instructions on
determining class statuses, would help avoid the common problems of forcing land reform and not trusting the masses.[55]

After identifying and taking root among potential activists, work teams
brought these future activists together in speak bitterness meetings, small
group settings where poor farmers were encouraged to discuss their frustrations and anger. Because many peasants were loath to publicly denounce
village elites, these meetings were essential to land reform. Such was the
case with Bao Yilin, a peasant militiaman. Far from militant, Bao later admitted that he felt guilty after struggling a village landlord who in the past
had treated him with kindness. According to Bao, despite the assurances of
local party leaders, forcing the kind landlord onto a village stage and curs-

ing him did not seem "fair."[56] For wavering activists such as Bao, speaking bitterness became an essential moment in rural revolution, useful for directing general peasant frustration and anger against newly identified class enemies. Once peasants were able to articulate their bitterness in small group settings, work teams focused their collective anger onto village landlords by suggesting how peasant bitterness was the direct result of landlord exploitation. As one report on the first year of land reform in North China colorfully explained, speaking bitterness allowed peasants to realize that the root of their poverty lay in the "blood-sucking devils" who lived alongside them. They would further realize that there were only two last names in the world: Rich (*Fu*) and Poor (*Qiong*). This knowledge, produced through speaking bitterness, led directly to action.[57] But speaking bitterness was not simply about generating anger and violence. Though the process of speaking bitterness, villagers narrated their lives within the context of the land reform campaign, making rural revolution meaningful on a personal level.[58] Decades of suffering and hardship were not simply a matter of fate but had an identifiable cause in class oppression and exploitation. As this suggests, work teams used speaking bitterness to reframe rural wealth. Because peasants had witnessed their neighbors' fortunes rise and fall over the years, many tenants accepted landownership as legitimate: hard work led to prosperity, while lazy famers sank into poverty. Through small group meetings, work teams endeavored to convince peasants that wealth and owning an excess of land was possible only through exploitation and thus was in fact an act of injustice.[59]

During these one-to-one and small group meetings, work team cadres taught Chinese farmers the new language of revolution, a process most captured vividly in land reform novels. In *The Hurricane*, for example, long impoverished Bare-Assed Zhao told Little Wang, a work team intellectual, of his desire to "fight until the end" (*gan daodi*), even if it meant sacrificing himself. While pleased with the sentiment, Little Wang corrected Zhao, instructing his peasant pupil to instead properly say that he would "carry the revolution through till the end" (*geming daodi*).[60] The educational value of these meetings was immense. In Zhou's tale of rural revolution, team leaders gave reports concerning the need for land reform, but they also told stories about Chairman Mao, the party, and the army's many successes in the war against the Japanese invasion. The affable intellectual Liu Sheng

IMAGE 7. A peasant woman speaks bitterness (*suku*). Source: *Zhongnan tudi gaige de weida shengli*, 109.

taught activists songs in praise of the party, including some drawn from popular land reform operas. During these meetings, peasants went through a "fermenting" process that armed them with organization, backbone, preparation, and assignments. Even the unlikely activist Old Sun had mastered the new vocabulary of land reform, telling his group: "Are we not following the revolutionary line? If we are following the revolutionary line, and see that the revolution is about to succeed, yet we still are full of fear, what kind of ideology is that?"[61]

As skillfully deployed by land reform work teams, speaking bitterness was essential in organizing farmers and spreading Communist power in the countryside. Work team members were instructed to "speak matters of the heart" in order to "use bitterness to draw out bitterness, connect bitterness with bitterness" (*yi ku yin ku, ku lian ku*). They also publicly displayed landlord property in "fruit exhibitions" (*zhanlan guoshi*) so that peasants could "point at objects and speak bitterness" (*zhiwu suku*), comparing their own pathetic existences to the easy lives of the landlord class.[62] Work team members shaped vague memories and a lifetime of rural hardship into concrete memories of detailed acts of exploitation and cruelty. They accomplished this during small group meetings by encouraging villagers to carefully rethink past events, turning impressions of repetitive acts into specific instances of bitterness, fundamentally altering how villagers thought of their neighbors and the past itself.[63]

Speaking bitterness with work teams, villagers were explicitly taught to reformulate their relationships with their neighbors. Social distinctions could be found in every village community. Some farmers had more property than their neighbors. Others were disliked for personal or moral reasons. Kinship and friendship networks overlapped in complex ways. All of these differences, under the guidance of visiting work teams, were reworked into a Maoist class system of moral peasants and exploitative landlords.[64] Furthermore, attending small group meetings marked activists as emerging village leaders; those denied entrance, conversely, were potential class enemies.[65] Speaking bitterness against class enemies, finally, helped generate anger while limiting potential feelings of sympathy and therefore helping legitimize the violence to come.[66]

Were work teams merely providing a forum for the poor and downtrodden to vent long-bottled-up frustrations, or were they coercing villagers to falsify complaints about potential struggle targets? Accounts of land reform present a peasantry that suffered no shortage of bitterness. And at times work team members also actively solicited complaints regarding local cadres. Such was the case with the Crooks, who observed a round of land reform that coincided with a campaign to reform local cadres. The team visited the village's poorest households and encouraged these peasants to speak bitterness, hearing complaints of cadre favoritism and unfair divisions of struggle fruits, which had left some farmers stuck with poor-quality land. As criticisms mounted, the team gathered peasants together in speak bitterness meetings, including one meeting of poor peasants chaired by team leader Lou Lin. According to the Crooks, small group meetings provided peasants with a safe environment to openly discuss their problems. At the meeting chaired by Lou Lin, for example, the work team discovered peasants had many complaints about cadres, including charges of sexism and immoral behavior.[67]

As the Crooks discovered, gender and power were intimately linked in village life. Party leaders, well aware of this, often sought to bring women into the process of mobilization for agrarian revolution. Deng Yingchao, Zhou Enlai's wife, strongly argued this point during a 1947 meeting on land reform policy when she declared that "women function as great mobilizers when they speak bitterness."[68] Examples of women speaking bitterness and telling life stories full of sorrow indicate that she was correct. Li Xiuying, a peasant woman who had ample bitterness to speak, emphasized how her youthful poverty compared to wealthy neighbors. After marrying into a poor family, she had been forced to bury one daughter alive and sell off one of her sons, eventually becoming a beggar herself. Despite her suffering, a local "moneybags" (*caizhu*) continually harassed her.[69] Even more extreme was the bitter tale of Lei Yuzhi, whose family had taken a leading role in their village's first attempt at land reform. When Nationalist forces took back the village in 1947, the land her family had taken from the landlord, Hu Zhensheng, was confiscated, and her mother was tortured and killed. Lei graphically described all of these sufferings as she spoke bitterness.[70] Believing these bitter tales to be excellent devices to organize farmers, the Communists often used women's associations, founded and run through the local party branch, as shock troops to attack the village elite. These women, having already broken with tradition by joining a village-wide organization, were thought to be natural participants in class struggle meetings.[71]

Documents issued by the Women's Federation explicitly called on activists to ensure that women understood their "special bitterness" in terms of class. Women met in groups, where female activists helped them prepare to speak in public, even role-playing as landlords to practice the art of struggle. Some argued that women, less involved in local power relations, were quick to speak out against class enemies. This was especially true of child daughters-in-law (*tongyangxi*), whose hardships moved the crowd. As one woman recalled, "They cried and the audience cried too."[72] The power of female tears was well respected: party reports praised female speakers of bitterness for easily breaking into tears and inducing tears among their audiences. Crying, in fact, was a true sign of a success. One county boasted that among 5,184 speakers of bitterness, 4,551 cried profusely. Among the bawlers, 12 fainted and 195 fell ill from their tears.[73] The party's emphasis on women during rural mobilization, however, was not always due to the belief that women were natural revolutionaries or excellent mobilizers. At least one party report warned that the organization of village women was essential because as "backward" elements, if not "hidden tails" of the landlord class, women were bound to hamper land reform by spreading rumors.[74]

Peasant women had many reasons to welcome the coming of Communist rule in the countryside, but many work teams found it difficult to mobilize women to publicly take part in village politics. Some cadres, discovering that women were more likely to be active in smaller, women-only meetings, suggested that work teams hold joint male-female land reform meetings only in areas that had been under Communist control long enough for women to have obtained a higher social standing. Local cadres and work team members active during the Civil War were encouraged to adapt to meet the needs of women, who had to regularly return home to cook, take care of family members, and carry out chores such as feeding livestock. Women were also more likely to be active in land reform if they could attend a greater number of shorter meetings as opposed to fewer longer meetings. When selecting female "backbones" to take part in land reform, work teams were instructed to find "proper" women of appropriate class backgrounds.[75]

After the founding of the PRC, the mobilization of women continued to be a priority for newly established local governments. Mobilization work, however, was highly dependent on local cadres. Some locals made sure to organize women during land reform, creating propaganda and activities to draw them into the campaign. In these villages, women joined peasant associations, with some promoted to leadership positions. In other places, however, village cadres ignored the mobilization of women, inviting harsh rebuke from party superiors.[76] The experiences of women in agrarian revolution defy any simple generalization. In Xiajia village in the Northeast, for example, women played an important part in its land reform campaign. But women generally met separately from the men.[77] In Guizhou's Five Mile Bridge, Wu Zhanxian's attempts to organize village women failed: when he came in the front door, the women of the household fled out the back door.[78]

At the dawn of the PRC era, with the Civil War finally over and with peace at hand, the prospects for mobilizing villagers seemed greatly improved. Peace proved short-lived, however. In summer 1950, American troops began arriving on the Korean peninsula to push back the forces of Kim Il-sung, who had once fought alongside the Chinese Communists in the Northeast. This news, accompanied by a constant stream of rumors of a renewed global military conflict, rattled the countryside. Investigation into rural society found widespread fears of American atomic bombs, and the party made an explicit connection between the threat of imperialist invasion and landlord resistance. According to party leaders in Hebei, landlords and rich peasants, encouraged by rumors that Chang Kai-shek had flown to the Northeast to "assess the situation," were said to be launching a counterattack against the party.[79] And in South Central China, landlords were said to be publicly speaking out against land reform, boldly registering the names of local cadres and instigating riots. With the countryside once again in turmoil, the fact that many work teams were staffed by cadres sent from North China became particularly troubling for locals. In one South Central village, local elites blamed a drought on the outsiders on the work team. Locals, angry that the work team members did not "believe in spirits" (*bu xin shen*), forcibly expelled the team from their village.

Despite these continued difficulties, the scope of mobilization expanded as the party returned to rural revolution in the early 1950s. The party hosted huge land reform exhibits in cities and towns, while also drafting urban residents into work teams to transform the countryside. Even in small rural towns, dockworkers and merchants were expected to learn about land reform, while elementary and middle school students created propaganda with their teachers.[80] Peasant associations, founded in the buildup to land reform, trained local leaders who could collaborate with work teams. In July 1951, for example, a work team hosted a two-day training session for peasant representatives in eastern Sichuan, feeding the future activists rice, porridge, and even a meat dish while discussing the urgent tasks at hand. Over a hundred peasant representatives, fifteen of them female, attended the meeting. Team leader Li, in charge of the work team, oversaw reports from each village and stressed the importance of investigating production, which would determine who gained and who lost during the campaign. Representatives vowed to carry out propaganda work after returning home, including mobilizing support for the Korean conflict and starting the difficult work of organizing women.[81]

The mobilization of the rural poor, however, remained the key to starting land reform. The end of the war with the Nationalists eliminated one major concern for work team members, but awareness of the topsy-turvy course of land reform from land to the tiller to the push for total equalization of landholdings created widespread confusion in villages awaiting rural revolution. One middle peasant wondered in fall 1949, "Party policy says middle peasant land will not be touched, but also says that there are some lands that will be touched, so what exactly is the policy?"[82] Work teams, meanwhile, did not always benefit from the party's many years of rural campaigning. When the suburbs of Beijing implemented land reform from 1949 to 1950, a mere 135 cadres with land reform experience were dispersed on work teams charged with bringing the revolution to 264 villages.[83] And despite the call for a slow and orderly land reform, mobilizing the masses remained a difficult process. In the months preceding the release of the party's final land law, Mao declared the upcoming campaigns for 300 million villagers a "hideous class war" between peasants and landlords, "a battle to the death."[84] Far less prosaically, a report from South Central China in late 1950 noted that implementing land reform would still take a "tremendous effort" (*feichang chili*).[85]

Many, however, woefully underestimated the scope of land reform in Mao's New China. In Sichuan's Nanchuan County, cadres touted their earlier successes and compared their upcoming land reform to the PLA's smooth crossing of the Yangtze River in the aftermath of the epic military battles of the Huaihai Campaign. With rent reduction and other mass campaigns already carried out in the newly conquered territories, these cadres boasted that carrying out land reform by finally distributing landlord property would be "no problem" (*mei wenti*).[86] Two Nanchuan cadres, Liu Tianzheng and Huang Kaiyu, brought their poor attitudes with them when they were transferred to nearby Fuling County to oversee land reform. In Fuling's Zengfu, Liu refused to accept local opinions and nearly destroyed the local peasant association. Peasants who dared question his methods were accused of standing with landlords. Huang, meanwhile, delighted in attacking village cadres, a practice known colloquially as "shaving beards." Tensions between the visiting cadres and locals exploded during a particularly contentious meeting; as a result, twenty-seven peasants were locked up until an investigation determined that the Nanchuan cadres were at fault.[87]

Despite the shifting context following the establishment of the PRC in 1949, the process of finding potential activists among the poorest peasants in a given village remained standard procedure throughout the party's campaigns to remake rural China. Speaking bitterness was firmly ensconced as the primary method of mobilization in the party's narrative of rural revolution. Du Runsheng, overseeing rural campaigns in the South Central region, praised speaking bitterness as nothing less than an "enlightenment movement of class consciousness."[88] Peasant activists vowed to aid land reform by "implementing speaking bitterness education" by following a set path: comparing, recalling, digging out the roots of poverty, and pouring out bitter water.[89]

In some cases, however, organizing potential activists became even more difficult during the final stages of land reform, which often took place in regions with a notable lack of local landlords. In the prosperous Jiangnan region surrounding Shanghai, for example, the rural rental system was highly commercialized and thoroughly impersonal. As a result, work teams found it difficult to stir up class anger among poor peasants, whose enmity was largely reserved for small-fry rent collectors.[90] The party's promise of class struggle and property redistribution, meanwhile, created a widespread sense of uncertainty among villagers. Yan Hongyan, speaking to cadres preparing to carry out land reform in Sichuan, connected this fear to the clashing interests of villagers. The poorest called for total equality, striking fear in the hearts of those who were even moderately wealthy. Landlords, meanwhile, could only fear for the worst.[91] And because agrarian revolution was by design a confrontational process, campaigns could and often did bring great violence to the countryside. Often it was not counterrevolution but the very actions of local activists that led to antiparty rumors.[92]

And just had been the case in the North, some work teams found it difficult to organize villagers who seemingly harbored no hatred for class enemies. Tan Qixiang, a historian helping carrying out land reform in 1951, confided in his journal that his team had faced great difficulty in generating peasant hatred toward landlords. Most peasants, in fact, were angry not with landlords but with local bullies and slackers.[93] Resistance to agrarian revolution was not limited to peasants. In Guangdong, confronted with local cadres largely opposed to harsh land reform policies, the party replaced village officials with North China cadres.[94] And while concern about outsiders had been a consistent theme throughout the party's agrarian revolution, mobilization was now particularly confounded by the well-developed lineages that often dominated villages in South China. In such cases, adopted sons and other fellow outsiders proved valuable allies for work teams looking to organize poor peasants. Poor lineage members, resentful over poor treatment from wealthy relatives, became heralded as exemplars for valuing loyalty to class over kin.[95] One land reform report went further, noting the importance of reaching out to "backward elements," treating such figures with respect and offering praise and encouragement, if not a good meal during meetings.

During the campaign in Guangdong's Zengbu, coming at the tail end of land reform, the work team still followed the accepted model of moving quickly to locate and meet individually with particularly poor peasants. In Zengbu, the team quickly gravitated to Liu Erbiao as a possible leader and set to mobilizing him through long talks about class exploitation. During these talks, work team members drew out bitterness and helped connect this bitterness to potential struggle targets. Liu Erbiao later confided:

> The work team explained why I worked all day long and could not make enough for two meals. They told me that the reason I was poor and had no money and could not make any was because the landlords—the local bullies who served as the managers of the ancestral halls—stole the ancestral land for their private use. They said that the ancestral lands and fishponds were plentiful but that they had been appropriated by the rich who used them for their own benefit. I believed them.[96]

In Zengbu, as was typical of land reform, struggle against landlords was preceded by small group meetings where cadres further educated peasants on how class enemies were in fact responsible for all of their sufferings before the Communists brought liberation.[97] Or as another Guangdong villager recalled of his time living with land reform work team members:

> They asked us to describe the circumstances of each of the households in the village. They taught us the nature of class relationships—who worked for whom, how the harvests were shared, who was enjoying the fruits of our labor. They seemed moved when we described the bitterness [*ku*] in our lives. Then they suggested that we must act to "grasp power in our own hands" against feudal exploitation.[98]

As this recollection suggests, work teams labored to connect personal bitterness with the very nature of the agrarian economy. Some went further. In the South Central region, teams were instructed to link personal sufferings to the actions not only of class enemies but of American imperialists as well.[99]

Drawing on years of experience, work teams sent to the countryside during the final years of the rural revolution had a clear blueprint for organizing peasants. In 1951, cadres working in De'wei, an administrative village in Jiangjin, followed a step-by-step formula for land reform, first descending on villages to explain what the campaign was, why it was needed, and who would take part. Within a week, all De'wei villages had held these informational meetings and moved on to smaller meetings for village cadres, poor peasants, women, and youths. Some villages also held special meetings for landlords to explain the legitimacy and rightness of rural revolution. But smaller meetings with poor peasants, where work teams explained the connections between rural poverty and economic exploitation, remained critical. In one such meeting in Shidao village, when one old peasant claimed his poverty was the result of bad fengshui, cadres pushed back by asking pointed questions: "Can a family be good or bad due to fengshui? Are families poor for generation after generation because of bad fengshui?"[100]

Because meetings with poor peasants served as the crux of the organizational process, land reform problems were often traced back to a failure to mobilize the rural poor to properly speak bitterness. One team, sent to Jijing village in Sichuan, carried out propaganda, held speak bitterness meetings, and even held a special leadership group (*zhuxi tuan*) meeting on the eve of confronting local landlords. Their careful preparation was not enough, however, and the confrontation ended in failure. Searching for answers, cadres blamed the collapse of the struggle meeting on the fact that the "the bitterness of the bitter ones did not become the bitterness of the masses."[101] A similar problem occurred in Wuxi County's Fenghuang, which had served as a testing ground for many of the party's campaigns in rural Sichuan. In Fenghuang a team of thirty cadres and activists, said to be of proper work style and clear class stance, conducted a full month of land reform without ever mobilizing the masses, to say nothing of holding a struggle meeting. According to the party, this team, while giving lip-service to the idea of fully exterminating the landlord class, simply did not know how to rely on the poor. By failing to "visit and link up with the bitter" (*fang ku chuan lian*), team members isolated themselves from locals. According to a party report, released to warn other teams against repeating their mistakes, they adopted a rather pathetic approach to rural organization. Upon meeting the masses, team members ignored middle peasants and simply asked poor peasants if they had bitterness (*ni you ku mei you*) and if they might be willing to struggle landlords (*gan douzheng dizhu bu gan*). Some poor peasants replied affirmatively, but when the team held meetings, these poor peasants begged off, claiming they were busy in the fields (*wo shengchan hen mang*). The work team lost faith in the masses, viewing them as backward and beyond hope. The masses, meanwhile, increasingly found ways to avoid meetings entirely.[102]

Work team members, outsiders laboring to understand local society, faced a difficult task in organizing villagers for rural revolution. The poet Shao

Yanxiang, who had left Beijing for land reform full of trepidation, learned this firsthand. Recalling his time in the countryside, Shao repeatedly noted how the lion's share of mobilization work had been done by Old Xu, a Gansu cadre. Shao lived with poor villagers but ate with their better-off neighbors. This allayed the fears of more prosperous farmers, while also allowing Shao and other cadres to eat noodles, pickled cabbage, red peppers, and even the occasional meat dish. Shao, however, was sincere in his attempt to bring himself closer to the masses, holding a get-together at night in the hopes of sparking up a conversation with the village poor. Waiting for some stragglers to arrive, the poet decided to try out a villager's water pipe, only to end up nauseated and bedridden as his guests awkwardly exited. Shao's real problems were less comical; unlike Old Xu, he did not speak the local dialect and could barely communicate with the villagers he was to lead in rural revolution.[103]

Cultural differences between teams and peasants took on new dimensions during the tail end of land reform, when the party moved to consolidate power in South and Southwest China, home to many ethnic minorities. The party, aware that that minorities had historically been oppressed by Han Chinese, first focused on developing local cadres before starting land reform. Linguistic issues, however, severely hampered the mobilization of minorities. Some work teams, anxious to jump-start class struggle, erroneously translated the term for "village headman" (*tusi*) as "village bully."[104] Other terms such as "backward" (*luohou*), having no local equivalent, had been translated as "thief" or "criminal," a practice that created much fear among locals. But the party's essentializing description of minority personalities (*xingge*) reveals a cultural chasm that made organization particularly difficult: "straightforward and simple, emphasizing practical action, attaches importance to emotions, assertive and tenacious, strong sense of self-respect, fond of praise and reward, and fearful of criticism."[105] One report on land reform in an ethnic Miao village directly insulted the Miao as culturally backward while simultaneously assuring its readers that the Miao hatred for the Han, who made up most of the village landlords, was "primarily a class hatred."[106] In other villages in the Southwest, minorities such as the Yi controlled the land and gave out high interest loans to Han tenants; yet because Han Chinese controlled the local governments and the Yi were considered an "oppressed" minority, it was impossible to easily locate an "exploiter" or "exploited" group to rely on in land reform. Work team members, well trained in previous rounds of land reform but still outsiders, continued to insist on following the class struggle method, even this meant forcing struggle on unwilling peasants.[107]

Even facing new challenges in China's socially complex minority regions, the key to mobilizing peasants remained consistent: speaking bitterness. Minority activists in the Northwest were told to emphasize how Hui landlords oppressed Han and Hui alike; one Hui activist, for example, was praised for her heartbreaking story of a Hui landlord burying a Han woman alive for breaking a porcelain bowl.[108] In retrospect, it is clear that these tales of suffering were essential to the success of Mao's rural revolution. As newcomers to villages, work teams generally discovered a significant reservoir of unhappiness among peasants, but this bitterness was useless unless work teams could transform memories of the past into hatred for class enemies. It was only through participation in these meetings that villagers learned to speak bitterness and dared to publicly struggle their neighbors. One county-level report on land reform argued that "without mobilizing to smash feelings and sentiments" (*dongyuan dapo qingmian*), villagers were likely to keep silent during struggle meetings.[109] But before class struggle could begin, the work team had to first oversee the next chapter of agrarian revolution: the division of villagers into their new Maoist classes.

3

DIVIDING

Creating Peasants and Landlords

Crafty Qian Wengui, long accustomed to getting his way by hook or crook, was running out of tricks. The Communists, now firmly entrenched in Nuanshui, enthusiastically watched as their network of peasant activists grew larger by the day. Land reform could not be stopped, and Qian knew that he was the work team's number one target. It was bad enough that the process of class division had made him a landlord. Once the work team branded him with the dreaded evil tyrant label, he knew that only drastic action might save him. Becoming an army dependent by having his son enlist and fight for the Communists had bought him some time, but that would not be enough to avoid the wrath of local activists. With few options remaining, he decided to use the women of his landlord household to shield himself from the new order. Qian first asked his daughter to marry Zhang Zhengdian, a village activist. The loyal landlord daughter was willing, and once Zhang was married into the family, he had no choice but to start protecting his new father-in-law. When his marriage and sudden lack of activism caused Zhang's reputation to suffer, Qian pushed his niece Heini to romance another rising village leader. The beautiful Heini, Qian figured, would make the perfect bait for his next trap. But Heini had been born to a peasant family and refused to take part in the nefarious plot.

Without the schemer's help from his niece, the walls continued to close in on him. Even the other landlords in the village turned on him in order to save themselves from struggle. They were landlords, true, but at least they were not evil tyrants! One landlord wife, at wit's end herself, went as far as to berate village cadres for not struggling Qian Wengui: "What kind of Communist Party is this bullshit? This is nothing but pretty talk, every day you settle accounts and get revenge, and all the while you protect a traitor and evil tyrant!"[1] With even his fellow landlords gunning for him, Qian was running out of time.

After arriving in Hanjiatuo, his work team's target village, Liu Quan of Peking University had overheard locals doubt the team could find a true landlord. Some even expressed outright disdain for class struggle. As he met with peasants in small groups, the reasons for their skepticism became all too clear. In Hanjiatuo, peasants revealed, very few villagers rented out land, and in any case it was impossible to make ends meet while solely relying on rental income. The Hanjiatuo villagers who rented out farmlands were far from bastions of feudal power: they all received money from relatives employed in the city, and it was this outside income that truly allowed them to survive. And, sure, there were some hooligans in the village, but they did not match the evil tyrants that the work team sought. In fact, one of Hanjiatuo's most prominent hooligans, villagers pointed out, had recently claimed to have reformed himself and was now serving as the secretary of the local party branch![2]

These doubts meant little to the work team and its leader, Zhang Li, who was determined to bring Mao's revolution to Hanjiatuo. Having already announced the start of land reform in a sleep-inducing meeting, the team followed the well-established precedent of moving in with local households in order to better understand the local society it planned to transform through fierce struggle. Liu Quan ended up staying with the Tangs, a middle peasant family. Always the dutiful revolutionary, Liu recalculated the family's property holdings and happily concluded that the Tangs were in fact middle peasants, not involved in any meaningful form of economic exploitation. According to the new state's land reform law, all of the family's property was explicitly protected. There was absolutely no reason, Liu decided, that his friendly hosts should be concerned about land reform.[3] But the naive Liu failed to figure in human greed. With his typical disregard for the peasants, team leader Zhang pushed for more landlords, more struggle, and more property to redistribute. Conspiring with local cadres, Zhang unjustly and illegally labeled the Tangs a landlord household. Villagers of course knew that their neighbors the Tangs were no landlords, just as Liu clearly understood that his work team was seriously deviating from the clear guidelines of the new land law. But no one dared to speak out against team leader Zhang, not even when the militia came to arrest the hapless Tang patriarch. Sobbing, his wife could only cry out: "He has never done a mean thing in his entire life, if you do not believe me then just ask. We are all neighbors, what could not be known?"[4]

In his writings on land reform, William Hinton waxed poetic about the seemingly eternal landholding system—"the quiet countryside" where "landlords continued to don long gowns, collect exorbitant rents, pay off the soldiery, manicure their fingernails, and eat white flour made from wheat."[5] He also made clear, however, that Long Bow landlords could hardly be considered wealthy. They were in fact rather poor. Anyone with real wealth had fled long before the Communists took power, and the small fry left behind were not particularly impressive. They wore silk garments on festive days but otherwise dressed like other villagers as they tilled the fields. The closest thing Long Bow had to a stereotypical landlord was Sheng Jinghe, whose long fingernails attested to the fact that he never worked his fields. Sheng was a frugal businessman, running and investing in distilleries. By the party's own class scheme, Sheng's role in rural industry meant that he should never have been labeled a landlord in the first place.[6] But during the round of land reform that followed the release of the May Fourth Directive, local cadres mislabeled Sheng as a landlord. Hinton was not in the village at the time, but the peasants who attacked Sheng's family during land reform told him of the landlord's evil crimes, which had left families broken and destitute.[7] It was natural for peasants to want more land, and Hinton saw nothing wrong if a family rented out a bit of its extra land to a neighbor. But a handful of families owning so much of Long Bow wealth was "in essence a form of armed plunder."[8] As for Sheng, Hinton never expressed doubt about his landlord status.

Hinton's work team arrived in the village long after the struggling of Sheng Jinghe. Following a narrative that assumed the village to still be controlled by feudal elements, the team shut down village organizations and moved to reassess the class status of every Long Bow resident. Using the method of "self-report, public appraisal," villagers made a case for their desired class status based on their lives over the past three years. With a potential redistribution of wealth looming, the stakes were high. Those classed poor would be able to take the property of those classed rich, and every villager claimed extreme poverty. But the truly poor "basic elements" in charge of the meeting were hoping to find more rich peasants so that they might finally find economic liberation themselves. The result was a push and pull that was only complicated by confusion over class labels. A landless builder was labeled a "village worker," which made no sense to Long Bow peasants. A blacksmith was accused of exploitation for providing shoddy goods. And a former opium-dealer-turned-poor-peasant was punished for his past crimes with the middle peasant class label. Much time was spent calculating the amount of income households gained through exploitation.[9] While Hinton was impressed by the ability of Long Bow's peasants to determine class labels, the result was disappointing: only one new rich peasant household was found, while over one hundred families lingered in unacceptable poverty.[10]

The party went to great lengths to explain the depravity of landlords to Long Bow peasants, and Hinton shared this education in rural classes as he observed the revolution in action. Operas featuring a mash-up of local music and Maoist ideology were among the party's most powerful propaganda weapons, and so it was that Hinton joined Long Bow peasants and took in a staging of *Red Leaf River*, a land reform opera depicting a depraved landlord who sexually assaulted women and drove families to financial ruin. The evening performance of the show by a Communist-affiliated drama troupe drew a massive audience that Hinton estimated in the thousands. Looking around him, he found the audience totally captivated by the drama:

> As the tragedy of this poor peasant's family unfolded, the women around me wept openly and unashamedly. On every side, as I turned to look, tears were coursing down their faces. No one sobbed, no one cried out, but all wept together in silence. The agony on the stage seemed to have unlocked a thousand painful memories, a bottomless reservoir of suffering that no one could control.[11]

Soon Hinton and the other male audience members joined the women in tears.

Class struggle requires class enemies, and Mao's tale of rural revolution was predicated on the belief that every village was marked by class conflict. During land reform, work teams had to identify those villagers who could be classed as landlords, making the concept of class (*jieji*) and the process of class division (*huafen jieji chengfen*) essential to the campaigns. This posed a tremendous challenge to land reform work teams. It was true that despite a deeply rooted longing for egalitarianism, societies in rural China were marked by varying degrees of social differentiation. Some households prospered, and others struggled to get by. But before the arrival of agrarian revolution, there were no "landlords" in China. Nor were there any "peasants." Both of these class labels, and the entire Maoist class system, were completely alien to the countryside. Even the very idea of class was foreign: early reformers had to recast *jieji*, which had previously meant "rank" or "level" in both Japanese and Chinese, for new purposes.[12] The pioneering reformer Liang Qichao had been at the forefront of this linguistic revolution. In 1899 Liang noted that European countries divided their nations into classes, while China did not. Later that year, he remedied this situation by creating China's first class system: capitalists and workers, men and women. Chinese who found this scheme lacking had to wait until 1919 for early convert Li Dazhao to formulate a more orthodox interpretation of class structure based on translations of seminal Marxist texts.[13] When land reform launched in 1946, the Communists had a fully developed rural class system based on multiple components: a villager's living standard and relationship to exploitation, the feudal or capitalist nature of that exploitation, and how past economic production had led to a villager's current economic situation.[14]

This foreign understanding of class status was unheard of in the countryside, where villagers used terms such as *stratum* (*jieceng*) to explain social differentiation.[15] It was only through multiple experiments with agrarian reform that Mao's unique rural class scheme slowly infiltrated the countryside. Landlords did not labor but instead lived off of exploitation. Rich peasant households engaged in farming while also earning income by exploiting the labor of others. Middle peasants represented the happy medium, living off their own labor on their own lands, avoiding significant involvement in economic exploitation. Poor peasants were exploited chiefly through land rents, and hired hands were exploited whenever they sold their labor. These were not the only class statuses given to villagers during the many years of rural campaigning. After the first summer of land to the tiller in 1946, for example, cadres in the Taihang Mountains formed guidelines to fully explain local society, acknowledging the existence of a diverse set of rural classes that included workers, merchants, vagrants, monks, nuns, traditional artists, and teachers.[16] But the detailed Taihang regulations were not widely promoted, and work teams rarely ventured outside the standard classes Mao promoted during his early days of agrarian revolution.

Maoist class labels were critically important to the process of agrarian revolution. All of them were also new to the countryside, ironically and tragically appearing just as land reform removed most markers of actual economic social differentiation.[17] The word for peasant, *nongmin*, was a Japanese creation based on classical Chinese, where it had simply meant "country folk."[18] The class label of poor peasant (*pinnong*), which emerged nearly simultaneously in Japan and China after Russia's October Revolution, was given to farmers who owned no or very little land, and instead rented their fields from wealthy neighbors. Along with hired hands (*gunong*), who could not afford to rent farmland and made a living from selling their labor, poor peasants were promoted as the proletariat of the village.[19] Or as Mao declared, these impoverished villagers, often ridiculed as "riffraff," were to be "the main force in the bitter fight" against feudal power in the countryside.[20] Narratives of rural revolution emphasized the bitter poverty that marked the lives of poor peasants and hired hands. In Zhou Libo's land reform novel, the poor peasant character Bare Assed Zhao owned a single pair of pants for his entire family. One popular land reform exhibit, meanwhile, displayed a tattered and worn pair of peasant pants, said to be 120 years old.

Middle peasant (*zhongnong*) was another late arrival borrowed from Japan. According to Mao in 1927, middle peasants always vacillated, fearful of what the revolution would take away from them. They joined peasant associations in great numbers, but took a wait-and-see approach.[21] By the start of first land-to-the-tiller land reform, double reduction campaigns had created massive numbers of middle peasants. These farmers often dominated village societies in the base areas yet stood to gain little from the redistribution of land.[22] But as Deng Zihui declared in 1946, the middle peasant class was by nature willing to compromise and could be considered an ally during land reform.[23] Sometimes called the "petite bourgeoisie of the countryside," middle peasants were typically thought to have enough land, labor, and agricultural materials to harvest quality yields and not go hungry. Because some middle peasants rented out some of their extra land, party

IMAGE 8. A "120 year old" pair of pants used to sym-
bolize the extreme poverty of China's peasants. Source:
Zhongnan tudi gaige de weida shengli, 55.

directives spoke out against activists who wanted to illegally raise middle
peasants into higher statuses.[24] In recognition of the diversity of rural landholding households, the party further divided middle peasants into upper-
middle, middle, and lower-middle categories. Lower-middle peasants did
not own enough land, and thus had to rent some of their fields.[25] Upper-
middle or well-to-do (*fuyu*) peasants were farmers who rented out a share
of their land, and this precise classification seemed promised to police the
line between rich and middle peasants. [26] But in practice the threat of the
"well-to-do" label helped create a widespread fear that all middle peasants
might face struggle and expropriation. As a result, the party had to regularly remind cadres that middle peasants were in fact allowed to have up to

25 percent of their income derived through land rents and other forms of exploitation.[27]

Rich peasant (*funong*) was yet another neologism borrowed from Japanese.[28] If the poor peasants and hired hands were the village proletariat and the "main force of revolutionary struggle," these peasants represented the "rural capitalist class."[29] While rich peasant households engaged in labor, a significant portion of their income was derived through exploitation, either though feudal exploitation in land rents and usury, or capitalist exploitation through wage labor and commercial enterprises. As a result, these farmers enjoyed good lives and accumulated profits thanks to their high level of agricultural production.[30] By the time Mao wrote about rich peasants for his "Hunan Report" in 1927, he had decided that this relative wealth made them enemies of the people. According to Mao, rich peasants were no friends of the peasant association and joined only under duress. Even after joining, they remained politically inactive, always uneasy with peasant activists.[31] By the time of the first land-to-the-tiller campaigns, this negative view of rich peasants was firmly established, with Deng Zihui declaring these farmers "selfish" and "full of tricks," wanting to "hog" the fruits of struggle.[32] As a result, rich peasants, unlike middle peasants, were typically not allowed to join the village party branch.[33]

Of all the class labels Mao gave to village residents, the most odious were landlord (*dizhu*) and evil tyrant (*eba*). The term *dizhu* has a long history, but only recently had come to mean a villager whose income came from exploiting the masses.[34] By the start of land reform, party theorists had developed a complex typology of landlords, starting with a distinction between large landlords, who effectively controlled one or more villages, and smaller landlords, who lacked true power over their neighbors. Managerial landlords (*jingying dizhu*), capitalists relying on hired labor to farm their lands, also exercised feudal power through renting lands, providing high-interest loans, holding political office, or cheating their workers. Bankrupt landlords (*pochan dizhu*) had lost their wealth due to drug addiction or bad business decisions, yet still managed to live the good life thanks to their family connections or outright trickery. Second landlords (*er dizhu*) were the agents renting out landlord land, making a living by taking a share of the collected rent.[35] Party propaganda, however, continually emphasized that the crimes of the landlord class went far

IMAGE 9. A poster depicts the connections of Longshan County landlords to the Nationalists, a right-wing youth league, spy organizations, and bandits. Source: *Zhongnan tudi gaige de weida shengli*, 40-41.

beyond mere economic exploitation. They were agents of evil, tied to the Nationalists and other reactionary elements.

Before the arrival of Communist power the term *dizhu* was unknown in the countryside. Villagers often simply called their wealthier neighbors "money bags" (*caizhu*).[36] The party even incorporated rural rhetorical preferences into propaganda: characters in land reform operas would use the term *money bags*, switching to *landlord* after receiving ideological training in their own fictional land reform.[37] Farmers in the Northeast, meanwhile, preferred the term *big grain household* (*da liang hu*) or, more colorfully, *big belly* (*da duzi*).[38] Critically, these terms merely implied wealth and were not by definition derogative. The "evil tyrant" label was reserved for particularly wicked local power holders in need of struggle as soon as villages came under Communist control.[39] The distinction between landlords and evil tyrants was left vague, leading Xi Zhongxun to complain about the fluidity of the evil tyrant label, which could be given to a villager who spoke too strongly or cut down the wrong tree, as opposed to someone who had "truly seized an area to bully the masses."[40] In practice, nearly any landlord, especially during the heat of confrontational class struggle, might be called an "evil tyrant landlord" (*eba dizhu*). The determination of landlord

IMAGE 10. A landlord's fur coat, featured in a land reform exhibit, provided a sharp contrast with the aged pair of peasant pants. Source: *Zhongnan tudi gaige de weida shengli,* 54.

class status was an essential moment in Mao's rural vision, dividing the village between friends and enemies of his revolution. One work team report, noting that class division was "complex and difficult," thus advised identifying and attacking landlords before ranking remaining villagers.[41]

Over the course of agrarian revolution, the party's treatment of rural classes constantly evolved, with sudden changes that often left local cadres perplexed, to say nothing of villagers trying to navigate life under the Communists. Experimenting with agrarian reform during the earlier land revolution, the party gave rich peasants land of the poorest quality and totally expropriated landlord property. A few years later, the party moved to protect rich peasants and landlords in order to facilitate a new alliance with the Nationalist Party. After the promulgation of the May Fourth Directive and the start of all-out land reform, those determined to be rich peasants stood to once again lose a share of their wealth, despite the directive's instructions to "generally" not touch rich peasant property. The treatment of China's rich peasants would become an essential question throughout the following years of rural revolution.

During the first land-to-the-tiller land reform campaigns, the process of class division was haphazard and varied widely. In the North China village of Wugong, the party branch quietly divided their neighbors into Maoist categories behind closed doors. Unable to find a single true landlord after years of Communist rule, the party branch arbitrarily labeled two households as landlords, creating class enemies in a community where nearly every household was in truth a middle peasant household.[42] Landlords could be hard to find even in newly liberated villages, especially when even the relatively wealthy took part in agricultural production. The result was a seemingly inevitable expansion of struggle from landlords to rich peasants and eventually middle peasants. During an early attempt at land reform in one Heilongjiang village, activists arbitrarily gave out class labels and persecuted more than 40 percent of the village population, creating landlords out of wealthy farmers who had dared to hire laborers. Any farmer who rented out land was considered a landlord.[43]

Divisions among the peasantry were already widespread during the land-to-the-tiller round of land reform. In theory, the party leaders hoped that after land had been given to the poorest villagers, middle peasants, the allied troops (*tongmeng jun*) of the rural revolution, could receive some property.[44] But some local cadres treated middle peasants roughly, handing out fines for political crimes such as not allowing children to take part in mass organizations.[45] Others saw middle peasants as not part of the basic masses (*jiben qunzhong*) but stubborn elements (*wangu fenzi*) to be kept out of peasant associations and perhaps in need of struggle. The result was widespread attacks on middle peasant interests. As one Communist observer lamented, the definition of the middle peasant class was simple, "but a simple definition cannot solve a problem."[46] Even poor peasants were afraid. According to one farmer, just having a "big mouth before land reform" was enough to earn a bad class label and persecution.[47]

The problem with rich peasants was even more acute, with the disjunction between the party's twin goals of economic development and revolution creating much confusion in class division policies. On one hand, party leaders understood the importance of rich peasants to the rural economy. Li Zipu, writing on the "middle peasant problem," thus recommended a cautious approach to rich peasants, reasoning that the natural "developmental future" of middle peasants was advancing to rich peasant status.[48] But during rural revolution, poor activists saw rich peasant wealth as an attractive target. Moreover, the party's own land reform narrative demanded that poor peasants and hired hands must receive land if a campaign was to come to a successful conclusion. In one directive announcing the implementation of land to the tiller, the Central China Bureau called for the preservation of the rich peasant economy and the distribution of a share of land to family members of all struggle targets, including traitors and local bullies. But this same directive also gave activists latitude to move on rich peasants, opening the door to the struggle of rich peasants by noting that the lands farmed by rich peasant households should only "usually" not be taken.[49] A subsequent directive from the bureau confirmed that lands rented out by rich peasants could be confiscated, while "exploitative" well-to-do middle peasants might be encouraged to donate their land.[50] The bureau, however, still advocated allowing rich peasants to keep the lands farmed by their own households, and party central explicitly endorsed this lenient path, advising work teams to yield (*rangbu*) to rich peasants, reasoning that a broad class alliance was needed to break the Nationalist offensive then threatening the base areas.[51] This approach, when followed, yielded positive results: During a successful land-to-the-tiller campaign in Beifengzheng, a village south of Shijiazhuang, activists settled accounts with rich peasants for past exploitation but left the fields they farmed themselves untouched.[52]

While some in the party promoted the limited protection of rich peasant assets, on-the-ground activism made this a tenuous proposal. Two months after the start of land to the tiller, the party was already receiving reports of poor peasants calling for equal division, or leveling, as the only means to economic liberation. This move to equalize holdings meant the confiscation of land from not only rich peasants but many middle peasants as well, a clear violation of party policy.[53] Some party leaders sided with land-hungry peasant activists. Investigating the leveling problem (*la ping wenti*) during the first summer of land to the tiller, Cao Huoqiu declared that the desire for equal holdings among the mobilized poor was "natural" (*ziran*). Foreshadowing the eventual call to equalize all landholdings, Cao called for leveling landholdings in newly liberated villages where over 60 percent of land was held by landlords; while some land would be taken from rich and middle peasants, Cao reasoned that most land would come from the landlord class.[54] With the Nationalist armies on the attack during land to the tiller, party leaders such as Deng Zihui increasingly saw the poorest members of rural society as true loyalists and affirmed their calls to equalize landholdings; although middle peasants were allies of the revolution, they were unreliable (*bu neng yikao zhongnong*).[55]

Matters were further complicated when party leaders recognized the vast changes that had occurred in base area villagers: not all rich peasants were equal. Leaders in the Jin-Cha-Ji Bureau, for example, noted that many rich peasants in their base area were "new" rich peasants who owed their high incomes to the party's own policies. These new rich peasants, the bureau insisted, must be considered part of the basic masses.[56] At the outset of land-to-the-tiller campaigns, some base areas also made concessions to the village elite by promising special treatment and high-quality fields to enlightened gentry and other longtime allies.[57] In Jin-Cha-Ji, leaders made a distinction between new territories where struggle was intense, and old areas where cadres were encouraged to work with landlords to ensure the quick transfer of land. In these "old liberated areas" as much as 80 percent of the population was composed of middle peasants, and only the most obstinate landlords needed to be subjected to mass struggle.[58] Jin-Cha-Ji leaders, while recognizing the natural and logical peasant desire for more land, insisted that equal distribution contravened the May Fourth Directive by taking too much from rich peasants and infringing on middle peasant interests.[59] The East China Bureau took an even more accommodating approach to rural classes in the "blank slate villages" where the party was bringing land reform. Small and middle landlords were allowed to donate land and keep more land than the average middle peasant, as well as their housing and tools.[60] In the chaotic Northeast, when work teams focused on struggling traitors and despotic landlords, most peasants who had served Japan's puppet regime in Manchukuo were allowed to apologize for their crimes and keep their lands. Small and medium landlords were allowed to directly donate their lands. The Northeast Bureau even instructed teams to give these landlords some "face" by letting them keep more land than the average village peasant.[61]

Given ample leeway by the vague May Fourth Directive, the Central China Bureau leadership moved steadily toward equalization. The "proper" land reform conducted by an elite Central China Bureau work team had equalized holdings, denying landlords and rich peasants an extra share of land in order to ensure that the poor received enough land.[62] Shortly after promoting the experiences of this work team, the Central China Bureau released its September First Directive, which promoted a simple model to solve the land issue: "don't touch the middle, level the two ends" (*zhong bu dong, liang tou ping*). The lands of middle peasants, who now approached half of all villagers in the aftermath of double reduction, were to be protected, but the holdings of the other village classes were to be largely equalized.[63]

In the aftermath of the September First Directive, land reform moved to a new stage with the call to "fill the gaps" of poverty, heralding an increasingly strident approach to rural class enemies. Leaders in Central China continued to promise a generous share of land to small and medium landlords, but fill-the-gap directives insisted that only after the masses had been fully mobilized and toppled the landlord class was it appropriate to even raise the issue of "taking care of landlords" (*zhaogu dizhu*). Directives also presented settling accounts with landlords through struggle as the simple solution to rural poverty. If the poor needed land, they would get land; if the poor needed housing, they would get housing.[64] By filling the gaps, work teams could reduce inequality among villagers without striking fear among middle peasants by raising the specter of all-out leveling. But rich peasants, still theoretically under the protection of the May Fourth Directive, were increasingly under attack from cadres and activists. Completing land reform in mid-1947, the Taihang base area confiscated property from landlords and rich peasants alike to "fill holes" among the poor.[65] The Central China Bureau, meanwhile, continued to promote its policy of leaving middle peasant land untouched while leveling the other rural classes. In summer 1947, the bureau thus lambasted the "rich peasant line" as it launched a combative land reform "reexamination" campaign that promised to ensure the poor had in fact gotten enough land. In this campaign, the land of landlords and rich peasants alike would be leveled with the village poor.[66]

Debates over the treatment of rural classes grew in importance over summer 1947 as Liu Shaoqi prepared to host a second land conference with an eye toward eventually compiling a land law to replace the vague May Fourth Directive. Writing on behalf of party central, Deng Zihui reached out to Liu in July, arguing for further attacks on landlords and rich peasants in line with the "don't touch the middle, move the two ends" approach.[67] As party central moved against rich peasants, the East China Bureau now pressured work teams to correct the lenient nature of land-to-the-tiller land reform during the ongoing "reexamination" campaigns. According to the bureau, landlords still had excess and high-quality land, while rich peasants still maintained all of the land farmed by their own households. Demanding a transformation of the rural economy, the bureau called on teams to once again settle accounts with rural class enemies who had "stolen the fruits of struggle." Previous policies had approved of donations and the peaceful transfer of land, and the September First Directive of 1946 had even allowed class enemies to keep extra land, housing, tools, and draft animals. But now "old" rich peasants and landlords would be given no more than the village poor. Far from denouncing the policy of sweeping landlords "out the door," the East China Bureau now advocated giving hated or "reactionary" landlords nothing.[68]

Confiscation of rich peasant property was officially approved with the Outline Land Law, released on October 10, 1947. As approved by party central following the Xibaipo land conference, this law claimed that landlords and rich peasants, while under 10 percent of the rural population, held as much as 80 percent of the land, a wild overestimation in North China. This figure was particularly untrue for the "old liberated areas" long under Communist control, which had already hosted double reduction and land reform campaigns. Even before 1937, land tenancy rates in Hebei and Shandong hovered as low as 10 percent.[69] Poor peasants would have to look elsewhere for wealth. But where? The law's sixth article called for equal land distribution, ensuring that landlords should receive a fair share of land. But this also meant that many middle peasants, and all rich peasants, stood to lose property.[70] After personally investigating rural conditions prior to the September land conference, Liu Shaoqi had intended to offer full protection to middle peasants. But just as the conference was coming to a close, Liu's original plan was disrupted by the publication of a newspaper article calling for the equalization of land, seen as an expression of Mao Zedong's views.[71] As a result, the sixth article of the land law called for equal distribution, giving landlord families the same share of land as families with sons in the PLA.[72]

Under the Outline Land Law, base areas launched a new round of land reform to equalize holdings. In order to help work teams correctly classify villagers, party central once again distributed copies of two articles Mao had written on rural classes back in 1933.[73] The articles' original call for poor treatment of rich peasants and landlords had been deleted, but this did little to stem the growth of what party central would soon condemn as "leftist" deviations in class division. These deviations are commonly blamed on the much-maligned Kang Sheng and his work in the Jin-Sui base area, where cadres brought politics into the process of creating economic classes, turning former Nationalist Party members into class enemies. Simply complaining about the new government was enough to be classed as a rich peasant or landlord. Cadres were also basing class statuses on the investigation into three previous generations (*cha san dai*), creating bankrupt landlords who had in fact labored their entire lives. The total malleability of what Kang Sheng called "shape shifting landlords" (*hua xing dizhu*) was compounded by secrecy in the class division process, with a small number of land-hungry activists divining class statuses for entire villages.[74] In Wugong in North China, a village stocked with middle peasants, the pressure to find class enemies remained strong enough for a work team to wrongly push seventy-one households into rich peasant status.[75]

With increasing violence in the push for equal holdings, some Communist Party leaders questioned the party's chaotic implementation of class division. In 1948, few spoke with more clarity and force than Xi Zhongxun, then stationed in the long-established Northwest base area, home to villages filled with middle peasants and new rich peasants. According to Xi, many villages lacked a single landlord or "old" rich peasant, and no more than 2 percent of villagers in the Northwest qualified as poor peasants. Relaunching land reform in these old areas for the sake of equal division, Xi argued, would turn the peasant masses against the party.[76] Xi wrote directly to Mao, warning him that a small number of hooligans, posing as activists, were now supporting a "poor peasant and hired hand line." These fake activists opposed what they called the "middle peasant line" and used deadly methods of struggle, causing a panic in the countryside. With labor heroes attacked because of their extra grain, peasants avoided production and feared prosperity. Xi even dared to question Mao's assumptions about rural classes. Noting that middle peasants were already the dominant class in the Northwest, Xi argued that many of those who remained poor were in fact lazy. Putting these peasants in charge of land reform had resulted in chaos. Whereas some party leaders had seen poor peasants as the only reliable rural class, Xi asked Mao to put his trust in China's middle peasants. They, alongside some but not all poor peasants, were the true basic masses.[77] As Xi would later say of the "complex" poor peasant class: "Some are poor because they love to eat, drink, go whoring, gamble, or don't want to work." As these hooligans accounted for 25 percent of poor peasants in the North-west, to rely on such men to run land reform and equally divide the land was to "seek death" for the countryside. According to Xi, it was far better to rely on peasant associations under middle peasant control; poor peasant activists were welcome to join once they were approved by their middle peasant neighbors.[78]

While Xi led the way, others in the party also moved to limit chaos stem-ming from the party's treatment of rural classes. In January 1948, party theoretician Ren Bishi delivered a speech on land reform that soon became required reading for work team members. As Ren emphasized, the party desperately needed a greater focus on accurate class division and a more nuanced view of village class structures. During the period of rectification that followed, the Communist Party attempted to correct class labels, pro-tect commerce, and make amends with those who had wrongly lost prop-erty, especially those who had been totally expropriated and "swept out the door" (*saodi chumen*).[79] Still, after the publication and distribution of Ren Bishi's speech, reports from the countryside confirmed that the treatment of rural classes remained highly problematic. In the Northeast, middle peas-ants had played a small role in struggle, allowing poor peasants and hired hands, overeager to class their neighbors as rich peasants and encouraged by slogans to embrace chaos, to beat, torture, and execute struggle targets in a never-ending search for hidden wealth. Many villagers classed as rich peasants were locked up, their property confiscated and "swept clean" (*yi sao guang*): they were left with nothing. Work teams and village cadres, meanwhile, looked the other way, not daring to contradict the will of the rural proletariat.[80]

In response, the party revised the call for equal landholdings in the Out-line Land Law in deference to middle peasants, allowing them to maintain their property if they did not agree to equal distribution. In practice, how-ever, the desire for equal distribution meant widespread infringement on middle peasant property until the party suspended land reform in summer 1948. Only a year later, with the end of the long war against the National-ists finally in sight, land reform and class division returned to the center of the party's rural policies. Two years to the day after the release of the Outline Land Law, the North China Bureau announced a new campaign to bring land reform to some 15 million newly liberated rural citizens. But there were hints that this would be a new land reform, with a new approach to class. This campaign featured a return to the "move the two ends, don't touch the middle" approach that had been discarded during the push for full equalization. Village intellectuals, including those from landlord and rich peasant families, were to be taught to "serve the people."[81] Leaders of the East China Bureau, noting that cadres dispatched from North China were facing challenges in their region, similarly suggested that young village intellectuals, leftist landlords, and enlightened gentry could make valuable contributions to rural work as village cadres.[82]

After the founding of the PRC, the process of class determination continued to follow the precedents established during Civil War campaigns, with an even greater emphasis on correct classification. No less of an authority than Mao Zedong had declared mistakes in class statuses as one of the primary problems with Civil War–era campaigns.[83] Work teams continued to use peasant associations as forums for villagers to collectively determine class status. Villagers would individually report (*zibao*) their class status, which would become official only with public agreement (*gongyi*).[84] As one village land reform report helpfully explained, this was a carefully plotted out process of "explaining the concept of class, learning the concept of class, advocating the concept of class, identifying classes, reviewing class status, finalizing class status, and finally approving the determination of class status with the higher level of leadership."[85]

Even in the relatively simple rural economy of North China, not every villager had fit neatly into Mao's rural class scheme. As the campaigns moved into the prosperous and diversified economies of southern and coastal China, Mao's classification system was tested to its limits. Shortly after promulgating the China Land Law in summer 1950, the party approved a host of new statuses for village residents: religious professional, practitioner of superstition, craftsman, peddler, independent professional, and merchant. In practice, however, significant problems with the division of classes remained. First, the land law strayed from a purely economic approach to class division. The law held that some rich peasants could be classed as "rich middle peasants" if villagers did not object, allowing public opinion considerable sway in the process of land reform.[86] The line between rich peasants and middle peasants, meanwhile, caused much anxiety, especially when attacks on rich peasants continued throughout the latter half of land reform. In land reform near Chongqing, for example, the phenomenon of equal distribution remained common, creating no shortage of chaos as cadres and activists illegally moved against rich peasants. Even middle peasants found themselves losing good land. Upper-level cadres wondered if this might be a landlord plot to dampen the desire for struggle among the masses, but also admitted that local cadres were to blame. Most did not see the "essence and evil consequences" of equal division, and some in fact fully supported taking property from rich and middle peasants in order to satisfy the needs of the poor.[87]

The process of class division, furthermore, remained a highly volatile affair. Outsiders on work teams had to rely on villagers to properly assess local economic relationships. The party called for the determination of classes to proceed through the investigation of the three years prior to liberation, but the messy process of class determination unearthed complex social relationships through recollections and accusations, reviving stories of parents and grandparents.[88] For those who understood the grounds for class determination, this could be an empowering moment—an opportunity to secure property and status under the new Communist order. One Sichuan nun, initially labeled a religious practitioner, was able to win reassignment as a poor peasant by insisting that she never begged and had instead relied on her own labor.[89] Open discussion of landholdings and past transgressions could also prove ruinous, even for the staunchest supporters of land reform. One peasant association vice chair found himself facing doubts over his past life as a bandit and charges that he had been too lenient to village landlords during a previous rent reduction. Might this former bandit be a class enemy in disguise? Fearing struggle, he committed suicide.[90]

There was good reason to fear struggle as class determination expanded during the first years of the PRC. Party leaders crafting the lenient class policies found in the new Land Reform Law had not anticipated how the outbreak of war on the Korean peninsula would create fears that landlords, already connected to the Nationalists in Mao's vision of rural China, might use the conflict to oppose the new order. Just months after fighting began, party reports made the ties between American imperialism and landlord deviousness explicit. Landlords, who had been praised for quietly accepting land reform in the immediate aftermath of the Civil War, were once again chastised as devious tricksters. In South Central China, Du Runsheng declared that with war in Korea, violent struggle was needed to tame class enemies.[91] Landlords were now accused of taking control of peasant associations, destroying production materials, and using their mastery of policy to attempt to influence the land reform process. One nefarious man, for example, argued against his rightful landlord status by proclaiming, "Chairman Mao has said that every extra landlord is an extra enemy."[92] Just a few months after party leaders had promoted working with the village elite, a Guangdong team was criticized for allying with the enlightened gentry to mobilize the rural poor.

With treatment of various classes still in flux, work teams could easily exacerbate rural anxiety. In Liangshan County, the team working in Jianshe village decided to bypass the peasant association, which was headed by a middle peasant, and held meetings with poor peasants and hired hands. Shut out, the peasant association chair grew nervous: "The poor peasants and hired hands hold meetings all day, and I have no idea what they are meeting about. Could it be that they are collecting materials for struggle?" As a result of the work team's secrecy, rumors began to fly that struggle would inevitably spread to rich and, finally, middle peasants.[93] Those classed as upper-middle peasants, in the nebulous zone between friend and enemy of Mao's revolution, generally feared land reform. One such upper-middle peasant, Lu Guosi, was so terrified by the prospect of struggle that he ran about his village, searching for any news of his fate. He also made sure to constantly complain about his own bitterness. Lu even tracked down anyone who owed him money to declare, "You don't have to repay me, that loan was my mistake."[94]

With so much at stake, villagers made the most of class division, often in ways that brought official rebuke. Investigations into class determination complained that villagers were ruled by self-interest, not revolutionary fervor or Maoist orthodoxy. Households, not surprisingly, tended to underreport their land in order to get better class labels. One study of three villages discovered that households had concealed over 20 percent of landholdings, leading investigators to declare, "Each household withholds information, each piece is untrue." While some blame was assigned to rich peasants and landlords who had previously hidden their land, the report admitted that peasants, hearing that distributions were based on current holdings, claimed to have pathetic landholdings, hoping to get more. Because this phenomenon was most associated with middle peasants, land-hungry poor peasants and hired hands suffered.[95] Reports on class determination also revealed that while some landlords were pleading for mercy, others schemed to avoid their class status, drumming up instances of labor. One Sichuan landlord attempted to pass off selling opium as labor.[96] A Guizhou landlord claimed

IMAGE 11. A peasant, chained by his landlord, works the land. Source: *Zhongnan tudi gaige de weida shengli*, 36-37.

he was too old to labor before villagers reminded him that he had never labored when he was younger. But middle peasants were also trying to pose as poor peasants in the hopes of getting more property.[97]

Despite the formal approval of new class statuses, fitting villagers into Maoist classes remained difficult. In the countryside surrounding Shanghai where villagers aspired to factory jobs, for example, most relied on nonagricultural income to make ends meet.[98] In Fujian's Yang village, peasants overseeing class division created an entirely new class status, that of the "usurious practitioner" (*zhaili shenghuozhe*), for two men who had no land or business but lived in the style of landlords by granting loans.[99] One work team, reporting a "struggle target problem" (*douzheng duixiang wenti*), admitted finding few true landlords.[100] Finding targets would have been even more difficult without the practice of considering economic relations during the three years prior to the arrival of Communist power. This practice unearthed some truly pathetic landlords, including the clearly impoverished Zhang Yuanxin. During his classification, Zhang argued that he should be labeled a poor peasant, reasoning, "Right now I live in the temple, with no land or house, what am I if not a poor peasant?" Activists rebuked Zhang, strongly reminding him that his previous wealth meant that in no way could he qualify as a poor peasant. Zhang, in the end, could only lower his head and accept his landlord status.[101]

Throughout the many campaigns of rural revolution, the theoretical basis of class division was economic: the definition of a landlord was based on the percentage of income derived through exploitation versus labor. Descriptions of landlord evils included tales of extreme peasant poverty caused by the economic crimes of the landlord class. As the Communists knew well, there was significant social disparity in many rural areas and no shortage of economic suffering. A report on Five Mile Bridge, a village in Guizhou, declared the economic situation there a "complete mess" (*lingluan*) where nearly everyone lived in a straw huts. One particularly pathetic case was that of Yang Minghua. Yang rented his farming land from Zhang Hanchang, but his rent was only part of what he owed his landlord. On various holidays and harvest days Zhang had to gift his landlord with fish, chicken, or home- cooked meals. He also had to perform a seemingly endless variety of free labor for his landlord, from chopping wood to running menial errands. As the report emphasized, all of this was unpaid, leaving Yang starving on the street after his landlord refused to feed him.[102]

But according to the party's revolutionary narrative as explained by its ever expanding propaganda army, being a landlord meant far more than prospering from the economic exploitation of the peasant masses. These men were cast as evil and corrupt. As a result, attempts to avoid the land-lord class status by selling off land and other properties took on sinister overtones.[103] Landlords were portrayed as a reactionary class attempting to derail the revolution, and records of landlords committing illegal acts to limit their losses abound in party records. One evil tyrant landlord in Wen-jia, an administrative village, was charged with illegally selling off much of his land before it could be taken away. Landlords also might spread ru-mors in the hopes of curbing peasant activism and class struggle. According to one landlord rumor, "The American soldiers have occupied Korea, the Third World War has started, soon the Communists will be gone, and when the Nationalist Party returns they will crack your skulls." Most brazenly, in the suburbs of Chongqing, an evil tyrant connected to the Nationalists

IMAGE 12. An evil landlord, upset over land reform, uses metal spikes to hurt a peasant. Source: ord. Source: *Zhongnan tudi gaige de weida shengli*, 113

teamed up with twenty like-minded elites to start their own peasant associa-tion to hamper the implementation of land reform. The evil tyrant claimed to have been a Communist for over ten years and promised that only those who joined his peasant association would receive land. Over two thousand signed up. Amazingly, this was not the only "fake" peasant association to spring up during the late rounds of land reform in Sichuan.[104]

While party propaganda generalized the evil nature of the landlord class, it was also certainly true that many landlords resorted to violence when faced with land reform. Even after the Civil War ended, there were cases of landlords poisoning wells or lashing out by destroying agricultural tools or cutting down forests.[105] These crimes against the new regime could be read as acts of self-preservation or desperation, yet the party universally portrayed these actions as the direct manifestation of the evil nature of the landlord class. The party further tainted local landlords by widely promot-ing stories of landlord crimes to demonstrate the depravity of the class as a whole. The landlord Liu Yuancong, struggled in 1951, was accused of over five hundred crimes. His underlings beat peasants to death over perceived slights and murdered others to cover their crimes. During a five-day mara-thon of charges in his local peasant association Liu was further accused of thievery, seizing property, making high-interest loans, and selling opium. In light of his crimes, one report concluded, "Killing him was really letting him off easy."[106]

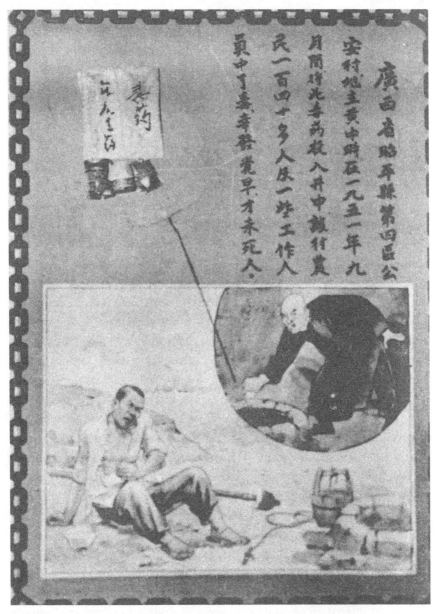

IMAGE 13. A landlord poisons a well to take revenge on peasant activists.
Source: *Zhongnan tudi gaige de weida shengli*, 105.

As discursively constructed by the Communist Party, landlords were ruthless exploiters. Living off the labor of the good peasant masses, they murdered to protect their lands and class interests. But that was just the start of landlord crimes. According to the party's countless tales of lecherous landlord men, they were by nature perverse sexual deviants. The sexual abuse by landlord men could take many forms, from raping peasant women to controlling the young women already within their households. Landlord women, meanwhile, were accused of using their sexuality to corrupt peasants and subvert the revolution. Through a skillful representation of rural gender relations, the Communists demonized the old order by portraying village power holders as lecherous sexual deviants preying on peasant women. Simultaneously, Communist propaganda presented the party as the sole savior of peasant women and, by extension, the peasant family.

Actual cases of landlord-as-sexual predator certainly existed, especially during the chaotic years preceding Communist victory. Jack Belden interviewed a woman who "was constantly forced to receive the attentions of a local landlord," who also headed the local Nationalist militia.[107] Communist propaganda ensured that the crimes of some landlords became indicative of the depravity of the landlord class as a whole. Such was the case with the vile Xuan Jingxiu, an accused evil tyrant and bandit. During his trial in late 1950, he was charged with the rape of Li Suqing in 1931, keeping her captive for two years before having her buried alive. This was only one of multiple charges of rape against Xuan, whose depravity seemed to know no bounds. According to the report, he raped and sodomized over two hundred women and children. And in the "counterrevolutionary territory" under his control, he claimed "first night rights" (*chu ye quan*), brazenly raping newlywed brides.[108]

For the party, the idea of landlords as sexual predators was an accepted truth. One report on the "feudal regime" in control of rural Sichuan declared that dishonoring peasant women was a standard landlord crime. The report offered an example of a sexually deviant landlord in Wenjiang county, Lei Fuhua, a wealthy landowner who served in a number of official posts, including school principal. Taking advantage of his wealth and position, Lei "constantly" raped peasant women: over thirty teachers, peasant wives, and students. As a result young women "didn't dare to go" anywhere near the landlord. Lei even took his running dogs to the household of the poor peasant Li Xinghua with the intension of raping Li's attractive nineteen-year-old daughter. Finding her not home, he sexually assaulted Li's thirteen-year-old daughter, ordering his running dogs to knife the girl to death when she resisted and cursed him. Threats of further violence kept her father quiet.[109]

Through skillful repetition in party propaganda, the horrific crimes of individual men such as Lei Fuhua became tied to the entire landlord class. The party, for example, offered powerful representations of new class identities in the operas that were staged throughout the countryside during the many years of agrarian revolution. Because the staging of evil landlords preying on helpless women proved highly effective in generating audience passion and anger, dramatists relied heavily on stock characters designed to promote class struggle. The landlord character Lu Chengshu of *Red Leaf River*, the opera William Hinton watched in Long Bow, is notable for both his love of cheating the peasantry and his predilection for sexual assault. Hardly limiting himself to collecting rent and interest, Lu was a sexual predator, cruelly raping Yan Yan, a young peasant girl, an act that led directly to her suicide. The connections between class and sexual assault became so pervasive that in some cases, all landlord and evil tyrant extramarital sex was simply deemed rape.[110]

Cadres and peasant activists, despite casual references to dividing the wives and daughters of class enemies, were almost never accused of sexual assault. The recent work of Tan Song, an academic and activist dedicated to recording the abuses of the land reform era, suggests that sexual misconduct among cadres and activists certainly existed and may have been widespread. Investigating the gang rape and killing of a landlord daughter over a half century after her death in 1950, Tan uncovered the details of the crime. A land reform work team, failing to get much from a local bank manager, called for the struggle of his daughter, a young teacher named Liang Wenhua. Some ten militiamen, sent to fetch Liang, gang-raped and killed her. In 2006, Tan's investigation revealed that one of the accused rapists, Li Chaozhao, was still alive. Interviewed by Tan, Li detailed the background of the crime, noting that the bank had been already taken over by the Communists, so naturally the manager had little cash to turn over. Li, insisting that he did not take part in the crime, admitted that the other militiamen were in fact guilty, although none were ever charged. As Li bluntly explained in graphic terms, activists overseeing female class enemies had nearly unlimited power.[111]

Agrarian revolution embedded the language of Maoist social classes deep within rural society. The famous philosopher Feng Youlan discovered this when he joined other intellectuals and traveled to a village just outside Beijing to join a land reform work team in early 1950. Later, Feng admitted that before participating in land reform, he had thought that the movement was "merely some sort of economic policy." After joining the work team, however, Feng witnessed strange events, including an old peasant woman who cursed her husband in the new language of class, yelling out, "You are a rich peasant, you are a landlord, and you are an evil tyrant!" Now, Feng wrote, he understood that land reform had to be understood as "a form of mass education."[112]

The introduction of the concepts of class, class labels, and class struggle into Chinese villages dramatically altered rural life for decades. The concepts of landlords and peasants, arriving in rural China during these seven years of agrarian revolution, became accepted as natural social categories. This was a moment of discursive explosion, a time when the campaign and its distinctive rhetoric spread to many narrative forms, from simple songs and slogans to full-length novels and operas. Under party direction, villagers were taught to see landlords as qualitatively different from peasants. Landlords were villains, determined to stop land reform at any cost. Landlords were also sexual deviants, capable of raping of young women and other reprehensible acts. Landlord women, meanwhile, used their sexuality to serve the impure interests of their class by seducing or even marrying local cadres. And the crimes of landlord elders were passed on to future generations without hesitation or question. In Wugong in North China, a visiting work team could find only one suitable class enemy to struggle: Li Yingzhou, a true bully whose actions had led to the deaths of multiple peasants. But because the man lay dying, the work team organized a brutal struggle of his only son, Li Dalin. This man, beaten and crippled by his neighbors during land reform, was guilty only of being his father's son. Not far from Wugong, meanwhile, a poor orphan girl was labeled a landlord so that she might serve as the village scapegoat for class struggle.[113]

Behind the narrative of liberation through class struggle, however, is evidence that some peasants actively sought to protect their landlords from struggle. During the height of the Civil War, many landlords found shelter and safety among family members in nearby villages.[114] The party generally blamed this phenomenon on landlord chicanery or ideological confusion. But the conspiracies local communities concocted during class division to convince work teams that village landlords were in fact laborers were impressive. In Guizhou, for example, a peasant association chair named Yang Taoxuan attempted to save his relative Yang Zexuan from being cast as a class enemy. The relative, Yang Taoxuan argued, had given him medicine to cure an illness and thus should be considered a doctor.[115] Many peasants, horrified at the prospect of struggling their neighbors, actively spoke out in favor of peaceful land reform. In Lu county in southeast Sichuan, peasants told work team cadres that their local landlords were actually rather poor, so there was not much to gain in violent class struggle. Some peasants also made it clear that they liked their landlords. As work team members reported, there was "not much hatred" (*chouhen bu hen*) to be found. One poor peasant wife insisted that their landlord was respectful (*gongjin*): when he came to the village, he wore grass sandals and never rode a sedan chair. A hired hand admitted that he had been exploited, but also declared it was no big deal. Work team members, through education, were able to correct these ideological problems.[116] The party could scarcely have it any other way. Without resentment toward landlords, fierce class struggle, the penultimate chapter of the party's narrative of rural revolution, was impossible.

STRUGGLING

Inside the Furnace of Revolution

Envisioning land reform in Nuanshui, work team cadres under the direction of Wen Cai never doubted the true nature of their campaign. As one cadre bluntly declared, "Land reform is to divide land, but there must be struggle!" Another responded, "Of course. Without struggle, how can there be reform?"[1] Some frightened Nuanshui landlords attempted to find accommodation with the new order. Hearing his tenants' demands to settle accounts, one meekly replied, "What, you still want to settle accounts! How could I not know that our village is to have land reform, this is a good thing."[2] Wanting nothing to do with struggle, the landlord directly offered up his land as a donation. The peasants wisely refused his offer: there was no room for donations if accounts were to be truly settled. The activist Guo Fugui took the lead, telling the landlord, "We are not going to settle old accounts, only those dating from the start of the Japanese occupation. That land of yours, how much can it produce in one year?"[3] Guo and his peasant brothers angrily calculated what the landlord owed them. When the bill was finally tabulated, the landlord had no choice but to hand over his land deeds in payment.

Other landlords did not back down so easily. Out of tricks yet obstinate until the end, Qian Wengui refused to go down without a fight. And so the middle peasant Old Wu, finally immune to the rumors of the return of the old feudal order, boldly roamed the streets of Nuanshui, banging his gong and calling for all to come to the village stage. In the past, Nuanshui peasants had gathered around this stage, dressed in their finest while peddlers hawked their goods, to take in operas featuring legendary gods and fair maidens. Today they still dressed up and merchants still wandered among the crowd, but this was a different type of performance. Preparing for the ritual enactment of fierce class struggle, Zhang Yumin, the most prominent Nuanshui activist, carefully arranged select villagers around the stage. Teacher Liu, meanwhile, led his students in song:

> Unite!
> Hey!
> Tillers of the land!
> The landlords have oppressed us, oppressed us for so many years,
> Let's . . . settle accounts, settle accounts![4]

Taking to the stage, Zhang called his fellow peasants to come forward and declare their grievances against the landlord and evil tyrant. "Today we are going to really struggle Qian Wengui," Zhang boldly declared. "Those with hatred will get revenge, those who have been wronged can right these wrongs."[5] One by one peasants mounted the stage, all revealing how they had suffered due to Qian's devious machinations. As the crowd reached a frenzied state of rage and anticipation, cadres saw their opportunity and moved to bring the struggle target to the stage so that he might finally face the wrath of the masses.

Qian Wengui's arrival at his struggle meeting changed everything. After loudly cursing the landlord and evil tyrant in absentia, peasants were now reluctant to speak. Just as the spirit of the meeting started to lag, Liu Man burst on the stage. A poor peasant activist, Liu had first learned the language of rural revolution by speaking bitterness with the work team's Yang Liang. Turning to the crowd, Liu told his well-rehearsed tale of woe, expertly detailing how Qian had led his family to financial ruin:

> My father had four sons, my brothers and I were all good workers, and relying on our own strength, we should have done pretty well. Before the war, we saved up over two hundred dollars and wanted to invest in some property. Unfortunately, we got involved with Qian Wengui, who said opening a mill was the way to big profits, and urged my father to open a mill, even helping him rent a building. He then got a friend of his to come in and be the accountant . . . within two months, the friend was nowhere to be seen. He took off with two donkeys and over a thousand *jin* of wheat and disappeared.[6]

Qian Wengui's trickery, Liu Man continued, had gotten one brother con-
scripted and almost certainly killed. Qian forced another of Liu's brothers
to serve as a tax collector for the Japanese. The psychological pressure of
collaboration with imperialist invaders had driven him mad. Liu ended his
tirade with a call for revenge, a call the crowd, now whipped into a frenzy,
heartily endorsed.

As the struggle meeting approached its climax, humiliation and violence
rained down on the once formidable landlord. Peasants, following Liu
Man's example, now shouted slogans at Qian and openly cursed him. Cadres roughly grabbed the devious Qian and dragged him to the front of the
village stage to play the role of villain in their drama. Pushed to his knees
in symbolic submission to Nuanshui's peasant masses, Qian's trial was not
yet over. As if following the exact script of rural revolution first penned by
Mao Zedong in 1927, cadres and activists humiliated Qian by forcing him
to don a dunce cap, his emblazoned with the slogan "Exterminate Feudal
Power." Some in the crowd continued to relentlessly curse him, while others vented by shouting slogans until their anger exploded into violence. A
swarm of peasants dragged Qian off the stage, where they mercilessly beat
him until cadres finally intervened. Bringing the landlord back to the stage,
they forced the beaten and bloodied man to kneel before the assembled
villagers and read aloud a humiliating confession.[7] The struggle of Qian
Wengui, landlord and exploiter of the peasant masses, was a total success.

Liu Quan watched the struggle of the Tang patriarch without joy, seeing
not liberation but only farce and tragedy. Farce for the blatant manner in
which his work team conspired with local Hanjiatuo cadres to orchestrate
struggle. One yelled out, "We need more from you Third Auntie Xia!
Louder! Clench your fist when you raise it! What do you think you are
doing, waving to someone on the street?"[8] And tragedy for the death of
the innocent peasants who were arbitrarily labeled as class enemies by
cynical team members and greedy activists. After being falsely identified
as a landlord, a middle peasant, Tang Zhankui, who had once welcomed
Liu into his home, discovered the true meaning of struggle. During the
mass meeting, Tang was violently attacked, his fellow villagers taking turns
beating him under work team supervision until he was senseless. After
undergoing this brutal ordeal, Tang was executed alongside other "feudal
landlords" (*fengjian dizhu*).[9] During the execution, team leader Zhang Li

made sure Liu Quan personally pulled the trigger to finish off one of the victims. Liu never saw the man's face, but he knew in his heart that he had murdered Tang Zhankui.

Tang was not the only Hanjiatuo villager to die during land reform. The work team had conspired with local activists to wrongly give several peasants the classification of landlord. Among those villagers so labeled, only Han Tingbang had been a true member of the landlord class. Because local cadres hoped to extract wealth from his family, Han, unlike the hapless middle peasant Tang Zhankui, was not taken to be legally executed. His suffering at the hands of village cadres, work team members, and peasant activists reached its most appalling levels as they tortured Han's wife to death in an attempt to uncover hidden wealth. The fact that the woman was six to seven months pregnant made their actions all the crueler. Her husband met a similar fate, dragged behind a cart until his skin and intestines littered the ground.[10]

William Hinton and his work team did not bring revolutionary struggle to Long Bow. That had happened long before, in the months following Japan's defeat in 1945. Local party members emerged to take over village power structures and called their neighbors together so that they could punish those who had collaborated with the hated Japanese. As peasants would later recall in conversations with Hinton and his interpreter, the village buzzed with excitement as Long Bow cadres brought former village head Guo Deyu before them, but his subsequent beating shocked the crowd into a stunned silence. Guo was just the first of many traitors struggled by Long Bow peasants. Those villagers who spoke up and denounced struggle targets received a share of the struggle fruits; those who remained silent got nothing.[11]

Early the following year, Long Bow cadres attending a district meeting were instructed to pivot their attacks to the landlord class. Excited, they quickly established a peasant association to settle accounts with Long Bow landlords. Due to mobilization work done by local cadres and the promise of economic gain through struggle, excitement ran high: "Women went so far as to bring food with them so that they and their families could stay right through the day and not miss a single minute."[12] Long Bow's two most prominent targets were beaten and tortured until they produced hidden wealth. After the two men fled the village, cadres moved to lesser targets, never afraid of using violence in the hopes of unearthing the wealth assumed to be buried by devious Long Bow landlords. Some were beaten to death; others were totally dispossessed, left with nothing.

The campaign to settle accounts ran for four weeks and according to Hinton nearly brought about the "destruction of the feudal land system."[13] But the party was just getting started in Long Bow. When news of the May Fourth Directive reached village cadres, they assumed that feudal exploitation remained a huge problem and that many peasants had yet to achieve liberation. Activists once again went on the attack, formulating a slogan to justify the torture used to unearth silver dollars and fine clothing: "If you don't beat down the drowning dog, he'll jump out and bite your hand." Because most heads of households had fled or been killed, struggle was often directed at women. Cadres quickly discovered that the surest way to break these women was to threaten their children. Each new discovery unearthed led to a call for more struggle targets, and activists began to search for "feudal tails": those who had benefited from exploitation in the past. Now even middle peasants found themselves attacked. Soon there were no new targets, and with no new wealth to be found, peasants had to be forced to attend Long Bow's final land reform meetings.[14] Some months later, William Hinton, wearing his heavy greatcoat, arrived in the village for the first time. It was time for his work team to bring revolution to the feudal countryside.

There could be no revolution for village China without what the Communists called *douzheng*: struggle. Intimately tied to the concept of class, the term *douzheng* was a linguistic creation of the twentieth century.[15] Introduced in the 1908 translation of the *Communist Manifesto*, *douzheng* helped explain the role of class struggle in the progression from one economic system to the next. In the everyday unfolding of the Chinese revolution, however, struggle referred not to the broad conflict between feudal landlords and capitalist farmers, but to the public denunciation of individual class enemies under the direction of the Communist Party. Enshrined as the critical moment in agrarian revolution by Mao in the 1920s, struggle was by design a confrontational affair. Actively taking part in struggle was viewed as the only way for peasants to get revenge (*baochou*) and avenge past injustices (*shenyuan*). Struggle also offered peasants an opportunity to settle accounts (*qingsuan* or *suanzhang*) by tabulating the total monetary amount lost through exploitation and demanding repayment. And while violence need not be involved, the use of struggle for economic gain, coupled with Mao's insistence that the masses be given free rein when confronting class enemies, led to the beating, torture, and execution of countless struggle targets during the many years of agrarian revolution.[16]

Throughout these years of campaigning, party leaders, following Mao's revolutionary narrative, remained firmly opposed to any suggestion of peaceful (*heping*) land reform. The Communists' land reform narrative demanded class struggle within every village regardless of local conditions. Land reform meant far more than seizing and redistributing landlord property. According to Mao's vision, peasants could not truly achieve liberation unless they personally participated in the overthrow of the landlord class by taking revenge for years of exploitation.[17] Work teams used highly ritualized mass struggle meetings (*da douzheng hui* or *kongsu hui*) as the means of liberating peasants through violent confrontations with landlords. Mass struggle meetings were nothing less than revolutionary rituals designed to transform farmers into class-conscious peasants.[18] Public events, struggle meetings were often held on stages; if the local temple did not have an opera stage, the work team might oversee the hasty erection of a temporary stage.[19] Taking part in fierce class struggle, work teams believed, gave peasants a chance to express their deep hatred of landlords and gain a true understanding of the power of the liberated peasant masses. For the party leaders, the very notion of peaceful land reform, which lacked class struggle and thus could not truly transform peasants and village society, was simply unacceptable.

The Communists advised work teams to carry out thorough investigations so that they "knew what was going on" before attempting to struggle village landlords.[20] Nothing was left to chance. Meticulous planning, carried out by local cadres and work team members, helped peasant activists enact predefined roles in the staging of rural class struggle. Because this ritual demanded a highly charged atmosphere, work teams encouraged activists to publicly denounce targets with repeated accusations of past crimes and exploitation. Humiliation often included violence, which ranged widely from beatings to torture and on-the-spot executions. While violence was publicly frowned on, especially during the final rounds of land reform, in practice struggle was often brutal, the threat of bodily harm an accepted tactic. One key shift over the many years of rural revolution, however, lay in the motives behind struggle. During early campaigns, activists, with the full support of the party, primarily engaged in struggle for economic gain. With impoverished peasants mistakenly thinking that landlords hid vast hordes of wealth, early mass campaigns in the North and Northeast were marred by brutality. The party attempted to restrict use of struggle for financial gains in later rounds of land reform by emphasizing the political and cultural liberation that struggle promised China's peasant masses. Throughout land reform, however, the party held fast to Mao's belief that only participation in public struggle could release pent-up anger, expose the truths behind the rural class system, and replace old village power holders with a new poor peasant elite.

The party's earliest forays into agrarian revolution were two campaigns that used struggle rituals for specific aims. The "antitraitor" campaign, launched in the aftermath of the eight-year war against Japan, represented the very start of the Communists' rural revolution. The first goal of the campaign was to punish the many Chinese who had collaborated with the Japanese. These collaborators, many attached to bandit gangs or secret societies, had carried out much of the violence against Chinese villagers.[21] As a result antitraitor struggle meetings were sites of considerable brutality, where pent-up frustrations and hatred vented with deadly results. The second objective was wealth extraction: activists funneled the property and weapons from collaborators to the party and its peasant supporters.[22] The subsequent settling accounts campaign widened the focus of struggle beyond collaborators, allowing peasants to begin the process of expropriating wealth from particularly exploitative landlords.

Both campaigns led to violent confrontations. In one story that emerged from North China, an accused traitor was led through multiple villages so that more peasants might have the chance to take their revenge. The result was a humiliating twenty-mile forced march: "Hardly had the traitor passed the first house when a crowd, armed with forks, hoes, pikes, and clubs poured toward him. One woman had a pair of scissors in her hand. 'I want to eat traitor's meat,' she cried."[23] Cadres were barely able to get the accused to the meeting in one piece. Once there, the crowd rushed the stage and beat him for hours. Fearing the situation had gotten wildly out of control, cadres took the struggle target away for a prompt execution. Villagers later found out where his body lay and continued to beat and stab the corpse until the head tore away from its body. Violence also marred the settling accounts campaign, during which poor activists used beatings, torture, and the threat of execution to encourage their targets to reveal new sources of wealth. The party, overestimating the amount of wealth in the countryside, pressed landlords and rich peasants to give up property that they simply did not have.[24]

Not every village saw violence during the brief lull in fighting that followed the end of the war against Japan. Recognizing that collaboration with Japan had been widespread, party leaders pushed cadres and activists to focus on only the egregious examples. In one Taihang region village, over 80 percent of households were implicated in collaboration, a fact that the village's "big traitor" used to threaten his neighbors into silence. The party resolved the potential crisis by making a point of only arresting the "big traitor" for struggle.[25] And nonviolent struggle could serve as an effective means of wealth transfer. In Ten Mile Inn, not far from Long Bow, peasants settled accounts with tax evaders during a campaign against unreported "black lands." These tax evaders, confronted with angry accusations and huge fines, had no choice but to hand over their farmlands. Land reform in Ten Mile Inn was a confrontational affair, but struggle meetings during the campaign against black lands were decidedly nonviolent.[26] Overall, however, the focus on violent revenge and wealth extraction that characterized these two campaigns would bleed into land reform.

When the May Fourth Directive officially launched land-to-the-tiller land reform in 1946, settling accounts through struggle was widely accepted as the prerequisite for the successful completion of agrarian reform. As later explained by Du Runsheng, one of the party's leading rural experts, to settle accounts during land reform was to

> mobilize peasants to wage struggle through the use of reason with landlords face to face, to expose one by one the landlord's economic exploitation of the peasantry, their political oppression of the peasantry, the facts of how in terms of human dignity they had humiliated the peasantry, in order to force landlords to admit guilt, so that they cannot but offer up their land, while the peasantry is in the legal and rightful position, and can feel proud and elated as they boldly and assuredly take possession of the land.[27]

The centrality of settling accounts ensured that the extraction of wealth from newly labeled class enemies remained the main focus of struggle meetings throughout the Civil War.

During the first land-to-the-tiller campaigns, however, some villagers temporarily forestalled violent class struggle by quietly negotiating the transfer of property to poor peasants. Such was the case with the first attempt at land reform in Wugong, a North China village where local cadres, free from the oversight of a work team, cooperated with patriotic landlords eager to avoid struggle.[28] Some party directives, meanwhile, suggested that enlightened gentry and other elite allies could avoid struggle if they attended meetings and voluntarily offered up their excess lands.[29] But the nonviolent transfer of property was rare: the arrival of work teams during the early rounds of land reform signaled almost certain public struggle for village elites. As Communist leader Chen Yi had quickly made clear, land to the tiller was "by nature a class struggle, an attack by the peasants on the landlords."[30] An August directive from the Central China Bureau noted that a summer of land to the tiller had seen a mixture of confiscation and donation, but declared donation appropriate only in villages where peasants had already been mobilized and achieved class awareness through settling accounts.[31] Later that same month, Deng Zihui praised a widely promoted Central China Bureau work team that had mobilized peasants to "struggle face to face" with rich peasants and landlords, giving the poor a "rice bowl" for the future.[32]

This praise for the Central China Bureau work team foreshadowed a broadening of struggle in the search for new sources of wealth. Peasants stuck in villages devoid of a wealthy elite, however, had difficulty finding proper struggle targets. In areas that had already carried out antitraitor or settling accounts campaigns, the start of land reform might be little more than the restruggling of formerly well-off villagers. Once there was no more wealth to be unearthed, activists turned to less-deserving struggle targets, including middle peasants. Party leaders were aware of this trend, with the Jin-Cha-Ji Bureau explicitly condemning endless (*wu xiuzhi*) struggle during land-to-the-tiller campaigns. Village leadership often passed to village hooligans (*liumang*) who used struggle sessions to enrich themselves; this was particularly the case when cadres distributed wealth to only politically active villagers. Questionable class determination methods, most notably the practice of tracing exploitation back three generations instead of three years, created new and increasingly poor struggle targets.[33] In poverty-stricken Ten Mile Inn, cadres claimed many middle peasants had "feudal tails" and were class enemies: 25 percent of village households were struggled in the vain search for more wealth.[34]

During the first land-to-the-tiller campaigns, party leaders allowed peasants a free hand in settling accounts, mandating that physical proof (*wu-zheng*) of exploitation was not needed; witness memory (*renzheng*) would suffice.[35] The violence of the campaign could be shocking. According to Jack Belden, in Shanxi's Stone Wall Village, activists strung up one struggle object so that he dangled in the air while peasants accused him of various crimes. He was later executed in a manner that Belden vividly captured:

> The crowd was on him like beasts. Their faces had turned yellow and their eyes rolled. A big farmer swung his pig knife and plunged it directly into the landlord's heart. His body quivered—even the tree shook—then slumped, but still the farmer drew his knife in and out, again and again and yet once again."[36]

The party's seminal land reform novels were penned during these years of chaos, embedding depictions of violent struggle in the party's narrative of agrarian revolution. In Zhou Libo's *The Hurricane*, work team cadres explicitly approved violence against the hated landlord Han Number Six as they prepared activists. The organizational work paid off: by the end of the struggle meeting, villagers had accused Han of killing seventeen peasants and sexually assaulting forty-three women. Accusations and curses were not the only things that rained down on Han Number Six. Irate peasants beat him throughout his trial. One woman relentlessly attacked the landlord with a stick. When her strength gave out, she dropped her weapon and jumped onto him, tearing into his shoulder and arm with her teeth to vent her hatred.[37] Only after all of his accusers had their turn did cadres put an end to the show with Han Number Six's execution. Land reform violence during early campaigns was intimately linked, of course, to the ongoing Civil War. When villages alternated back and forth between Communist and Nationalist control, both sides carried out horrific acts of brutality.[38]

Public struggle of class enemies to settle accounts during the initial rounds of land-to-the-tiller land reform meted out revenge and extracted wealth, but perceived weaknesses in the campaign left leaders and peasants alike unsatisfied with early results. Party leaders in the Northeast Bureau described the "half-cooked" results of their 1946 land reform campaigns: activists were disliked, the masses were not fully mobilized, and landlords still held on to village power. Land reform, including the mass struggle of class enemies, would have to be investigated and redone as needed.[39] While early efforts at land reform proved disappointing, party leaders never wavered in their shared belief that mass struggle held the key to agrarian reform and posited that full peasant participation in these rituals would bring about a successful campaign. After a lull during the 1947 spring planting, the party's reexamination campaigns aimed to bring the masses fully into the rituals of struggle. Given a variety of colorful names, such as the campaign against "air raid shelters" in the Taihang Mountains, they aimed at uncovering hidden landlord wealth. In the Northeast, a similar campaign sought to "chop down feudal trees and dig out treasures."

Even Ten Mile Inn, which had so far avoided violent struggle, was not immune from land reform excesses. During a 1947 campaign to "divide the family," cadres classed village struggle targets into three grades based on past levels of exploitation and tyranny. The worst offenders were forced to wear a patch identifying themselves: "Landlord/ First Class Struggle Object/Underminer of the Democratic Movement."[40] During a later campaign against "air raid shelters," Ten Mile Inn activists beat struggle targets in the search for wealth. Many landlords had indeed stashed away valuable property, but the ferocity of reexamination campaigns was also due to famine conditions in many parts of China, particularly in the Northeast, where many were without livestock or seed. A slogan popularized in one Northeast village summed up the attitude of many peasants: "No horse and no cow, so keep on struggling out money and valuables."[41]

As rural revolution deepened, the arrival of land reform work teams increasingly heralded violence, humiliation, and possible death. One party report, from the Taihang Mountains, made the desperation of landlords in 1947 clear. There, both landlords and rich peasants were subject to struggle, with landlords not even allowed to speak during struggle sessions. Sun Peiwu, thinking to ready himself for the coming ordeal, had his wife string him up; the painful experiment encouraged him to hand over all of his property. Other landlords were said to soil their pants at the mere mention of a mass meeting. But for poverty-stricken peasants in Communist base areas, struggle promised the means to obtain a better life. The poor peasants and hired hands of the Taihang Mountains, for example, were said to want to struggle anyone who had more wealth than they did.[42] Peasants in the Northeast, suffering through famine in summer 1947, were motivated to "dig out treasures" by the fervent belief that landlords sat on stockpiles of grain so vast that they were going to rot. Later party documents claimed that landlords had mocked the supposed liberation of the poor.[43] Party leaders attempted to control the peasant impulse to "dig out" wealth, insisting that activists throughout the scattered base areas limit their targets to only the largest and most exploitative landlords and to stop "digging" once these landlords had given up enough grain, clothes, tools, and seeds to satisfy the needs of the poor. Activists were instructed to use "soft" and "hard" methods. Negotiation with family members and friends, as well as promises that landlords could keep some of their buried loot, was to be combined with mass meetings and fierce struggle to force landlords to reveal their "treasure cellars" (*caibao dijiao*).[44] Party leaders hoped that this approach would reduce the endless struggle that led to rural killings and suicide.

The impulse to use struggle for economic gain and cadre enthusiasm, however, ensured continued violence in the countryside. Some party leaders were unconcerned. Kang Sheng, always an advocate of unrelenting attacks on rural class enemies, preached that all landlords, even those who appeared bankrupt or enlightened, were not to be trusted and must be subjected to public struggle. With seeming total disdain for landlord lives, Kang Sheng actively encouraged violence in the pursuit of hidden wealth.[45] After many favorable reports, these and other aspects of Kang Sheng's land reform methods were transferred to other base areas, bringing considerable violence to reexamination campaigns. In a "pulling landlords" movement that spread through parts of North China, for example, struggle targets were tied up and pulled apart at the limbs to force confessions of hidden wealth.[46] The reexamination campaigns sought to ensure the equalization of wealthy and poor households, rectify local Communist Party branches, and fully mobilize the peasantry. But even more than the first wave of land-to-the-tiller land reform, reexamination tended toward violence. In Shandong's Shanghe County, more than a thousand were beaten to death.[47] In Hebei's Fuping County, where over three hundred were killed during a brief reexamination campaign, activists attempting to extract wealth from wealthier villagers buried some of their victims alive.[48] This trend toward what would eventually be labeled "leftist deviation" coincided with increasing violence on the battlefront. When Nationalist forces or homecoming regiments returned, land reform and Civil War violence blurred.[49]

With the Civil War raging during summer 1947, party leaders endorsed the broad use of struggle to bring their revolution to village China by fully releasing the power of the peasant masses. In practice, giving poor villagers a free hand led to an upsurge in economic struggle: using struggle techniques to extract wealth. The party wanted economic benefits for its supporters, but the push for wealth overwhelmed political struggle: using struggle to overthrow feudal power and remake rural societies. As one experienced rural revolutionary noted in mid-1947, "'Struggling money and valuables' can increase determination, but economic struggle is not equivalent to political consciousness; therefore in 'struggling money and valuables' one must be wary of the trend towards economy-ism [*jingji zhuyi*"[50] The party encouraged land reform work teams to focus on raising political consciousness through the discovery of class hatred, but teams still had to find new sources of wealth to extract if peasants were to ever find economic liberation.

The Outline Land Law, released in October 1947, enshrined the equalization of landholding and instantly expanded the number of potential struggle targets in the countryside. During the subsequent land equalization campaigns, the rural poor fully embraced economic struggle. Party leaders understood the potential problems of economic struggle. In the Jin-Sui base area, where Kang Sheng had pioneered his brutal approach to dealing with landlords, party directives warned against allowing opportunists (*touji fenzi*) masquerading as activists to kill landlords and wreck the distribution of property. The Jin-Sui Bureau, demanding spontaneous (*zifa*) struggle, recognized that in fact many of the movements popping up to equalize landholdings were initiated by village cadres with impure motives that included "atoning for one's crimes through meritorious acts" and "taking advantage of a crisis for personal gain."[51]

The cadres leading the Jin-Sui Bureau called for a balance between releasing the energies of the masses while maintaining party control over rural revolution. As party central would shortly decree, releasing the masses did not mean embracing "tail-ism" (*weiba zhuyi*), that is, abandoning the responsibilities of leadership.[52] But in practice, violence permeated the land equalization campaigns. While some village cadres were reluctant to start land reform, violent attacks on class enemies became the norm once mass struggle began. Party leaders attempted to push back. One late 1947 directive called for lenient treatment for the enlightened gentry and other elite allies in established base areas, who would lose their excess lands but avoid the fierce struggle now demanded of other class enemies. According to party central, work teams and village cadres had to walk a fine line during struggle, never throwing cold water on the masses but also convincing activists to limit beatings and oppose spontaneous executions. Not for the last time, party central issued a reminder that the goal of land reform was to exterminate landlords as an economic class, not landlords as individuals.[53]

Despite such warnings, beatings and executions became increasingly common as the range of struggle was continually expanded during land equalization campaigns. Middle peasants, cadres, and women of ill repute scorned as "broken shoes" found themselves facing mass struggle.[54] A desire for wealth drove the push for ever greater struggle, but many acted out in fear of being seen as politically backward. Villagers also rushed to extract wealth from local class enemies before any property could be claimed by outsiders and then went on the road themselves in search of new targets. The party frowned on the practice of visiting other villages in search of wealth, known colloquially as "cleaning out the temple" (*sao tangzi*).[55] Particularly troubling for party leaders, villagers began to show up in urban areas seeking to struggle out what they saw as their rightful share of wealth.[56]

Violence was particularly acute in the Northeast, where farm ownership was often highly concentrated, leaving as much as half of the rural population as landless laborers.[57] These poor villagers had used threats and violence to force struggle targets to reveal hidden sources of wealth in a "digging-out-treasures" campaign. During the subsequent "swept-out-of-the-house" campaign, struggle targets in the Northeast often lost everything. This campaign started with a single mass meeting in December 1947, a massive affair with over six thousand peasants in attendance. These peasants then returned home to their own villages to struggle their own landlords, now seen as a source of seemingly unlimited wealth. As the campaign quickly spread throughout the Northeast countryside, activists pushed for the total expropriation of landlord households and repeatedly used struggle to force their victims to produce hidden valuables, leaving struggle targets with nothing.[58] Violence was not limited to the Northeast. According to the party's own accounting, in 1947 alone some 250,000 rich peasants and landlords were killed in the land reform campaigns of North China.[59]

As mass violence threatened to derail agrarian revolution in early 1948, some party leaders began to speak out against land reform struggle. In the Northwest, Xi Zhongxun noted how activists had falsely created landlords, resulting in manufactured struggle (*zhizao douzheng*). Campaigns that appeared spontaneous had in fact been jump-started by impure elements with dubious motivations. Activists in one poor peasant league, for example, had threatened to stone villagers to death if they did not take part in struggle; elsewhere, a work team ordered the local militia to string up landlords and beat village cadres. And at many mass meetings, activists hired thugs to "tie up, string up, beat up, and flog" villagers, leaving the countryside in a panic.[60] Writing personally to Mao, Xi was unflinching in his description of the extremes of rural revolution. In five days of land reform in Shaanxi's Jia County, hooligans drowned victims in vats of salt water; they also poured boiling oil over the heads of struggle targets, burning them to death. Local cadres and their families were strung up and beaten in the search for wealth. Struggle even spread to a school for party children. There, teachers and students as young as seven years old were singled out as landlord running dogs. While these events were rare, Xi argued that they deeply affected rural society: peasants were so afraid they did not even dare to bury the dead.[61]

Xi Zhongxun, long an advocate of middle peasants, was not alone in pushing for a reevaluation of land reform struggle. As Ren Bishi announced in early January 1948, the party would now attempt to protect middle peasants and cadres from struggle. And in a retreat from what was now lambasted as the "poor peasant line," struggle targets were guaranteed a share of property. With these new policies in place, the land reform campaigns of 1948 saw a slow but decisive shift from economic struggle toward political struggle. Landlords still stood to lose property, but a guarantee of livelihood promised a halt to the never-ending search for wealth. Middle peasants and other class allies who had earned the wrath of the masses could still be struggled, but this struggle was to be political, not economic. Struggle targets were to be fewer, and work teams were instructed not to use beating or torture in the search for wealth.[62]

In the Northwest, Xi Zhongxun, emboldened by the move away from all-out equalization, continued to promote an alternative path to land reform in 1948. That summer, sending work teams to newly liberated areas, Xi had discovered that rushing land reform under the slogan "determine fast, distribute fast" (*kuai ding kuai fen*) had empowered hooligans to indiscriminately beat, struggle, and kill, leaving many households "swept out of the house." Xi instead promoted the model used in Huanglong, where the party carried out only double reduction, promising to start land reform as needed in a year or two. Noting that lands given up by nervous Huanglong landlords had been accepted and distributed without struggle, Xi scoffed at the idea that his work teams were being too charitable. In the past, Xi argued, "formal struggle" (*xingshi shang de douzheng*) was always considered the most revolutionary, but in reality this was a "very bad tactic" (*ji bu celue*).[63]

The brutality of the first years of agrarian revolution is now well known.

In the 1990s, party leader Bo Yibo admitted that rich peasants had been targeted throughout the base areas, especially where peasants and cadres sought the equal distribution of land.[64] In one Shanxi village, activists murdered all of their local landlords in a single evening.[65] The ferocity that characterized struggle during these first rounds of land reform would be hard to shake. Even after party leaders finally moved to tamp down struggle in 1948, the party continued to reward zealous activists with promotion after promotion; those who shied away from aggressive confrontations saw their careers stall.[66] Party central, after receiving a report from the Northeast Bureau in late April 1948 documenting widespread cruelty and growing casualties in the search for hidden treasure, agreed that using torture to struggle out wealth had to be stopped. But party leaders chastised the Northeast Bureau for wanting to protect hidden wealth from future distribution. Instead, peasants should be encouraged to use nonviolent means to find landlord loot.[67] In the short term, struggle declined over the course of 1948 as work teams focused on correcting class labels and returning property to those who had been unfairly struggled, including landlords who had lost everything during the swept-out-the-door campaigns. Land reform was declared complete in the old base areas, and after a disastrous experiment of attempting land reform in newly claimed territories, the campaigns were put on hold during summer 1948.

When agrarian revolution returned the following year, violent struggle remained an essential part of rural campaigns. Tangshan cadres, thinking that it was "better to be left than right," argued that it was impossible to mobilize the masses unless they beat landlords. Some insisted that beating and killing were the only way to "solve problems."[68] Working in forty villages in rural Shunyi, now a Beijing suburb, work teams dispatched by the North China Bureau committed a host of what were termed "leftist" errors in late summer 1949: indiscriminate imprisonments, beatings, and struggle. Teams forced peasants to take part in struggle and left victims with nothing, once again using the swept-out-the-door method.[69] But the North China Bureau decisively moved to squash indiscriminate corporal punishments when settling accounts. The most egregious tyrants were to be sent to local courts for trial and possible execution, while the vast majority of landlords and rich peasants were to be struggled through the "speaking reason and talking policy" method. The bureau also banned the practice of "digging out" hidden wealth, now seen as a surefire way to incite violence. Work teams were instead to encourage landlords and rich peasants to voluntarily hand over their hidden wealth by allowing them to keep as much as 30 percent for themselves.[70]

The test run at land reform in Shunyi, by drawing attention to the problems of violent struggle, helped pave the way for a much larger campaign for the rest of the Beijing countryside. Running from October 1949 to March 1950, this campaign, carried out with "leadership, planning, and organization," was remarkable for the relative absence of violence.[71] Even villagers seemed particularly well versed in the party's land policy. Landlords, knowing that beatings were illegal, declared themselves eager to simply put land reform behind them.[72] During this campaign, which brought the revolution to some 640,000 rural citizens, work teams focused struggle on 130 evil tyrants, 40 of whom were handed over to the courts. Seven of them were executed. Work teams proved essential in limiting violence. Noting that the three villages that had started land reform on local initiative had witnessed violence and struggling of peasants, the city government had instructed teams to "resolutely prohibit spontaneous struggle by peasants in land reform."[73]

More lenient handling of landlords and rich peasants became official policy with the promulgation of the Land Reform Law of the People's Republic of China in summer 1950. In accordance with the new law of the land, work teams were to limit struggle targets and oversee nonviolent and legal struggle meetings. Law-abiding rich peasants were formally exempt from struggle. Landlords would still lose excess property, but the party demanded fewer struggle targets in order to unite peasants in opposition to a limited number of landlords. The party instructed work teams to avoid the indiscriminate use of struggle, now deemed "illegal struggle" (*weifa douzheng*). One land reform directive reasoned, "We must point the spear of struggle at big landlords and a select number of stubbornly resistant medium landlords." The party now advocated a resolute attack on the core of the landlord class, which would force medium and small landlords to lower their heads and accept land reform. By guaranteeing the property of rich peasants and promising a fair share of land to landlords, the party limited the economic gains that could be made through class struggle. But with struggle still promoted as the essential moment in land reform, would cadres and activists grasp the policy that "not beating has reason" (*yi bu da wei youli*)?[74]

In the immediate aftermath of the release of the new Land Reform Law, there were hints that the country would follow the example set in rural Beijing and limit struggle, especially in its most violent forms. In its own experiments with land reform in autumn 1950, the East China Bureau touted the use of a new struggle method (*douzheng fangshi*) and a new struggle form (*douzheng xingzhi*). In test point villages in Zhejiang, work teams sent true evil tyrants away for trial while meeting with landlords to discuss Mao's generous policies toward them. Meeting no resistance from landlords, the East China experiments in nonviolent land reform were declared a total success.[75]

Following the outbreak of the Korean conflict, however, party leaders quickly denounced peaceful land reform as a deviation due to fears that class enemies would use the conflict to push back against the new regime. After combating "leftist" deviations, the pendulum had now swung too far toward accommodation with the old rural elite. As 1950 came to a close, party reports began to again speak of "half-cooked" land reform and "rightist" deviations. According to the South Central China Bureau, cadres had mistakenly believed that landlords would embrace land reform. However, the landlords had instead made copies of their land deeds, started riots, and tried to pass themselves off as middle peasants. For the bureau, this proved that teams must rely on poor peasants and hired hands to "mobilize a fiery dawn, a hurricane" and carry out land reform.[76] In May 1951, Du Runsheng, ruminating on the 90 million South Central China villagers who had already "entered struggle," argued against southern exceptionalism: the idea that "in the North we had to emphasize struggle, but in the South we must emphasize peace."[77] For Du, the fact that landlords had embraced peaceful land reform as "worth it" (*hua de lai*) proved that such an approach was bound to fail. Noting that activists had strung up and beaten class enemies in most villages during the region's first round of land reform, Du insisted that the number of victims was still relatively small.

Giving a speech to cadres preparing to oversee rural revolution in in 1951, Deng Xiaoping agreed that class struggle was still an essential part of rural revolution. And while he instructed work teams to help peasants carry out private and nonviolent "speak reason struggle" (*shuoli de douzheng*), they must always remember that land reform was a great mass movement, and not a moment to be "refined and gentle" (*sisiwenwen de*). Chaos, Deng announced, was inevitable. Echoing Mao's 1927 "Hunan Report," Deng declared that China's peasants were to "surge like a tide" (*chaoyong*), impossible to stop. Ideally no one would die. But ever the pragmatist, Deng admitted that such an outcome was unlikely: "If some tightfisted land-lords hang themselves, does that mean that our policies are wrong? Are we responsible?"[78]

In order to facilitate class struggle, work teams during the final rounds of land reform typically asked landlords to give self-reports. Those deemed honest, remorseful, and compliant might escape struggle completely. Land-lords who balked at handing over their property were struggled, but with a renewed emphasis on political over economic forms of struggle, many land-lords saw only speak reason struggle: calculating exploitation and settling accounts, often in private. Landlords illegally hiding valuables, attempt-ing to purchase influence, or pretending to be poor were accused of their wrongdoings during public struggle meetings. Despite the party's explicit attempt to limit class struggle, these meetings could be quite common dur-ing the final stages of land reform. Among landlords in one northern Sich-uan county, 50 percent took part in speak reason struggle, 30 percent were subjected to public struggle, while only 20 percent avoided all struggle.[79] By this time, of course, most truly wealthy landlords had long fled the country-side, if not the country itself. For some villages, finding true landlords, as opposed to their running dog underlings, was a true problem.[80]

New emphases on political struggle, speak reason struggle, and private struggle diversified land reform experiences, but violence remained a stub-born problem. During one of the final rounds of land reform, future party reformer Hu Yaobang still had to clarify that the call to "annihilate" (*xiao-mie*) the landlord class meant to take landlord land, not landlord lives. But while Hu insisted that work teams never "use beheadings to solve prob-lems," he also argued that the execution of evil tyrant landlords was correct and just. As for counterrevolutionary landlords who refused to submit to the new order, Hu simply declared, "It is entirely they who force us to kill them."[81] In 1951 Chai Zemin, who decades later would serve as the PRC's first ambassador to the United States, explained to work team cadres that if, in the heat of the moment, activists beat up landlords, it was "not con-sidered an error." Work teams, instructed not to encourage such violence, nevertheless tended to fear peaceful land reform more than violent land reform.[82] Land reform exhibits, meanwhile, proudly displayed images of defiant peasants standing up to their landlord oppressors. Fierce class strug-gle remained essential to land reform and the party's narrative of agrarian revolution.

IMAGE 14. Confronting a landlord. Source: *Zhongnan tudi gaige de weida shengli*, 113.

Party documents reveal how work team members attempted to release the peasant masses while also maintaining control over the rituals of class struggle. Reports on land reform in the Chongqing area, for example, called for a controlled struggle at the outset of campaigns, suggesting work teams struggle only three or four landlords per administrative village. Only then would teams turn their attention to other landlords, making sure to treat large and small landlords differently.[83] Initial struggle meetings at the administrative village level were to be highly controlled to serve as model examples (*shifan*) for future meetings in smaller hamlets.[84] Another report discussed how to balance struggle with negotiation (*tanpan*). While by no means the primary method of struggle, negotiation had a place in the land reform process, at least for compliant and smaller landlords. By first struggling large landlords and evil tyrants, work teams scared these more docile landlords, allowing land reform to continue through negotiation. Land reform campaigns that eschewed any negotiation for all-out struggle ran the risk of a continuous broadening of struggle from representative big landlords to smaller fry. Given the tendency for violence and torture, struggle-

IMAGE 15. A mass struggle meeting. Source: *Zhongnan tudi gaige de weida shengli*, 111.

heavy campaigns guaranteed increased rates of suicide among landlords.[85] A similar report, noting how the tense atmosphere of an urban campaign targeting "counterrevolutionaries" had enveloped the countryside in panic and unease, instructed work teams to follow the law and replace violence with logic when they directed peasants who were struggling landlords. But with work teams well versed in the land reform narrative of liberation through fierce struggle, the violence of the early campaigns easily returned.

The party, in fact, was sending contradictory messages as the scope of agrarian revolution reached its zenith during the massive final rounds of land reform. The party instructed work teams to promote speaking reason and negotiation, especially when dealing with enlightened personages (*kaiming renshi*) who willingly turned over property, followed the law, and encouraged their peers to do the same.[86] Teams were also encouraged to work with landlord intellectuals; one work team was praised for mobilizing an educated landlord daughter to get her household to disclose hidden wealth.[87] Peasant associations vowed to focus on truly powerful class enemies and to never beat, abuse, or physically punish landlords. Such actions were to be left to the courts.[88] At the same time, however, the party still firmly opposed any suggestion of peaceful land reform and continued to promote narratives of liberation through fierce class struggle. As a result, violence continued long after the Civil War had ended in victory for the Communists. Some cadres, suffering from what was deemed a "struggle method problem," felt that it was "impossible" to produce wealth without beating, locking up, or killing landlords.[89]

A May 17, 1951, directive for a land reform reexamination campaign admitted that "once again there has been a rise in hanging up and beating people." As a result, incidents of "going all out for revenge at the risk of one's own life" were on the rise. Many landlords, unable to see a future for themselves in Mao's China, committed suicide. Reminding cadres to focus on evil tyrants, the directive explicitly called for the end of cursing, beating, and corporal punishments.[90] But the lure of wealth was hard to ignore, especially when greed or the desire for revenge could easily be glossed over with a sheen of peasant activism. Borrowing rhetoric from Civil War–era campaigns, activists continued to torture class enemies in the hopes of uncovering "hidden treasures." Some villagers were illegally "swept out of the house."[91] And peasants used the "settle accounts" slogan as an excuse to indiscriminately struggle smaller landlords and expropriate commercial enterprises such as noodle houses and paper shops. Jealousy of middle peasants, meanwhile, led to conspiracies to raise their class statuses in order to force a transfer of wealth.[92]

With activists seeking wealth continuing to carry out ferocious attacks on class enemies, violence remained an essential part of agrarian revolution. Events in Sichuan's Jiangjin region serve as a powerful example of the continued danger of struggle as land reform came to a close. There, after the execution of an evil tyrant named Huang Qingyun, his widow refused to return the deposits that the household had collected from its peasant tenants. Cadres turned to local party boss Lin Song, who gave them free rein to follow the will of the masses, adding that "with such an obstinate big landlord, we need to let masses shake things up, strike a few blows against the landlord's spirits." This call to violence produced a massive haul of gold from the widow. Enthused, activists expanded their reign of terror, beating and torturing class enemies at will. Not until hundreds had died did Lin Song move to tamp down the violence. Brought to task for his failings as a leader of rural revolution, Lin asked for further education.[93]

Lin Song's casual attitude to violence would have its most devastating effect in Jiangjin's Dazu County. In Dazu's Fourth District, a local party boss named Duan Mingzhu had initially overseen a peaceful campaign to reduce rents and return deposits in the lead-up to land reform. During a mass struggle of two powerful landlords, an angry crowd began beating the two struggle targets. Instead of channeling this anger, Duan ended the meeting, a decision that was said to dampen activism and give hope to landlords. After attending a February 1951 meeting, however, Duan became convinced that Lin Song was correct: violence was the key to remaking local society. When he returned to his Fourth District, he ordered local cadres to beat three big landlords. Hearing the three had been beaten to death, Duan casually remarked, "If they are dead so be it" (*dasi jiu dasi*). Given free rein, local cadres expanded their search for wealth, with each score pushing them to find new targets to beat.[94]

Encouraged by their party superiors, local activists competed to be revolutionary heroes and beat up and hung villagers in the search for wealth. Poor and middle peasants took the brunt of the abuse. Landlords committed suicide en masse. Rich, middle, and poor peasants were also killing themselves to avoid the terror. The problem was particularly severe in Dazu's Second and Fourth districts. In the Fourth District, Duan actively promoted violence, with deadly results. In one village, local cadres competed for Duan's favor by beating class enemies, resulting in six deaths. In the Second District, party committee vice secretary Sun Yulong was just as bad, teaching peasant association representatives how to beat and then hang class enemies. After this training session, representatives adopted a casual attitude toward revolutionary violence. One remarked that "beating one or two people to death is no big deal." Said another, "If speaking reason does not work, then let the fists speak."[95]

Duan Mingzhu and Sun Yulong, under the direction of Lin Song, oversaw campaigns of terror and torture. But because struggle remained essential to the land reform narrative, party leaders were slow to rein in violent activists. Dazu county's party secretary, Guo Zhongxing, when informed of the terror shaking his county, said only that "this is not very good." And because beating was actively promoted as the only correct mode of struggle, opposing or simply not advocating violence was dangerous. Activists could charge pacifists with improper class stances or with harboring landlords. As a result, local cadres feared criticism or, as locals called it, "getting their beards shaved." With no good options, these cadres felt that they had no choice but to take part in beating and torturing villagers. Former bandits and other "bad elements," meanwhile, posed as activists in order to take revenge. Some cadres used violence to cover up their crimes. In the Second District, local cadre Yu Qing had illegally beaten a landlord woman; fearing that his crimes might be exposed, Yu used a bayonet to stab her to death.[96]

County party secretary Guo Zhongxing would later admit in his own self-criticism that local activists were simply using struggle as a means of wealth extraction. Guo claimed that he did nothing to quell the violence because he feared "pouring cold water on the masses" and dooming the revolution. The result? Activists had used nearly forty different methods of torture, leading to hundreds of deaths in the Second and Fourth districts. Even in his confession, Guo still saw little problem with killing landlords. Upon learning that eleven landlords had been "forced" (*bi*) to death in the Fourth District, Guo remained indifferent: "Beating peasants to death is wrong, but beating landlords to death was not really going against policy."[97] The Dazu investigation revealed Guo to be an "arrogant and impetuous" man who found ways to promote violence. While Guo never directly ordered cadres to beat struggle targets, his casual comments to his underlings made his views on torture clear. Guo had publicly noted, for example, how mass violence in nearby Anyue County had been helpful in bringing agrarian revolution to a successful close. Hearing about a beating in Dazu's Seventh District that led to the discovery of wealth, Guo remarked, "Beating is very useful, a single stick can beat out eighty copper coins." Guo even asked cadres how many landlords had "voluntarily" (*zijue ziyuan*) died in their districts, while threatening cadres who had not beaten enough landlords to death. As he said to the Third District party secretary, "You are too rightist, how can you develop work and complete your tasks?" The result of all this was this a "secret" directive: "If the masses want to beat and hang people, they must not be stopped."[98]

The mass use of torture frightened and upset Dazu villagers, who complained about changed party policies, "once sweet, now bitter." They openly doubted that such a cruel government could last. Many villagers seemed sadly resigned to their fate. As one remarked after a landlord was beaten to death, "Well the guy is dead, there's really nothing more to say, we commoners should get out of here."[99] Dazu was an extreme case, but the party's commitment to fierce class struggle meant that the countryside, no stranger to violence, saw extreme acts of brutality during land reform.[100] In nearby Yongchuan, death was so common that party leaders insisted that all "accidental deaths" needed to be investigated before burial. The top-down push for struggle is particularly well documented in reports from Shijiao, an administrative village in Yongchuan. There, cadres oversaw seven struggle meetings over two weeks, with cadres vexed by both peasant indifference and cases of extreme violence. During one struggle meeting, a village cadre admonished the crowd to not act as if they were "asking for favors" because they were giggling or quarreling, but to instead conduct a "serious struggle." As leaders from Shijiao's various hamlets met to discuss their difficulties in carrying out revolution, the diversity in their experiences came on full display. Each neighboring community had taken a different approach to forcing landlords to pay fines, ranging from outright beating to exposing them to the elements.[101]

As these last examples suggest, after years of campaigning, rural struggle remained essentially linked to the search for wealth. In Jijing village, not far from Dazu and Yongchuan, local cadres, by allowing torture in the search for hidden treasure, reenacted the "deviations" that had marked the most violent days of land reform in the North and Northeast. Jijing cadres faced many familiar problems, starting with lackluster struggle meetings. They had carefully prepared activists, even holding special meetings on the night before initiating struggle to plot out their approach to toppling feudal power. But the "bitterness of the bitter ones" (*kuzhu de ku*) had not sufficiently moved the crowd, which was watered down with disinterested peasants and schoolchildren looking for excitement. As a result, cadres took things into their own hands, dousing landlords with cold water and exposing them to the elements or forcing them to kneel on broken porcelain.[102] In Shenping village, cadres struggled an evil tyrant landlord and his entire family, both male and female, for eleven days until they finally produced seven boxes hidden in a wall, buried porcelain, and gold jewelry stashed away in a pigpen. Village militiamen were said to subscribe to a "martial struggle ideology" (*wu dou sixiang*) that compared landlords to walnuts: they needed to be cracked open by force. Militiamen in Houping secretly tortured a landlord by rolling him up in a bamboo curtain, holding him upside down, and pouring hot pepper water down his nose in search of hidden wealth. According to county party leaders, such torture was "very common," and at times work team comrades actively conspired with village militiamen.[103]

Unsurprisingly, the violence that so marked China's agrarian revolution spread in unexpected ways. In the Chongqing region, some landlords attempted to skirt land reform by giving away property, perhaps in the hope of getting it back when the campaigns had ended. Instead of educating villagers to turn over what landlords had asked them to hide, local cadres labeled peasants as running dog collaborators and subjected them to fierce struggle in hopes of digging out as much wealth as possible from these landlord "air-raid shelters" (*fangkongdong*), yet another term revived from Civil War–era campaigns. Many peasants committed suicide in a desperate attempt to avoid struggle.[104] An investigation into land reform in Youyang revealed that poor peasants with "bad records" (*lieji*) were also committing suicide.[105] In Hechuan, a trained peasant activist killed himself, fearing that his past association with a secret society would expose him to struggle.[106] And peasants continued to seek to bring struggle to urban areas in search of wealth: in 1951, thousands of peasants marched into Guangdong's Huicheng demanding compensation from town-based estate managers. Even in the last stages of land reform, work teams failed to curb the "leftist excess" of emphasizing the economic uses of struggle.[107] In the countryside surrounding Chongqing, peasants with a "simplistic economic perspective" disregarded political struggle and, in an all-out pursuit of landlord wealth, marched to the city in search of workers, teachers, students, and office workers with ties to feudal families.[108]

Even during the final rounds of land reform, newly labeled landlords continued to avoid struggle at all costs. Some, such as the landlords of Fuling County's Xinmiao village, were successful for a time. Taking control over the local peasant association, they posted guards at the door while struggling other landlords with pleasant conversation, later staging a struggle meeting to fool a visiting land reform work team. In nearby Fengjie County, land reform was similarly hampered by peasant associations found to be largely controlled by middle and rich peasants. One report on forty-four villages found that only eighteen had peasant associations run by poor peasants and hired hands. And the party found extreme cases. In Jintian, for example, the village peasant association was secretly run by Zhou Zhaokang, an evil tyrant, in collaboration with secret society members and hooligans. When it came time to struggle the evil tyrant, the peasant association chair, Zhou Zuwu, cut off the "bitter people" attempting to speak bitterness, snapping that "you two will not speak off his head."[109]

Many peasants, including those hungry for landlord land, also shunned struggle. In Hunan, where land reform was underway in 1951, one peasant argued that if the point of the campaign was to help the poor by giving them more land, "why doesn't Chairman Mao just print some banknotes, buy the land from the landlords, and then give us our share?"[110] Even some rural cadres were in favor of peaceful land reform: experienced cadres wanted to avoid chaos and making mistakes, while newer cadres might believe local landlords were enlightened.[111] Many peasants wished to peacefully divide the land. While the party blamed this on the "numbing methods" (*mabi banfa*) that landlords used to trick peasants, it was clear that financial motivations were critical. When they sensed there was little to gain, middle peasants were particularly uninterested in struggle. Many poor activists, meanwhile, took part in struggle not to topple feudal power but for material wealth. For these activists, land reform struggle was not about creating Mao's New China but simply plowing the most productive lands and living in the best houses.[112]

Peasants wanted more than peaceful land reform. They also took action to avoid having to struggle their landlord neighbors under the direction of outsiders, as the case of the Sichuanese landlord Huang Anming shows. When the work team ordered villagers to struggle Huang, his tenants instead competed to treat him to a meal. When the work team asked the village militia to guard Huang, they instead turned him over to a tenant, Zhou Fushan, who again treated Huang to a meal. Village cadres all insisted that Huang was a law-abiding landlord; the work team had to ask cadres three times before they finally agreed to struggle him. After having Huang kneel for an hour, village cadres sent him home, declaring, "In the past we never struggled him, but this time we punished him by making him kneel." And yet even this brief moment of struggle was too much for village cadres, who felt as if they had wronged the beloved Huang. The landlord was known as a fair man who set reasonable and consistent rents and even sent tenants clothes during the winter months.[113]

For the party, any attempt to avoid struggle was unacceptable. Xi Zhongxun, long skeptical of struggle in the countryside, remained a true outlier. Reporting to Mao Zedong on the final stages of land reform in his Northwest Bureau, Xi once again found himself arguing against Mao's grand narrative of rural revolution. Accepting the centrality of releasing the masses and struggle for raising class consciousness, Xi nevertheless insisted that the party not abandon leadership of land reform. Xi instructed the forty thousand cadres and activists under his direction to mobilize poor and middle peasants together, so that they might use speak reason struggle and prohibit chaotic beatings.[114] Working in Gansu and Qinghai, Xi's work teams had discovered serious disputes between Han and Hui populations that had greatly complicated land reform. Xi proposed embracing peaceful land reform, at least for the moment. By working with Hui elites and treating landlords well, work teams in the Northwest were successfully transferring land and power to the peasantry. Later, Xi would describe this "somewhat peaceful" (*heping yi xie*) approach to land reform as "uniting with the feudal to combat the feudal."[115] But Xi was a rare voice, and even he made concessions to Mao's vision by arguing that this peaceful approach would "numb the enemy" and facilitate an eventual strategic attack on the landlord class.[116] And indeed before the end of 1951, the Northwest Bureau issued directives calling for the mass struggle of minority landlords, instructing work teams to develop Hui cadres and mobilize Hui peasants to speak out against Hui landlords.[117] Fierce struggle was essential to land reform and Mao's grand vision of rural revolution. For the many who may have found such violence abhorrent, Chinese intellectuals were ready to provide a theoretical justification of class struggle.

In 1927 Mao Zedong enthused over rural class struggle in his "Hunan Report," but even at this early date, he understood that many observing these confrontational rituals would feel revulsion and turn against the revolution. The problem of selling class struggle, already evident to Mao during the peasant movement, became a defining problem of the land reform campaigns. In 1927, Mao claimed that those who did not accept the necessity of the violent class struggle embedded in rural revolution would be left behind. But as Communist power grew in the late 1940s, culminating in victory in the Civil War, the belief in the need of class struggle was far from universal. Many urbanites had family ties to rural landlords, and some dared to argue that the restructuring of village property holdings could be accomplished without violence. After participating in land reform, Hu Shihua, a professor of philosophy at Peking University, recalled the initial reaction of his colleagues to the continuing campaigns. As one of his friends fretted: "Right now the countryside is so chaotic. Landlords are being hung up and beaten! During struggle, they will make landlords strip bare in the freezing cold or force them to wear cold wet clothes. And they even make landlords eat cow dung." Another friend summed up the case against violence toward landlords when he wondered, "If there is going to be land reform, then just have reform. Why must there be struggle!?"[118]

Crafting essays on their own experiences of participating in agrarian revolution, intellectuals offered their readers a multifaceted explanation for the necessity of confrontational and ritualized class struggle. For Hu, land reform was by definition a series of fierce struggles. The ritual of struggle, moreover, was required in order to mobilize the peasantry to overthrow the landlord class. And if violence occurred, as it did while Hu was in the countryside, this was simply a natural reaction to past landlord abuses. Violence, Hu argued, was beneficial to the formation of peasant class consciousness and thus helped the peasantry stand up to the landlord class and obtain liberation. It was simply illogical to feel sorry for landlords. After reminding readers of the many crimes of the landlord class, the philosophy professor, echoing the words of Mao's "Hunan Report," declared, "If we are to say that the peasants should not [do the same], and say that the peasants are going too far against the landlords, I think this is not fair! This is not rational!" Hu added a more practical excuse, noting that if these criminals had been formally arrested, they probably would have been executed anyway, so "those landlords who were beaten to death cannot feel they were treated unjustly, as the peasants were not incorrect in beating them."[119]

For Hu Shihua, class struggle grew out of class hatred and increased peasant class consciousness. Li Junlong, an intellectual who observed land reform in Hunan during early 1951, similarly noted how struggle sessions changed the way participants viewed the landlord class. "We participated in many large meetings where landlords were struggled," Li recalled,

> and when a normally very authoritative local despot landlord is led into the meeting by the people's militia for speaking bitterness and struggle, when it is explained how he exploited and cheated the peasants, how he stole land and wives, how he plotted to plunder and murder, as long you have a bit of a sense of justice, you will naturally stand with the peasants and know that to say "landlords are criminals" is not going far enough![120]

The process of struggle made the crimes of struggle targets public and encouraged class hatred, which, Li further reasoned, made violence logical and understandable.

Zheng Linzhuang, a professor of agricultural economics at Yanjing University, drew on the land reform narrative to rationalize rural violence: struggle was necessary due to the deep roots of the feudal system, the devious temperament of the landlord class, and the need to force landlords to confess their heinous crimes and submit to the peasantry. In his essay "Do Cadres Incite the Struggling of Landlords?" Zheng argued that violent class struggle was simply the natural outgrowth of the immoral nature of the landlord class: "There is not a single honest landlord, nor is there a single landlord who does not act like a tyrant (*zuowei zuofu*) and specialize in cheating and bullying the peasantry." According to Zheng's reasoning, all peasants rationally desired revenge through struggle, yet generations of landlord ideology had conditioned them to "meekly submit to oppression."[121] Work teams thus had to teach peasants about the nature of landlord exploitation; this was not incitement but education.

For intellectuals helping the Communists carry out the transformation of the Chinese countryside, the use of confrontational and ritualized struggle in land reform could easily be explained. By both creating class consciousness and altering village power relations, struggle held the key to what the Communists called *fanshen*: the liberation of the peasantry that followed in the wake of land reform. The intellectual Cheng Houzhi thus praised a village-wide meeting where he observed peasants denouncing and struggling village landlords: "This mass meeting was not only an important procedure for land reform, but also a revolutionary exercise of profound political and educational significance. Without it, peasants would not experience *fanshen*, and would not feel hatred towards landlords."[122] Chinese intellectuals had put their faith in Mao's narrative of revolution, but one question remained: Would fierce class struggle truly lead to *fanshen*, the liberation of China's peasant masses?

TURNING

The Promise of Fanshen

The decisive struggle meeting brought Nuanshui's revolution to its final chapter. Through fierce struggle, the peasant masses had toppled the hated Qian Wengui and found what the Communists called *fanshen*: economic, political, and even cultural liberation. Land reform transformed the village from a bastion of reactionary feudal power into a beacon of hope. As meetings came to a close, newly emancipated peasants rejoiced. Their cries, filled with excitement and a sense of their vast collective power, reverberated throughout the village. The end of land reform heralded a new era for countryside. Soon village cadres carefully oversaw the division of the fruits of struggle, gathering Qian's many fine belongings for redistribution to the needy masses. Cadres did not let Nuanshui's peasants forget that they had all been fundamentally changed by the revolution. When two farmers began arguing over the division of land, they were sternly reminded that the masses must be of one heart: "To lose unity over land the size of a sesame seed, what kind of fanshen is this?"[1]

Even Wen Cai found new life through land reform and class struggle. Despite his previous studies and self-reflections in the Communists' Yan'an capital, team leader Wen had still found it difficult to embrace revolutionary practice and truly become one with the masses. As an intellectual, casting off his deeply seated reverence for formal study and traditional learning for folksy peasant wisdom had proved almost impossible. Only through personally observing fierce class struggle in Nuanshui did the power of the masses correct his arrogance, finally jarring him away from his sanctimonious intellectual ways. Throwing himself into Nuanshui's revolution, Wen was now happy to provide any small assistance, working an abacus for peasants who otherwise did not really need his help. He had also learned to respect his underlings on the work team, accepting that they rightly had more authority among Nuanshui villagers because their work style spoke directly to the masses. As he gradually reformed himself, however, team leader Wen could not fully cast off his stinky intellectual airs. Some habits were simply too hard to break.[2]

In the months and years following the publication of *Sanggan River*, Ding Ling repeatedly emphasized that characters such as Qian Wengui and Wen Cai developed organically through her time carrying out land reform in North China. A brief glimpse of a beautiful yet forlorn landlord daughter in Hebei's Xin village, for example, inspired the creation of Qian's niece, Heini. Ding Ling's nuanced treatment of Heini, suggesting that landlord crimes should not be passed on to their children, would prove one of the most controversial aspects of the text.[3] Critics charged that Ding Ling "only saw how the peasants' houses were so dirty" while conversely seeing landlord daughters as beautiful, which led her to sympathize with landlords and rich peasants.[4] But for Ding Ling, it was important to create an accurate portrayal of rural China. Thus, she did not make her poor peasant activists perfect characters, and her scheming landlord villain was far from the stereotypical large landholder.[5]

Ideology, however, weighed heavily on Ding Ling's mind as she wrote in support of rural revolution. After *Sanggan River* won a Stalin Prize, given to outstanding works of socialist art, she humbly insisted that all thanks were due to Joseph Stalin and Mao Zedong: "While working in my heart I am often thinking about them, it is like they are standing right in front of me. In this way, I try my best to work according to their ideologies and in terms of their likes and dislikes."[6]

And so *Sanggan River* praised the triumph of peasant liberation. In actuality, the village that Ding Ling used as a template for Nuanshui was taken by Nationalist soldiers shortly after her land reform work team had left. As Ding Ling lamented, her beloved peasants would "suffer reprisals from despotic landlords."[7] Their true liberation would have to await another work team.

Tang Zhankui, by law a middle peasant, was executed for being a "feudal landlord" by village cadres greedily eyeing his properties. The work team, under Zhang Li, had happily gone along with the illegal class division in order to produce more struggle and more struggle objects. Liu Quan, believing himself responsible for Tang's murder, now watched the village prepare to divide the fruits of struggle taken from the hapless victims of land reform. The confiscated items were collected and displayed in the village's largest courtyard, but because the village had only one true landlord, most of the items up for grabs had been wrongly confiscated from mislabeled peasants. To make matters worse, corrupt village cadres devised a method to ensure that the best items fell into their hands. Led by the "reformed hooligan" Li Xiangqian, the cadres decided against drawing lots for property, slyly arguing that under such a system, peasants might not get what they really needed. Proceeding instead from the vague principle of "providing what is needed" (*que shenme bu shenme*), each household was asked to indicate what items they lacked. Small discussion groups then debated and decided who would be given each item, a system rigged by a small number of village cadres. They gave most peasants old and damaged items, of little use in raising their standard of living. One incredulous peasant received only an old clock, the minute hand broken off. The items desired by all, truly useful implements such as plows, were allocated to corrupt village cadres and activists.[8] For the peasant masses, there would be no liberation.

Liu Quan left Peking University for the countryside fully aware of his limitations. He lacked revolutionary practice, but he honestly believed he would be able to transform himself by taking part in agrarian revolution. He had gladly played his role in land reform, moving in with the friendly Tangs in order to learn from this peasant family and get closer to the masses. His experiences in the countryside had indeed changed him, but not in the way the party had intended. Arriving in Hanjiatuo, he had overheard villagers discussing class struggle with doubt and disgust. He had watched as the work team had used the false label of landlord as a pretext to arrest and execute the Tang patriarch. Attending the execution, team leader Li had pressed Liu to personally dispatch one of the landlords. Liu never saw his victim's face, but he was sure it had been his former host. Now, seeing the belongings of honest middle peasants carried off by village cadres and activists, Liu came to a truly bitter realization: land reform was simply about killing people and seizing their goods.

Carrying out land reform was Liu Quan's introduction to life under Communist rule. He still had much to learn. In subsequent chapters of *Love in Redland*, Zhang Ailing detailed Liu's experiences as both a propagandist in Shanghai and a soldier in Korea. According to literary critic C. T. Hsia, this wide-ranging approach allowed Zhang to "render with full justice the manifold aspects of Communist tyranny."[9] After his initial disillusionment during land reform, Liu's degradation and disillusionment at the hand of the Communist Party continued, reaching a peak during an anticorruption campaign when he was wrongly imprisoned and nearly executed. After his release, Liu requested a transfer to the Korean front, believing that death was preferable to remaining in the PRC. Liu, who considered himself the only member of the "voluntary force" to actually volunteer, had little choice: "His only thought was that he could not go on living in Mainland China, he could not even breathe. He thought the further away he was the better."[10] Yet after getting captured, he reversed course and chose to return to Mao's China with the hope of finding others to stand against the Communists. This ending, surely inspired by the outline that American agents had given to Zhang to structure her book, revealed that she, no less than Ding Ling, balanced her own experiences in the countryside with ideological concerns. In the American Cold War imagination, liberation in the Chinese countryside was inconceivable. But unlike the hugely influential *Sanggan River*, *Love in Redland* was quickly forgotten.[11] The world would have to wait for another gifted writer to cement the global understanding of China's rural revolution.

Embedded in the work team, William Hinton was uniquely suited to explain to Western readers what it meant for a peasant to obtain fanshen. In his classic formulation, fanshen in its most basic sense was the taking of land and other property of a class enemy, but the term also implied a profound personal transformation. As Hinton later translated in *Fanshen*, his "documentary" account of Long Bow's revolution, this was a complex concept:

> It meant to throw off superstition and study science, to abolish "word blindness" and learn to read, to cease considering women as chattels and establish equality between the sexes, to do away with appointed village magistrates and replace them with elected councils. It meant to enter a new world.[12]

This inspiring definition of fanshen was Hinton's greatest contribution to the popular understanding of Mao Zedong's rural revolution. Hinton never shied away from describing the violence that racked Long Bow during land reform, but he shared Mao's belief that in the end, peasant liberation justified class struggle. His poetic explanation of fanshen has become truly foundational: one recent history of land reform published in the PRC translated the previous quotation into Chinese in order to best explain how Mao's revolution had transformed China's peasants.[13]

But when exactly did the peasants of Long Bow obtain their fanshen? Hinton arrived in Long Bow long after villagers had already received the fruits of struggle from three distinct mass campaigns, including a round of land reform following the release of the May Fourth Directive. Newly empowered cadres, however, quickly transformed into bullies, shamelessly stealing property and sexually assaulting village women. One of the biggest tasks facing the work team was the investigation of local cadres, who now had to pass the "gate" of public opinion. Finally observing rural revolution in action, Hinton was impressed by how peasants fearlessly criticized the many wrongs of the new village elite. Declaring this an important moment for the "political fanshen" of the village, he would later write: "It had already created a new climate of opinion, and new political atmosphere, a new relationship between the Communist Party and the people, and a new relationship between the people and the Border Region government."[14]

Even as Long Bow's peasants seemed to be gaining a political awakening, however, they were having trouble making ends meet. Land reform had been carried out, but the work team declared the previous campaign a failure and promised to find enough wealth to allow all of Long Bow's remaining poor peasants to obtain fanshen. A renewed classification of the village had yielded only one new rich peasant household, with over a hundred households yet to fanshen. To make matters worse, the team realized that many of Long Bow's earlier struggle objects had been incorrectly classed and would have to be repaid.[15] The team tirelessly reclassified the village yet again, hoping in vain to find new sources of wealth to make good on their promise of universal economic liberation, only to be flummoxed by an abrupt policy shift. To ensure agricultural production, widespread confiscation of property was no longer tolerated. Accordingly, the local county party secretary announced that earlier evaluations of the rural scene had been wrong. Peasants had in fact obtained fanshen, even if they did not realize it at the time. Hinton knew what this meant: there was nothing left to redistribute. After boldly promising further fanshen, the work team sheepishly moved to return property to those who had previously been dispossessed. During yet another round of classification, any household with an average amount of land and housing was declared to have obtained fanshen. This round of class determination was overseen by Long Bow's newly elected People's Congress, and here Hinton found the start of something special. Noting how the congress had solved a taxation problem though fair and democratic means, he realized that his work team was no longer needed.

Land reform was only the first step for Long Bow peasants. Through the painful process of rural revolution, they had "transformed themselves from passive victims of natural and social forces into active builders of a new world." For Hinton this was the "essence of fanshen."[16] And as the Communists rushed to victory in the Civil War, soon all Chinese would follow their Long Bow brothers down "the great road to fanshen."[17] As for William Hinton, he eventually made his way home after the Korean War ended, but found his passion for Maoism an ill fit with McCarthyism. Zealous custom officials seized the copious notes he had taken while in Long Bow, depriving him of the chance to tell the epic story he had observed in China. A long legal battle gave him almost two decades to ponder his time in Long Bow before his notes were returned. In 1966 his account of rural revolution, the boldly titled *Fanshen,* finally made it to print. In the decades following its publication, the book sold hundreds of thousands of copies. Translated into ten languages, no other book has had a stronger impact on the global understanding of Mao's rural revolution.

In a literal sense, the word *fanshen* simply means "to turn the body." At the outset of Zhou Libo's novel *The Hurricane,* for example, the evil tyrant landlord Han Number Six lay on his back smoking opium. Hearing of the sudden arrival of a work team, Han "threw down his opium pipe, turned over (fanshen), and hastily asked" if this frightful news was indeed true.[18] This was the only type of fanshen for landlords in the land reform narrative. For peasants, conversely, "turning the body" was the prerequisite for the successful completion of agrarian revolution. In contrast to many terms popularized during land reform, *fanshen* was no neologism, but firmly rooted in the Chinese tradition.[19] The party had been speaking of fanshen for years during double reduction and other rural campaigns, but mass propaganda from grand operas to simple slogans ensured that

IMAGE 16. Peasants receiving their new land deeds. Source: *Zhongnan tudi gaige de weida shengli*, 126.

"turning the body" would become synonymous with land reform. Fanshen represented the total emancipation of the peasant masses through fierce struggle. This was partly an economic liberation: in the stories that the Communist Party told about land reform, peasants found financial security by taking possession of the fruits of struggle: the property confiscated from toppled landlords and other class enemies.

This promise of material benefits motivated many villagers to enthusiastically take part in land reform; with the ownership of farmlands in question, few dared to ignore the campaigns. The transferring of land deeds, however, could not compare to the spectacle that accompanied the distribution of the landlord's movable property (*fucai*), when the fruits of struggle were publicly staged and selected by the village poor. Villages used a variety of methods to distribute movable property. In some villages, cadres decided allotment in closed-door meetings.[20] More popularly, work teams arranged the fruits of struggle in a landlord courtyard or other open space, creating a makeshift revolutionary bazaar for peasants to come and lay claim to desired items. Party reports typically proclaimed struggle fruit harvests to be truly bountiful. In the Taihang region, a party investigation into almost three thousand villages found thirty-three distinct types of struggle fruits, including land, draft animals, housing, grain, clothes, agricultural tools, furniture, coins, and silver.[21] In the Northeast, regional party leaders boasted of distributing more than 1,000 kilograms of gold and 23,650

IMAGE 17. A happy family after land reform. Source: *Zhongnan tudi gaige de weida shengli*, 121.

kilograms of silver. In the aftermath of rural revolution, peasants in the Northeast were said to have ample land, with some families enjoying the services of two draft animals.[22]

Touting fanshen, the Communists promised a decisive end to peasant poverty and freedom from landlord exploitation. This process began through double reduction and other mass campaigns launched in anticipation of land reform. These campaigns adjusted rents and interests to favor tenants, returned hefty deposits to renters, and generally weakened the power of village elites. While party directives insisted on the importance of these first rural campaigns, it was only through land reform and the redistribution of the fruits of struggle that peasants could truly obtain economic fanshen by owning enough land and goods to prosper in the transformed countryside. For the party, these economic changes simply represented the start of fanshen. As work teams knew well, land reform also had to result in the political and cultural transformation of village China.

Empowered by the gift of fanshen, peasants were said to embrace education and reject all things feudal. Once again the land reform narrative drew on Mao Zedong's 1927 blueprint for rural revolution, which insisted on the link between village politics and culture. As Mao had boldly declared in his "Hunan Report," "The moment the power of the landlords was overthrown in the rural areas, the peasants' movement for education began."[23] Or as one popular land reform saying held, "If you want to turn the body, you have to turn the mind (*fanxin*), turn from the head and the feet will follow."[24] According to Peking University professor Yang Rengeng, fanshen changed the very nature of the peasantry. Once peasants obtained fanshen, they "quickly accepted political education and can understand a very high level of political theory. They can think, and they can think well; they can speak, and they speak correctly." And during small meetings, "when they use new terms they do not make mistakes."[25] The cultural transformation associated with fanshen was the true conclusion to the land reform narrative and its class struggle plotline: every step of mobilization had been designed with this end point in mind. One party report from the first days of land reform explained the connections between the various chapters of rural revolution in colloquial terms: "Digging out the poor roots to spit out bitter water and settle accounts is the key to turning minds."[26]

For some observers, these political and cultural aspects of fanshen were far more important than economic concerns. Li Guangtian, intellectual observer of land reform, declared that this was in fact the real meaning of fanshen. Economic liberation freed peasants from exploitation and allowed them to increase production, providing the foundation for a new peasant society. While a critical first step, this was not true fanshen. Not until peasants seized political power, rejected superstition, and embraced Mao and his revolution were they truly liberated. Li claimed to have seen real fanshen during land reform. When a village co-op quickly sold out its inventory of three hundred portraits of Chairman Mao, those who arrived too late and returned to their families empty handed were greeted with curses.[27] Such was the transformative power attributed to fanshen. And as the party made clear, the true liberation of the peasant masses was dependent on a successful land reform campaign. If land reform was done poorly, peasants could only "turn an empty body" or "half turn the body."[28]

The Communists carefully explained how fanshen transformed the countryside. Villages, once culturally and economically static, were now declared to be alive with revolutionary change. During the Civil War, party reports emphasized how peasant families, prosperous and politically active after land reform, happily sent their sons to battle Chiang Kai-shek and the Nationalists. At one such parting banquet, a father proclaimed to his son, "I toast you this cup of wine, so that when you return you might bring me Old Chiang's head."[29] Meeting to discuss the division of land, peasants put aside their personal interests for the betterment of the masses.[30] In the grasslands of Heilongjiang, hamlets once named after prominent elites now adopted proper revolutionary names: Liberation village, Democracy village, Prosperity village, and even Fanshen village. Production rose, peasants prospered, and the old "bare stick" bachelors got married. Villagers claimed that after land reform, even the climate had changed.[31] This, in addition to greater access to agricultural tools and new motivation derived from landownership, led to increased productivity in the grasslands.

Observers were also quick to note political and cultural transformations. According to Li Junlong, then an advisor to the Government Administration Council:

> Whenever we passed through villages or towns, we saw countless peasants wearing "people's militia" armbands, carrying spears, large knives, or rifles, leading criminal landlords to the peasant association or the district government. At night there would be patrolling people's militia everywhere, guarding against bandits and spies who might engage in activities such as destroying telephone lines. On the main village roads, groups of men and women happily converse, discussing issues. If they are not inspecting the fields, they are attending meetings; if they are not struggling landlords, they are repairing embankments and engaging in production. Big character slogans of "Long Live Peasant Fanshen," "Long Live Chairman Mao," and "Long Live the Chinese Communist Party," can be seen everywhere.[32]

One work team noted that after land reform, villagers no longer worshipped bodhisattvas. Instead they venerated images of Mao and praised him for delivering the peasant masses from their bitter lives.[33] Observers declared that the desire for a cultural fanshen led to "millions upon millions of peasants studying under burning lamps" in winter schools. Blackboards could now be found in nearly every village. Peasants no longer drank, played cards, fought, or "associated with women of ill repute" (*pao poxie*). "Nowadays," one report claimed, "their interests include dancing the new-style *yangge*, performing new operas, reading the magazine *New Country-side*, and listening to education officers read the newspaper."[34]

One of the best ways to understand the Communists' vision of fanshen was to visit one of the many hamlets now renamed Fanshen village in the aftermath of rural revolution. Yi Su, a visitor to a Fanshen village in Jiangsu, recalled resting on a hot summer's day at the house of Wang Chunxi, a peasant who obtained oxen, hogs, and fanshen through land reform. Wang had proclaimed that he could never "really compare today with the past, I never even dreamed I could be as lucky as I am now."[35] Residents of this village enjoyed literacy classes for adults and children alike. They even had health care from the popular village doctor, Xu Yulin. According to the doctor: "Nowadays many more villagers come to seek treatment, in the past if they got ill they would just muddle from one day to the next, but now their lives are better, and if they have even the smallest problem they will come for treatment."[36] Huang Jinshan, a landlord new to farming, reported to Yi, "I never labored before, but now I am fit and have energy." Everyone was happy in Fanshen village. Nine Buddhist nuns formerly attached to a local temple had been given their own farmlands so that they might engage in agricultural production. As one nun told Yi, because it was wrong to only eat, everyone should labor: "Nowadays under the leadership of the people's government, everyone has to produce, and if you don't produce you can only eat the northwest wind."[37]

The party did not forget about the difficulties nuns and other women faced in rural society, promising female villagers a "double fanshen": one as a peasant and one as a woman.[38] Like peasant men, they would have an economic fanshen by obtaining land and movable property through the fierce struggle of rural class enemies. The Communists heralded cases such as that of Guo Shuzhen, a Liaoning woman who gained a modicum of fame for her activism during the late 1940s. First mobilized during a 1947 land reform campaign, Guo and her family received land, two horses, a mule, and a cart.[39] But for peasant women, fanshen was also portrayed as a feminist awakening. During land reform, they were expected to overthrow traditional assumptions about a woman's role in society, and party accounts of land reform highlight how the campaign signaled a new life for peasant women. For Guo, obtaining land was only the first of many changes. Politically awakened during land reform, she joined her local party branch, headed her local women's association, organized literacy classes, and took a leading role in organizing production.

The feminist transformation of women through fanshen started with the call to eliminate a host of traditional marriage practices, now derided as feudal. In their place, free marriage would blossom.[40] Widows, previously strongly discouraged from remarriage, would now be free to find new husbands.[41] Bride-prices were also to disappear. Perhaps most dramatic was the introduction of divorce, which seemed to offer an escape route for many women trapped in unhappy unions. Reports on land reform did not shy away from suggesting what the introduction of divorce might mean for a class-stratified society turned upside down, and emphasized how rural revolution facilitated the flow of women from landlord to peasant households. In an account promoted from the Jin-Sui base area, for example, a peasant woman named Xue Qiaohua divorced her landlord husband, but not before publicly struggling him during land reform. She later remarried, this time to a peasant. Her new union did not end her political activism. After joining the village *yangge* dance team, she even composed a song describing her liberation from her ex-husband.[42]

The elimination of feudal marriage practices was just the start. After land reform, women were to take political roles in the village and be judged by the "height of their political consciousness" as well as the "correctness of their politics."[43] Party voices emphasized how women gained new power in their families during land reform. Chen Xianfan's husband would not allow her to attend meetings, insisting that she claim illness. With the support of village leaders, Chen fought for her right to attend meetings and won widespread admiration. Even Chen's mother-in-law accepted her new political activism, cooking for the family when meetings ran late and proclaiming that "as long as everyone thinks highly of her and she is helping everyone, then that's great!"[44] Hui women in the Northwest were said to have a particularly meaningful liberation. By first winning over elder generations, the party gave Hui women not just land but "freedom over their own bodies" (*renshen ziyou*). As a result they embraced the revolution and rushed to attend meetings.[45]

The party presented land reform as an unqualified boon for peasant women, a time when they gained land, freedom from feudal customs, and even a political voice within families and communities. In a 1947 land reform campaign in Hebei's Ding County, not only were women active in land reform, they went on to form a good part of local leadership, composing over half of the membership of local peasant associations.[46] In Shanxi's Lingqiu County, meanwhile, over 90 percent of the area's women were active in land reform, proving invaluable when "struggling landlords and searching for movable property."[47] Yet while the party addressed some key problems for women during land reform, it ignored and even suppressed other important issues. Land reform, by rebuilding the traditional family-based peasant economy, tended to reinforce patriarchal power in the countryside.[48] The redistribution of land served to buttress the family, firmly under the control of its male head, as the foundation of the Chinese economy. In theory, rural revolution represented an explicit threat to patriarchal village society through the promise of land rights to women, as well as the opportunity to participate in the public process of land reform. But in practice, only widows and divorced women received their own land deeds, and a woman's political voice was generally subordinate to others in her household.[49]

Even the 1946–1947 land reform campaigns near the party's capital of Yan'an failed to truly transform the status of women. To be sure, women there benefited from having a government actively committed to ending foot binding, infanticide, and the buying and selling of women.[50] But while the Communists called for women to receive land, few women had any real farming experience. Despite pleas from female party leaders to provide peasant women with adequate agricultural training, little was done. And in a striking contrast to promises of cultural and social liberation, the party limited the range of complaints permissible while speaking bitterness. Yan'an area women were not allowed to discuss the very real oppression they suffered at the hands of men within their own households. Frustrated, many women did not actively participate in land reform.[51] This proved an enduring problem. During the final campaigns in the far Southwest, work teams were still silencing women eager to speak bitterness about the patriarchal oppression they endured daily. One report disdained such women because they "do not see class oppression, only their in-laws and husbands."[52]

Agrarian revolution promised women a meaningful chance to participate in public life, with peasant associations aiming at a 30 percent female membership. Land reform directives explicitly called on women to get their own share of land, which they could handle (*chuli*) themselves when they married or remarried.[53] But while fanshen promised women a share of land and a political voice, in practice the Communists failed to deal with the cultural and practical obstacles facing potential female landholders. Limited by patriarchal norms, few child care alternatives, and inexperience in agricultural production, peasant women were unable to stake a claim to their land and in practice did not receive property rights. Party policies failed to address the patriarchal realities of rural society, where families controlled marriages and private life. The arrival of Communist power, meanwhile, brought new forms of patriarchal oppression. In East China land reform, for example, during widespread attacks on local temples, the newly mobilized masses forced nuns to leave their orders (*huansu*) and take husbands.[54]

Upon first arriving in the countryside, intellectuals serving on land reform work teams had been on the lookout for any signs of peasant bitterness. Preparing to leave, it behooved them to find evidence of peasant fanshen, and indeed their reports on land reform endlessly praised the power of the transformed peasantry. In discussing changes among rural citizens, intellectuals often returned to a favored theme: the superiority of peasants to their educated organizers. Chen Zhenzhou, after leading a small group meeting of peasants to discuss the division of landlord property, framed the comparison clearly: "Intellectuals who lock themselves in the library will naturally be arrogant and look down on the laboring peoples, but coming out and joining the masses they cannot help but understand the power and knowledge of the masses, and only then realize their own insignificance." Luckily for Chen, peasants were not the only ones who could be transformed by land reform. Having previously questioned class struggle due to his old class loyalties, land reform "educated" Chen so that he "no longer takes any pity on the landlord class, only feeling hatred."[55]

The full transformation of intellectuals on work teams was predicated on the experience of class struggle. Without personal knowledge of struggle, they were only "half intellectuals," with questionable class stances. The great scholar of philosophy Feng Youlan explained that his participation in land reform allowed him to struggle landlords as well as his own "hidden emotions" for landlords and thus "speed up my own progress."[56] By learning from cadres and peasants, as well as seeing and participating in class struggle, intellectuals overseeing agrarian revolution found the opportunity to transform themselves into party loyalists. Thus, Dang Qiaoxin noted that while previously his hatred of landlords was only abstract, in this "great furnace of fierce struggle," he truly understood the crimes of the landlord class. Seeing peasant anger triggered his own feelings of rage: "I already utterly detested my own landlord family, despised my father, and I kept thinking about the peasant brothers in my hometown, greatly fearing that they had let my family off the hook."[57]

Some went as far as to describe their time on rural work teams as nothing less than an "enlightenment."[58] Qinghua University professor Yuan Fang put his training in sociology to good use as he expertly analyzed how agrarian revolution promised to change intellectuals. Looking at the twelve comrades on his work team, he counted five "old cadres" and seven "new cadres." Of the old cadres, three were of worker-peasant origin, while two were "intellectuals who had been made into worker-peasants, having long ago cast aside their old landlord class and entered the ranks of the proletariat." This was a transformation open to the new cadres, all students and professors from Qinghua. As he bluntly concluded, "Land reform can change intellectuals. This is the best occasion for intellectuals to become worker-peasants." If they followed the path of the reformed intellectuals on the work team and cast off their original class characteristics, "such as pitying landlords and viewing problems abstractly," they too would be changed by land reform.[59] The party's rural campaigns were thus not just a moment of peasant fanshen, as intellectuals were to be transformed as well, an idea that informed their subsequent writings about the campaigns. One report written by young intellectuals from landlord families rhapsodized that taking part in land reform was like waking up from a dream.[60]

Waking up was especially important for landlord children seeking to join the revolution. Hu Du, a self-described "intellectual youth born to a landlord family," admitted that throughout his early life, he was surrounded by and supported by the landlord class. For him, land reform represented an "ideological struggle."[61] Hu visited his family as land reform was being carried out in his home village and spoke out against his extended family members, demonstrating that his "ideological struggle ended in victory."[62] Li Hua, a Qinghua student, still felt affection for landlord family members despite having received a revolutionary education. A viewing of a single performance of the revolutionary opera *Liu Hulan*, however, changed everything. Overcome with guilt and determined to change, Li embraced land reform. Taking part in a campaign, Li heard how peasants had suffered as they turned over their harvests to exploitative landlords and understood a fundamental truth: peasant grain fed landlord children. Thus, Li proclaimed, "I was not raised by my parents' family . . . peasants are my real parents." With this new understanding of the nature of class and class exploitation, Li firmly stood with his true family, the peasant masses, as they carried out land reform.[63]

Chinese intellectuals insisted that taking part in rural revolution had indeed been a life-changing experience. Looking back on these reports, however, it is hard to ignore how they were produced in an atmosphere of limited intellectual freedom. Recalling their times on work teams, China's urban elite were simply not free to question the basic contours of the land reform movement. Ye Duyi, a prominent member of the Democratic League, observed the campaign for eight months following the establishment of the PRC. Witnessing poverty, suicide, and disturbing acts of interfamilial terror, Ye was shocked by the violence and horrors of agrarian revolution, but he could only parrot the party line that such excesses were necessary. To object would to be to invite suspicion on himself and his class background.[64] Ye remained silent, but reports on land reform made it clear that many work team members abhorred Mao's rural revolution. For example, most members of the three work teams that carried out land reform in sixty-four Sichuan villages in one of the final land reform campaigns overcame language and lifestyle differences within a few weeks to provide real leadership for local cadres. Realizing the folly of peaceful land reform, they joined the peasantry in the fierce crucible of class struggle. But while some team members had to restrain themselves from beating landlords, others were frightened by peasant violence and did not even dare to attend struggle meetings. Team members were also accused of not wanting to work, maintaining a distance from the peasant masses, and looking down at local cadres.[65]

The Communists, meanwhile, suggested that many intellectuals had dubious motives. One party report on educators studying land reform policy claimed that in fact, relatively few "saw the importance of land reform." Far from active in their support of agrarian revolution, most had "goldplated thinking," simply attempting to learn what was needed to guarantee their current positions. Those with landlord backgrounds, meanwhile, often hoped to help their families by mastering the intricacies of the party's ever evolving rural platform. Even more troubling, some openly doubted the need for agrarian revolution. Had not the United States, one free thinker dared ask, industrialized without these campaigns? A few even questioned

the moral judgments buried at the heart of Mao's rural class system, arguing that "there are bad peasants too, who like to eat but avoid work, while
some landlords work hard and pinch pennies their entire lives."[66]

Another internal account of "democratic personages" and students taking part in land reform in Sichuan openly questioned the transformative
value of the campaigns for urban citizens. These team members also had
questionable motives. Some wanted to collect enough material to write a
report, while others focused on increasing their political capital. Even after
a two-week study program, one intellectual still impetuously suggested that
landlord resistance was not due to an inherently evil nature but a misunderstanding of party policy. Others were criticized for being selfish, undis-
ciplined, and using the study period to have improper sexual relations. Sent
to carry out agrarian revolution, team members were assigned to areas with
weak leadership and ultimately were underused.[67] The party had recruited
urbanites to carry out rural revolution with a promise of transformation,
not just for China's peasants but work team members as well. They embraced the challenge and insisted that their ideological transformation had
in fact been achieved. The Communists, however, remained dubious, foreshadowing decades of tensions between the party and China's educated
elite. What, then, of the transformation of the peasant masses, which began
with their economic liberation?

In the aftermath of land reform and the redistribution of village fields,
many peasants indeed prospered. The turn from rural revolution to regular
agricultural production generally resulted in increasing harvests and rising
incomes.[68] Besides the obvious benefit of the end of decades of warfare and
chaos, the enthusiasm of new land owners drove production. One report
boasted, "For liberated peasants, the first time they labor on their own land,
their desire to produce increases dramatically. They work from morning
till night, forgetting their pain, and create their own happy life."[69] As early
as the first land-to-the-tiller campaign, some peasants spoke of getting rich
(*facai*) from their bountiful harvests.[70] But the party faced an intractable
problem in regard to giving the peasant masses true economic liberation:
there was not enough land and property to go around. This issue plagued
the entire land reform effort. In summer 1946, party central was already
warning base areas that the poorest villagers had not received enough
land.[71] After the completion of agrarian revolution in Shanxi, most peasants

still did not own enough land to make ends meet and survived only through sideline employment.[72]

The problem of scarcity during land-to-the-tiller campaigns was compounded when the PLA or the new government demanded a share of struggle fruits, a move that infuriated the masses. In parts of North China, as much as 15 percent of struggle fruits was lost in such a manner.[73] The problem was even more acute in the Northeast, where at times the state commandeered (*guigong*) the majority of struggle fruits.[74] In one Northeast village, for example, opium, gold, and silver seized from class enemies were all taken by the country government, leaving some activists with little more than their new fields.[75] And party leaders had no easy solutions when confronted with economic disparities between rich villages (*fucun*) and poor ones (*pincun*). During land to the tiller, peasants living in poor villages with not enough land had moved to bring struggle to other villages, leaving party leaders flummoxed.[76]

As land reform came to a close in the old base areas during the Civil War, party reports praised landlords for accepting a poor peasant share of land and welcoming the new order. In the Taihang region, for example, the Communists conducted a surprise military exercise simulating the arrival of a homecoming regiment. Hearing this news, many landlords fled alongside peasants, and some even killed themselves than rather than face the return of the Nationalists and their allies. But other landlords, "swept out of the house" during land reform, now lived in village temples. Impoverished landlords were not the only Taihang villagers living in poverty: "filling holes" had failed to raise all Taihang villagers to middle peasant prosperity.[77] Frustration with the continued existence of poor peasants had resulted in the Outline Land Law, which said that up to 80 percent of rural land was still in the hands of class enemies. In reality, most villages, especially in the old base areas where the Communists had already carried out reform for years, lacked a true exploiting class. In North China's Wugong, the party's insistence on its vision of rural landholding had left a work team no choice but to ignore local realities and unjustly expropriate farming households.[78] Later, after a second work team returned most of the wrongly confiscated land, local cadres reclassified villagers until the village books matched party ideals.[79] The push to equalize holdings, furthermore, often depressed rural production: farmers had little desire to increase their yields when they feared future rounds of redistribution.[80]

The rise in rural violence driven by extreme poverty had been a leading factor in the move to shut down land reform in summer 1948. When campaigns resumed the following year, restrictions on violence seemed to make economic fanshen impossible. Cadres in the Tangshan region complained that landlords and rich peasants were getting off too easy. Upset, some called the new policies "rightist" and openly wondered, "How can the masses fanshen?" Tangshan cadres also grumbled about abandoning equalization and suggested that middle peasant lands would be needed for the poor to have a true fanshen.[81] The results of land reform in rural Beijing, however, offered an example of a peaceful campaign that left peasants content. True, the Beijing campaign, which ran from October 1949 to March 1950, was unique. Much of the land in question belonged to absentee landlords who rented through agents. Proximity to Beijing had resulted in a diverse and highly commercialized agricultural economy, along with a good share of industrial development. Most striking, work teams turned confiscated rental lands over to the state. Some of these lands were given out to farmers, who paid not rent but agricultural taxes. Other lands were earmarked for industrial development, overjoying peasants now given the chance to become true members of the proletariat.[82] And it was not just peasants who prospered: surveys of landlords found many had become successful farmers, while others had moved into the city for employment.[83]

But positive reports from the Beijing countryside were overshadowed by a broad failure to truly transform the rural economy. Work teams in the field following the establishment of the PRC discovered that campaigns designed to force landlords to return deposits mostly helped middle peasants, leaving poor peasants bitter over their continued poverty. Poor peasants illegally pushed for a share of what was due to their middle peasant neighbors. A resulting 1950 directive to protect middle peasant interests railed against this return to the "poor peasant and hired hand line" and quoted Liu Shaoqi, who had declared that changing land systems, not curing poverty, was the explicit goal of land reform. As this 1950 directive admitted, land reform would not be able to solve the fundamental economic problems of the peasantry.[84] And indeed some villages found that the fruits of struggle were rather pathetic: not even land but old clothes and the like.[85] A land reform team working in Sichuan somehow had to divide five oxen among over one hundred poor peasant and hired hand households.[86]

One persistent problem was the status of poor peasants. After the campaign was finished in the South Central region, poor peasants commonly lacked production materials.[87] And despite the call to rely on the poor peasants and hired hands, many peasant associations in Mao's New China were dominated by middle peasants. Even when most members of associations were poor peasants, leaders came from middle peasant households. Some poor peasant activists were in fact meeting experts (*kaihui zhuanjia*) acting on the behalf of middle peasants. This problem was particularly acute during campaigns to reduce rents and return deposits, which primarily benefited middle peasants. Cadres gushed over activist middle peasants while disparaging poor peasants who had little to gain from the campaigns. As one cadre remarked of the poor, "Their clothes are so crappy, how can they even work?" Some poor peasants agreed. In North Sichuan's Sihe village, middle peasant leadership not only looked down on their poorer neighbors but cheated them out of their proper share of the fruits of struggle. In a resigned response, one poor peasant lamented that "we muddy feet folk" could not compare with the middle peasants and intellectuals who ran the peasant association.[88]

Yet at the same time, other work teams and local cadres were going out of their way to discriminate against middle peasants. Desperate to get the poor to fanshen, some peasant associations forced middle peasants to "donate" the struggle fruits they had just gotten in land reform. Following a campaign to return rent deposits in Sichuan's Ba County, one middle peasant was forced to hand over 73 percent of the grain he had received to his peasant association. The party considered middle peasants allies, but poor peasants often saw them as simply wealthy and jealously eyed their share of the struggle fruits. As one peasant representative bluntly proclaimed, the only way to raise the "spirits of the poor peasants and hired hands so that they unite with middle peasants and topple the landlord class" was to first distribute fruits from middle peasants to their poorer neighbors. Middle peasants, fearing struggle, reluctantly turned over their property to local peasant associations. Others spent their struggle fruits before they could be redistributed. One peasant spent his returned deposit on food, booze, and clothes. His state of mind is neatly summed up by his final purchase: a casket.[89]

With not enough land to go around, tensions flared. According to one 1951 directive, despite the great alliance between workers and peasants, land reform's redistribution of property had revealed unexpected class tensions, particularly in suburbs, factories, and mines. Unemployed workers returning to their home villages found it difficult to get an equal share of property. Workers and miners renting from evil tyrants might see their houses distributed to peasants.[90] Some peasants, seeing their landlord targets go bankrupt, marched to cities in search of relatives to pay up. Urban residents with few ties to the countryside, finding themselves potentially liable for charges of agrarian exploitation, had to fight against a forced deportation to their ancestral homes. Cadres attached to the new government in Zhong County, for example, demanded that two young women attending school in nearby Chongqing return to answer for the crimes of their landlord father. Party officials, reasoning that the two students were not supported by their father, ruled that the women could remain in school after providing their would-be jailers with some money to cover their failed expedition.

In a similar manner, two landlord sons working for the Chongqing Public Security Bureau found themselves nearly dragged back to their home village to answer for the crimes of their father, even though one of them had reported the father for fleeing their home village in the first place.[91] Investigation into this stream of peasants flowing into the city to calculate exploitation bills (*suan boxue zhang*) revealed that the root of the problem lay in the countryside, where peasants had demanded too much grain from their landlords. Unable to get payment, peasants turned to urban relatives, some of whom committed suicide when confronted with exploitation bills.[92] Party officials, recognizing that land reform had linked city and countryside, were in a bind. On one hand, peasants "running back and forth at will" to "indiscriminately arrest" urban landlord relatives was unacceptable. But on the other hand, forcing peasants to return home empty handed might lead to rural unrest. As a compromise, urban landlord relatives were encouraged to donate what they could to peasant bill collectors. Only the truly counterrevolutionary were dragged back to the countryside to answer for their crimes.[93]

Agrarian revolution had resulted in a complex and uneven rural economy. In northern Anhui, land reform left every new rural class with specific worries that impeded production. Rich peasants refused to hire workers or lend out money in fear of future charges of exploitation. Middle peasants feared standing out (*maojian*) and produced the bare minimum. Poor peasants wanted to find new struggle targets so that they might continue to "eat struggle food" (*chi douzheng fan*): grain confiscated from class enemies. Hired hands, increasingly unable to find work, pushed for the equal division of land. Village cadres, meanwhile, often abandoned political work or neglected production after completing land reform.[94] Overall yields did not rise as quickly as expected because many peasants feared future rounds of confiscation and redistribution. Middle peasants, now dominant in the countryside, often preferred to eat excess grain instead of bringing their harvests to the market.[95] Disturbingly, a report from Hunan noted that some peasant households had been better off before land reform.[96]

Agrarian revolution did not solve China's land problem, but for decades, the party continued to promote land distribution as the major accomplishment of land reform. Over half a century later, Du Runsheng, who had overseen land reform in the massive South Central region, would finally admit that there simply "wasn't a lot of land to be distributed." According to Du's assessment of recent studies of his party's agrarian revolution, "The results of the reform were that peasants received an insignificant plot of taxed land."[97] For Du Runsheng, the party's failure to solve peasant poverty during land reform did little to diminish the broader impact of land reform, most notably the political and cultural transformation of rural China. Economic change, after all, was only the start of the transformation of the countryside. Deng Zihui, praising the first land-to-the-tiller campaigns, declared that after solving the land problem "all work and all responsibilities can be easily completed without great effort."[98]

But in the political and cultural realms, the party again found major problems, starting with local cadres, many of whom struggled to remain focused on the issues that so concerned the Communists. In Hunan's Shaoyang and Wugang counties, for example, most local cadres ignored political work. Instead, these cadres "lowered their guards and took the enemy lightly."[99] Many peasants, fearing that political responsibilities would interfere with farming, refused to serve as local cadres.[100] One Shanxi party branch declared that with the Japanese, the Nationalists, and the landlord class uniformly defeated, the revolution was essentially over. As a result local cadres dissolved their party branch.[101] The extent of this problem is suggested by the reaction to an article about slacking cadres that appeared in *New Hunan*. Seeking to generate discussion about leadership problems on the village level, this article introduced readers to Li Sixi, said to be a typical village cadre. Li believed that with land reform complete and the landlord class toppled, there was simply "nothing left to do" and retreated from politics in order to focus on production. The paper received 1,088 letters in less than a month, confirming that the existence of "Li Sixi Thinking" was "extremely common."[102] A report from East China further emphasized the tendency for cadres to focus on production rather than politics. As one East China cadre described his growing aversion to political work, which kept him away from home, "Even when it is raining and windy, meetings run to the middle of the night. My wife used to be afraid of me, but now I am afraid of my wife."[103]

Disinterested and henpecked cadres were bad enough. Widespread corruption among newly empowered village cadres and activists exacerbated the problems of rural scarcity. During early campaigns during the Civil War era, new village leaders often rose to power after denouncing former elites; because many of these men were essentially uneducated ruffians, they often abused the power that fell into their hands through fierce class struggle.[104] Local cadres, for example, might hoard the best property for themselves as a reward for their militancy against the old order, scandalizing peasant families grieving the loss of their sons in the wars against the Japanese and the Nationalists. Overseeing the distribution of property confiscated from landlords, local cadres certainly had ample opportunities for corruption. In Da Fo village, the local party committee leveraged the auctioning of confiscated land to ensure they got the best fields and later distributed furniture in a closed-door meeting. Poor villagers without strong political connections got little or sometimes nothing.[105] During land-to-the-tiller campaigns, the distribution of struggle fruits also tended to favor those active in struggle, further skewing holdings in the aftermath of land reform.[106]

In North China, the connections between the first land reform campaigns and local cadre corruption were unavoidable. Launching the fill-the-gaps campaign in fall 1946, party leaders noted that village cadres, activists, and militiamen had taken too many struggle fruits during land to the tiller.[107] The following year, a Central China Bureau report admitted that cadres and activists taking an unfair share of redistributed property was "an unavoidable problem in land reform."[108] In East China, such fruits had also been distributed through the logic of "those who settle it get it."[109] Land reform following the Outline Land Law of 1947 was thus often run in concert with anticorruption campaigns. These attempts to combat local party malfeasance faced a daunting task; in some villages, things had gotten so bad that peasants longed to struggle their local officials.[110]

After the founding of the PRC, party leaders demanded continued vigilance against corruption. One founding peasant representative conference vowed that village cadres must have a clean history, an "upright work-style," and never take an unfair share of the fruits of struggle.[111] Peasant associations, however, were frequently lambasted as potential hothouses of immorality, where new village leaders stockpiled confiscated goods for their own gain. In Mawu, an administrative village on the outskirts of Chongqing, investigations revealed a diversity of landlord goods confiscated in mass campaigns and now illegally held by peasant associations: cash, clocks, gramophones, porcelains, and silver coins.[112]

Another investigation also found serious corruption problems among peasant associations, often involving the distribution of struggle fruits. In one grievous example, village cadres gorged themselves on confiscated food night after night, eating over three hundred pounds of smoked pork belly. Meanwhile their poor peasant neighbor Li Caiwu, given a few empty jars, cried for three days.[113] In Jiangsu's Qindong township, the "vast majority" of peasant association leaders and village cadres had been corrupted by offers of grain, wristwatches, and gold rings. Some, "seduced" by the "pretty women" in landlord families, had agreed to lower the classifications given to village class enemies.[114] Sexual misconduct among village cadres was in fact a widespread problem, although party documents tend to discuss these relationships in terms of class relations, an approach that served to downplay the possibility of sexual assault. In Sichuan's Nanchuan County, for example, village cadres were essentially described as peasant Lotharios. Ye Yunfei, known locally as a "big king of romance" (*lian'ai da wang*), confessed to writing inappropriate love letters to at least eight women. Men such as Ye Yunfei were further accused of letting landlord family members into positions of power as part of their flirtations.[115] As this suggests, problems with local cadres were often blamed on class enemies. One investigation into malfeasance in peasant associations denounced rich peasants and landlord elements for taking over village governments. Some of these elements had found ways to be classed as poor peasants and take direct control of their local association, but more commonly, they used their status as teachers, secretaries, propagandists, or female cadres to seize power and cause chaos.[116]

Despite corruption, many villages prospered after land reform, proving that economic fanshen, while far from universal, was in fact real. But in places where incomes rose, the party found a new problem, or rather the return of the original problem that the revolution had promised to solve:

growing economic disparity among villagers. Many rich peasants and well-to-do middle peasants welcomed the party's promise to preserve the rich peasant economy and embraced production. They did well, as did middle peasants old and new. Initially fearful of accumulating excess savings or grain, they now proudly hung couplets on their doors proclaiming "Protect Private Property, Enjoy Eternal Benefit." But poor peasants, still lacking land, remained impoverished and bitter, and it was not landlords but their better-off peasant neighbors who produced their enmity. "They just put on rich peasant skin," the poor grumbled, "and look at how well they eat!" Other peasants were seen as bad farmers. These lackluster farmers were shunned from village cooperatives and doomed to poverty. One peasant caustically remarked, "They like to eat but not work, they cannot be helped."[117]

The result was the seemingly inevitable return of the hiring of labor and renting of land. In Shanxi, wealthy peasants brazenly used the guise of the party's mutual aid teams to cover the rehiring of agricultural laborers.[118] A report on class division in the Taihang Mountains noted that this practice was "equivalent to changing outer appearances to cover the exploitation of hired labor."[119] In Sichuan's Wenjing village, the number of households renting out fields in the aftermath of land reform rose from thirty-two to seventy-two in one year. Almost 10 percent of Wenjing's households were renting out land, and Dazu County's Chengdong village saw a similar spike in renters, as well as the return of the high-interest loans that had symbolized the feudal countryside. With growing hardship among the poor, some had no choice but to sell off their newly won fields. Even worse, some local cadres embraced these changes. "Buying land is correct," a district cadre proclaimed, "that's how you establish yourself!"[120] This cadre was subsequently determined to be ideologically confused.

For many peasants, fanshen meant quickly moving on from land reform and class struggle. The poet Shao Yanxiang recalled that during his time in the countryside, he made much progress with a local activist who vowed to join the party. Some months later, Shao learned that his peasant friend, wholly focused on farming, now ignored village affairs.[121] After the completion of land reform in 1950 in Henan, Xuchang peasants similarly focused on production. Party observers were far from pleased: villagers cared only about "safe and sound production" and refused to attend meetings or keep tabs on landlords. Local cadres, misinformed on current events, failed to educate peasants about the growing threat in Korea. This led to some truly disturbing trends. Peasants did not hate America as much as they hated Japan or Chiang Kai-shek. Some even went as far as to express great admiration for the aid, churches, and hospitals provided by the United States. Xuchang peasants were more interested in production than revolution. The source of this disturbing problem lay in the recent land reform campaign, which "emphasized economic gain, such as the distribution of struggle fruits and engaging in production, to mobilize the masses, while ignoring political and ideological mobilization." For the Communist Party, this was unacceptable. Xuchang would use the upcoming distribution of land deeds to rectify these mistakes.[122]

As this suggests, the party found it difficult to convince liberated peasants to value state goals over personal interests. Prosperous farmers welcomed economic liberation by focusing on farming and ignoring politics. The party might have learned this lesson during the Civil War. During the early rounds of land reform, peasant support for the war effort was often due to fear of reprisals if the Nationalists returned. Peasants aided the war effort locally, but after receiving land largely opted to farm and declined to join the PLA.[123] This tendency to value production and profit continued during peacetime. In 1951, Hunan's urban markets saw reduced grain because peasants were not enthusiastic about selling their harvests, preferring to wait until prices rose or to sell in more distant and lucrative markets. Ominously, this problem was partially blamed on land reform for "putting the ownership of grain in the hands of the peasants."[124]

But economically liberated peasants often preferred to enjoy their good fortune instead of focusing on production or politics. The Communists criticized peasants for spending their money on food and "fanshen wine" (*fanshen jiu*). Expenditures were up for weddings and holidays as well. One administrative village in northern Sichuan, with a population of 16,500, slaughtered oxen and fifteen hundred pigs in preparation for the upcoming Spring Festival.[125] In East China, meanwhile, many peasants hoped to rely on the government or reasoned that any economic gains would be wiped out with the coming of socialism. And so they too spent their money on food and wine, not the much-needed oxen and agricultural tools.[126] Such thinking was common in Jiangxi, where many peasants believed that socialism meant total collectivization and assumed that soon the entire village would work and eat together, and even all wear the same style of clothes.[127] Other peasants took a passive approach to politics, thinking "the land is divided, as have the [struggle] fruits, landlords are toppled, and so that's that."[128] The lack of peasant mobilization was typically blamed on land reform campaigns that had been too peaceful.[129]

Party leaders, aware of the many problems plaguing the countryside in the wake of agrarian revolution, often blamed landlords. One report noted that contrary to land reform accounts that stressed a humbled and defeated landlord class, intense class conflict still lingered. Some landlords refused to submit to the peasantry and employed new tactics, such as the "political assassination" of their enemies.[130] For the Communists, the rise of counterrevolution was the natural corollary to the political backsliding of cadres and peasants; with former activists focused on production or enjoying newly found wealth, it was only natural that landlords, still stigmatized as evil by nature, would return to their reactionary ways. In the Hanyang area, for example, when political work regressed following land reform, some landlords began "counterattacking" peasants through physical assault or by demanding rent.[131] Some landlords, employing a different strategy, promoted the concept of "agricultural socialism": an egalitarian society free from class labels.[132]

As these landlords would learn, the Communist Party was not yet ready to part ways with the Maoist class structure now imposed on Chinese villages. When the party first carried out class determination in the Taihang Mountain base area in 1942, villagers were told they would be able to change their class statuses in three years. Taihang leaders repudiated this policy in 1946, arguing that more time was needed to truly change the thinking of landlords and rich peasants. These villagers were now labeled as "lowered landlords" and "lowered rich peasants" to acknowledge their declining fortunes while also keeping them isolated from the peasant masses.[133] At the end of the following year, party central also raised the idea of landlords and rich peasants from the old base areas being eligible for new class statuses; landlords had to labor for five years, rich peasants for three.[134] This offer of adjusting class statuses became a frequent but never fulfilled promise. As late as a 1952 reexamination land reform campaign in Guangdong, the party continued to promise landlords a chance to change their class statuses after five years of labor.[135]

In 1953, barely a year after the end of land reform, the party called on peasants to turn over their newly won land to collective farms. A high tide of collectivization in 1955–1956 destroyed China's private landholding system. Maoist class labels, however, were here to stay. A few peasants were able to leave the countryside and transcend their class labels through service to the party or the new state, but for the vast majority of rural families, these labels were passed on to children and grandchildren. Those labeled poor peasants became the new rural elite, while the social and political status of middle peasants remained ever ambiguous. The families of those labeled landlords and rich peasants became village pariahs for generations.[136]

As early as 1948, Xi Zhongxun had warned against applying class labels and bringing struggle to entire households. In reference to the label of evil tyrant, Xi personally warned Mao Zedong that it was wrong to pass this label to the wife and child of a hated class enemy. To bring struggle to future generations would result in "evil fruit." Instead of endless struggle, Xi argued, what the peasant masses truly desired was democracy (*minzhu*) and fair burdens (*fudan gongping*). There was a reason, he hinted, that the masses were so quick to bring struggle to their village cadres.[137] This warning, which went unheeded, proved sadly true. In 1951, Du Runsheng, denouncing the idea that "one battle would change the world," had instructed work teams to not rush land reform and the elimination of the landlord class.[138] Du was right to suspect that the landlord class would not simply disappear overnight, but its longevity was ultimately due to Mao and his insistence that China never forget class struggle. Economically, in Mao's New China, the members of the landlord class had lost most of their land and property and were typically the most destitute members of rural society.[139] Condemned as remnants of feudal power, they and their offspring would eat bitterness for the remainder of the revolutionary era.

CONCLUSION

Agrarian Revolution in Retrospect

Stories, which transform complex and messy events into tidy narratives with linear plotlines, are essential to the craft of history. Historians in both China and the West have embraced narrative arcs, character development, and dramatic denouements to enthrall generation after generation of readers. This shared narrative approach to making the past sensible and readable has bequeathed a surprising number of similar stories.[1] These, however, are simply smaller tales in the much larger story of history, the metanarrative that gives meaning to the vast stretch of time now covered by the historical record.[2] In modern China, history has largely been written by reformers and revolutionaries attempting to legitimize their political actions. As a result, the past has been viewed primarily through two grand narratives. Historians affiliated with the Nationalist Party favored a narrative of gradual progress toward Western modernization under the stern political tutelage of Chiang Kai-shek. Those working with the Communists, by contrast, promoted a tale of revolution against the twin forces of feudalism and imperialism.[3] Both sides attempted to faithfully recreate history, but the primacy of ideological concerns and a commitment to a straightforward course toward modernity resulted in histories that owe as much to literary fiction as to historical realities.

The natural inclination to narrative, however, has also deeply affected the course of history. This book has explored how the tales of revolution spun by Mao Zedong and his comrades in the Chinese Communist Party defined the course of their greatest enterprise: the transformation of the country-side as the party came to power and cemented its hold over one-quarter of humanity. Party leaders, following the dictates of Marx and Lenin, had ini-tially tied their fates to China's tiny proletariat, only to see their dreams of a proper urban revolution dashed in the Shanghai Massacre of 1927. Cast out into the countryside and forced to reimagine a path to socialist uto-pia, Mao Zedong forecast a novel revolutionary storm that would bring his party to power. According to his vision, the Communist Party would lead the peasant masses through a fierce storm of class struggle. Once liberated, China's peasants would surge forth like a hurricane, sweep aside the forces of feudalism, and recreate the world as Mao envisioned.

This story had its origins in 1927 when Mao Zedong returned home to Hunan to observe firsthand the turmoil then roiling the countryside. His de-tailed survey of village life, framed as objective and truthful, quickly became the basis for the Communist Party's narrative of peasant revolution. This story was never intended to be confined to the page. In 1945, after eight years of fighting off Japanese imperialists, the party moved to bring Mao's narrative to life, dispatching a vast army of work teams to remake rural society through a series of revolutionary campaigns, the most important of which was land reform. Party authors taking part in the early rounds of agrarian revolution penned narrative accounts of their time in the country-side, creating textual models for future work teams. The chapters of this book have followed their narrative structure, starting with the mobilization of urban intellectuals to join seasoned rural activists in the party's many work teams. Work teams arrived in rural China intent on transforming the countryside by bringing Mao's tale of peasant liberation to life through fierce class struggle. Team members sought out impoverished villagers and taught them how to speak bitterness, always sure to carry out ideologi-cal training so that newly identified activists understood that landlords and other class enemies were behind their suffering. Once mobilized, activists assisted work teams in dividing villages using Mao's class structure, a con-tentious affair that simplified complex and fluid social structures into fixed groupings of peasants and landlords. The arrival of these Maoist class cat-egories, previously unheard of in the Chinese countryside, would have mo-mentous consequences for future generations.

Mao's narrative of agrarian revolution reached its denouement when peasant activists, trained by the party's work teams, took part in highly ritualized enactments of class struggle. Work teams viewed the public and confrontational struggling of landlords as the means to peasant emancipation, but during early campaigns, poor activists used the ritual to beat and torture their neighbors for economic gain. Later campaigns promised a more nuanced approach to class division and property redistribution, but never shook the violent origins of class struggle, ensuring that agrarian revolution remained true to Mao's narrative of liberation through violence. Many, of course, benefited from the arrival of Communist power. Recalling his time on a work team, the poet Shao Yanxiang noted with pride how the campaign wrapped up before the New Year, so that villagers could celebrate not just the holiday but their fanshen as well. When the team left, the peasants he left behind seemed genuinely happy, many planning long-hoped-for marriages.[4] But the party was unable to deliver on the promise of fanshen and provide universal peasant emancipation. The poorest gained new property from their wealthier neighbors, but party leaders were well aware that land reform alone could never truly transform the rural economy. The violence of the campaigns, meanwhile, left many villagers and work team members traumatized. And while Mao promised liberation through class struggle, land reform bequeathed a legacy of bitterness that endured for decades by fixing the statuses of class enemies. Decades after taking part in agrarian revolution, the poet Shao Yanxiang could only wonder if violence was truly the only way to solve the land problem.[5]

Mao Zedong's vision of agrarian revolution, brought to life during these years of campaigns, dramatically altered the Chinese countryside. In late September 1952, future minister of agriculture Liao Luyan praised the monumental accomplishments of land reform during the PRC era. Fielding as many as 300,000 work team members for every year of campaigning, the party had brought the revolution to some 300 million peasants in three years. The result, Liao proclaimed, was an enthusiastic and productive workforce, of which as much as 70 percent had received property distributions. Peasants were happy, politically active, and raising their cultural levels.[6] Scholars have agreed that land reform was effective in transferring land; some 43 percent of land was redistributed and over 10 million landlords expropriated.[7] But the exact death toll of agrarian reform will never be known. With some 1 million villages in China, one assumption was a death rate of one class enemy per village; recently, scholars have estimated that it is possible that as many as 2 million died as a result of Mao's land revolution.[8] To this accounting, historians must now consider the problem of sexual assault, long ignored by the party. While this issue demands further investigation, at the moment it seems sadly reasonable to assume that sexual assault was just as common as the killing of class enemies in China's rural revolution.

In recent years, the party has quietly tried to downplay class struggle, preferring instead to highlight the party's role in promoting rural economic development. One account of the Communists' role in agricultural development, published by the party's history press, argued that bringing about the end of feudalism as an economic system represented the true significance of land reform.[9] But Mao's revolutionary narrative and its promise of peasant liberation has never been forgotten. The foundational study of land reform edited by senior party official Du Runsheng, who personally led massive campaigns to transform rural China, offers a succinct party take on the events discussed in this book: "Land reform was not only a profound economic transformation, but a profound political transformation as well, a prelude to the establishment and construction of a new China."[10] Du defended the legacy of land reform by arguing that the Communists' agrarian revolution was not simply about creating a more equitable division of land but about transforming peasants and laying the very foundations for the political modernization of rural China. As Du strongly reminded his readers, to one-sidedly judge the revolution "by how much land was distributed" can only result in a "neglect of the tremendous achievements in the political and social realms."[11] Unique among Maoist-era campaigns, land reform is firmly tied to the notion of the liberation and emancipation of the peasantry and represents the cornerstone of party legitimacy in the countryside.[12]

This is not to say that all Chinese accept the party's narrative of peasant liberation through land reform. Tan Song, a university professor obsessed with documenting the violence of land reform, has conducted extensive fieldwork to unearth the horrors of rural revolution. His work includes a reevaluation of the case of Liu Wencai, perhaps the most infamous evil tyrant of the early 1950s, notorious for exploiting and torturing peasants, even coercing new mothers to breast-feed him so that he might extend his own life. Liu's own grandson, Liu Xiaofei, has pushed back against these charges, bringing his family's tale to global attention in 2016. According to Liu Xiaofei, his grandfather, in fact a kind man, personally financed a Communist guerrilla force.[13] Fittingly, novelists have also pushed back against the party's narrative; Fang Fang's 2016 award-winning novel *Soft Burial* (Ruan mai), inspired by one of the stories unearthed by Tan Song, told the shocking tale of an entire family driven to suicide during land reform.[14] The party, however, has systematically pushed back these challenges. Tan Song lost his job for his outspokenness, Liu Xiaofei's grandfather remains a notorious villain, and Fang Fang's novel was quickly banned.

In the decades following agrarian revolution, the party continued to use land reform methods, most notably a heavy reliance on class struggle, as the driving force behind the politicization and mobilization of Chinese citizens. Struggle meetings appeared in Chinese cities in the early 1950s when urban workers adapted the rituals of land reform to attack urban merchants.[15] Struggle also remained an important part of rural political life, with landlords regularly humiliated and abused in accordance with the needs of the party. As seen in this account of a rural struggle meeting during a 1965 campaign against corruption, even village cadres could be struggled as if they were land-reform-era landlords:

> To open the session, the "master of ceremonies" whips the crowd into an emotional frenzy by portraying the person's crimes in as lurid a light as possible. From the crowd, carefully prepared activists scream out cursing cries of rage. Others get caught up in the enthusiasm and start yelling out as well. Then the accused is led out by the local armed militia. . . . He is often made to wear a heavy placard branding him a traitor, class enemy, and so on. . . . People from the crowd "spontaneously" bring forth evidence that amplifies his misdeeds and shows that these are part of a whole despicable pattern of wrongdoing. Shouted curses fill the air. Sometimes strong young militiamen rise from their seats and beat the enemy of the people. This is not officially permitted, but depending on the purposes of the session it is sometimes informally encouraged and tacitly condoned. The guilty person stands facing the people during his whole ordeal (which can last several hours); he is an object of the struggle by the people, not one of the people. When the session is over, he is dragged away in total disgrace. He has been symbolically destroyed.[16]

While the struggle objects in this case were corrupt cadres, not landlords, all of the key features of land reform struggle are present, including the use of small groups to prepare villagers, the public explication of evil deeds, the shouting of politically charged rhetoric, and the use of humiliation and violence. Mao's Cultural Revolution furthered the model of struggle perfected in agrarian revolution, now firmly entrenched in urban political culture. According to one recollection, prior to the struggling of two teachers, students explicitly discussed the importance of following Mao's "Hunan Report," which had detailed the use of dunce caps and the parading of class enemies.[17] Cultural Revolution struggle sessions featured slogans, humiliation, violence, and other familiar features. Many elements of struggle were taken to extreme degrees during the course of the Cultural Revolution; one struggle object wore "a five-meter-high dunce cap decorated with paper cutouts of skeletons, monsters, turtles, and ox heads" during a parade.[18]

In 1981 Communist leadership, rethinking the party's long and tumultuous history, explicitly rejected the Cultural Revolution and its rhetoric of class and rituals of struggle. Agrarian reform, which had first popularized the enactment of class struggle, was still considered a major success.[19] Because land reform and the liberation of the peasant masses occupy hallowed grounds in the party's tale of revolution, the campaigns have never been discredited. Alongside the war against Japanese imperialism, agrarian revolution represents the foundation of party legitimacy. During subsequent rural campaigns, work teams attempted to associate themselves with the legitimacy of land reform by consciously practicing the three togethers: eating, working, and living with the peasants. Villagers may have blamed the party for the pains of collectivization, the disasters of the Great Leap Forward, and the chaos of the Cultural Revolution. But despite its violence, land reform represented something unique: a treasured moment of cooperation between peasants and the party.[20]

Today agrarian revolution remains a treasured moment, seemingly immune to the criticisms often directed at other PRC mass movements. A true reckoning of China's massive agrarian revolution must wait until the day when the campaigns are no longer needed to help legitimize the PRC government. When placed in its proper perspective, agrarian revolution is not something to be lionized as it is in PRC histories, but neither is it worthy of wholesale denunciation. Given widespread rural poverty, the promise of fanshen gave land reform a powerful appeal—not just for poor peasants in desperate need of land but for Chinese elites seeking to create a stronger nation. After land reform, many members of the rural poor, empowered through agrarian revolution, overwhelmingly put their faith in the party.[21] It would be unwise to discount the many peasants who fondly remembered the arrival of Communist power, recalling a time when the party worked with farmers to improve rural life. Yet in evaluating these years of difficult campaigning, it is essential to remember that in Mao's narrative of agrarian revolution, liberation was always predicated on struggle: without class labels, without fierce struggle, there could be no transformation of the peasantry.

If the concepts of class and class struggle were discarded with the leveling of the rural classes, Mao's agrarian revolution would certainly have a different meaning in retrospect. But the class labels handed out during these years of campaigning became a patrilineal inheritance, entirely divorced from economic realities. Future generations of peasants became the dominant social grouping in Chinese villages, serving as local cadres and enjoying political privileges. Descendants of rich peasants and landlords, scorned as members of the "four bad types," were kept under surveillance and excluded from village politics unless needed as scapegoats for future campaigns.[22] Even the rich peasants who had been allowed to keep their excess property during PRC-era rural campaigns were subjected to decades of systemic social and political discrimination.[23] Many landlords feared leaving their homes; when they did venture out into the village, they made sure to make way for village cadres and activists, humbly bowing when greeting their economic and political superiors.[24] Not until the 1980s did landlords reenter village society as equals.[25] The demise of Maoist classes, however, was hardly an unqualified boon for Chinese villagers. Deng Xiaoping's move against "egalitarianism" in the late 1970s resulted in the total abandonment of the long-held goal of eliminating differences between urban and rural populations. Largely left behind in Deng's push to modernize during the "opening and reform" era, China's rural citizens are now disdained as a problematic population, mostly notable for their supposed low "quality" (*suzhi*).[26] In today's China, villagers suffer no shortage of indignity, with little hope besides escaping to cities where they labor as underpaid and poorly treated migrant workers. Peasants, as a social category, have become scapegoats for China's perceived weaknesses.

This bothered Shao Yanxiang, the poet who took part in land reform. Reflecting on his time on a work team a half-century later, Shao gushed over the peasants he worked with, who deeply impressed him with their attention to policy, their ability to organize, and especially their self-awareness during elections. Who, Shao asked, can truly say the peasants are low quality and cannot take part in democratic elections?[27] The juxtaposition of the promise of rural liberation embedded in the Communist revolutionary narrative and the realities of contemporary village life leaves Xi Jinping, now China's most powerful leader since Mao Zedong, in a unique position. Xi's father, the pragmatic Xi Zhongxun, was one of the few party leaders to question Mao's framing of rural classes and methods of agrarian revolution. Xi Jinping, furthermore, is no stranger to village life, having spent many of his early years as a "sent-down youth" in rural China during the Cultural Revolution. Xi Jinping, however, continues to insist on clinging to Mao's revolutionary narrative to bolster the party's legitimacy. Despite his own years in the countryside, his party has shut down attempts to move toward a more accurate representation of agrarian revolution. Economically, Xi and his comrades have pushed for rapid urbanization, while also moving to increase state control over farmlands and rural credit markets. In the countryside, where his father once advocated democracy and fair treatment for rural citizens, Xi seeks, above all else, to maintain power. In retrospect, it is little wonder that many elderly villagers fondly remember Mao's grand attempt to remake the countryside through agrarian revolution. In reality, these campaigns were complex, uneven, and prone to violence. The stories told about agrarian revolution, however, remain just as compelling as they did in 1927, when Mao returned home in search of a rural path to revolutionary glory.

Major Land Laws and Rural Campaigns

May 4, 1946: May Fourth Directive

- During experimental land-to-the-tiller land reform, activists quickly move toward equalization of holdings.
- September First Directive, issued by the Central China Bureau, calls for "leveling" the holdings of rich and poor peasants. The shift from land-to-the-filler to fill-the-gaps land reform occurred in fall 1946
- Summer 1947: "Reexamination" land reform seeks to ensure the poor received enough land.

October 10, 1947: China Outline Land Law

- Subsequent land equalization campaigns attempt to level holdings.
- December 1947: "Swept out of the house" campaigns start in the Northeast; excessive violence and expanding struggle threaten the Civil War effort.
- Early 1948: Reexamination campaigns now seek to repay the wrongly expropriated.
- Summer, 1948: Land reform was halted.
- October 10, 1949: The North China Bureau calls for new campaigns using the "move the two ends, don't touch the middle" approach.
- Late 1949: Beijing suburbs experiment with relatively peaceful land reform.

June 30, 1950: Land Reform Law of the People's Republic of China

- 1950: Campaigns against Nationalist "bandits" and "evil tyrants" took place.

· Land reform typically was preceded by campaigns to reduce rent and interest; in some places, it was also preceded by campaigns to return deposits held by landlords.

· The first campaigns with the final land law start in autumn 1950 and were often followed by reexamination campaigns.

NOTES

Introduction

1. Mao was not the first to propose the idea that peasants could be true revolutionaries. The idea of peasant revolution has been traced back to 1907 with the work of Liu Shipei, a Chinese anarchist then writing in Tokyo. His views, however, were far from mainstream. Day, *The Peasant in Postsocialist China*, 18–19.

2. For views on the land problem during the 1930s, see Tawney, *Agrarian China*. For an early discussion of the land problem by a Western scholar, see Buck, *Land Utilization in China*.

3. Quoted in Harrison, *The Long March to Power*, 72.

4. Equally important to Mao at this early date was Peng Pai, active in the Guangdong countryside. Peng, like Mao, was a May Fourth intellectual drawn to both Marxism and the countryside. For more on Peng Pai, see Hofheinz, *The Broken Wave*; Marks, *Rural Revolution in South China*; and Galbiati, *Peng Pai and the Hai-Lu-Feng Soviet*. For Mao's early work in Hunan, see McDonald, *The Urban Origins of Rural Revolution*.

5. Harrison, *The Long March to Power*, 73. The Nationalists eventually turned away from land redistribution, instead promoting agricultural development as the key to solving the country's rural problems. Not until the Nationalists fled to Taiwan did they seriously address land reform. For more on Nationalist Party views on land reform, see Pepper, *Civil War in China*, 230–231. For a look at land reform in Taiwan, see Strauss, "Regimes and Repertoires of State Building."

6. Pantsov with Levine, *Mao*, 165–166.

7. See, for example, Hunt, *Politics, Culture, and Class in the French Revolution*, 176–177.

8. Mao Zedong, "Report on an Investigation of the Peasant Movement in Hunan," 23–24.

9. Ibid., 27.

10. Ibid., 37.

11. Ibid., 38.

12. For more on Chinese villages and their relationships to the outside world, see P. Huang, *The Peasant Economy and Social Change in North China*, 23–32.

13. For an example of the difficulty of finding class enemies, see P. Huang, "Rural Class Struggle in the Chinese Revolution," 114–116. Recently, Frank Dikötter has implied that landlords were a Communist fiction. In his study of the early PRC, Dikötter, describing the countryside before the party's arrival, wrote, "Nowhere in this profusion of social diversity could anybody called a "landlord" (*dizhu*) be found." Due to Dikötter's choice of phrasing, many readers believe that he is arguing that there were no landlords in China. His citation, however, refers to my UCLA dissertation, where I discuss how the term *landlord* (*dizhu*) was an alien word in the countryside. See Dikötter, *The Tragedy of Liberation*, 70. There were, to be sure, many landlords in China. See Esherick, "Number Games."

14. Quoted in Gao Wangling and Liu Yang, "On a Slippery Roof," 20–21.

15. Xiaojia Hou has further argued that the unruly peasants Mao had observed were in fact attacking quasi-government officials over market concerns, not feudal landlords. See Hou, *Negotiating Socialism in Rural China*, 37.

16. In 1927, party central released a flurry of directives in an attempt to halt rural violence. In 1928, Mao himself doubted the use of terror in the revolution. Perry, "Reclaiming the Chinese Revolution," 1157.

17. Ding Shu, *Yangmou*, 8.

18. In later years, the Nationalists, unwilling and unable to return to rural reform, squandered the advances the two parties had made in the countryside during their brief alliance. Nationalist land policies, primarily concerned with tapping rural revenue streams, typically increased landlord power at the local level. Reformers working with the Nationalists attempted to implement "rural reconstruction" and offer a true alternative to Mao's path to modernity through class struggle. For a recent look at rural reconstruction, see Merkel-Hess, *The Rural Modern*. Many intellectuals affiliated with the Nationalist Party, meanwhile, put their faith in the historical process of modernization, to be carried out not through revolution but a strong centralized state led by enlightened elites. See Huaiyin Li, *Reinventing Modern China*, 46–47.

19. Stalin hoped that rural radicalism might push left-wing Nationalists closer to the Communists. In actuality, however, violence in the peasant movement helped finally sever ties between the Communists and their Nationalist Party sympathizers.

20. For an analysis of land laws during this era, see Hsiao, *The Land Revolution in China, 1930–1934*, chaps. 1 and 2.

21. Pantsov with Levine, *Mao*, 212.

22. The early success of the party's rural turn owed much to the efforts of rural elites. But some local party members attempted to sabotage or subvert the effort to redistribute land. Averill, "Party, Society, and Local Elite in the Jiangxi Communist Movement," 294.

23. The December 1928 Jinggang Mountains Land Law.

24. The Xingguo Land Law of April 1929 still forbade the purchase or sale of land. In a concession to the demands of party central, however, the law did reduce the number of targets for expropriation. For more on land laws during

the Jiangxi Soviet, see Ling Buji and Shu Long, *Zhonghua suweiai gongheguo shi*, 274–278.

25. Quoted in Pantsov with Levine, *Mao*, 223. This third land law, the February Seventh Land Law of 1930, was inspired by Stalin's criticism of the Chinese Communists for their supposed leniency toward rich peasants. The law did, however, repeal the ban on buying and selling land.

26. Hou, *Negotiating Socialism in Rural China*, 41.

27. For an overview of Western scholarship on this era, see P. Huang, "The Jiangxi Period."

28. Mao Zedong, *Report from Xunwu*, 157.

29. Pantsov with Levine, *Mao*, 247.

30. Bo Yibo, *Ruogan zhongda juece yu shijian de huigu*, 114.

31. The Land Law of the Chinese Soviet Republic (Zhonghua suweiai gongheguo tudi fa), passed on December 1, 1931, at the First All-China Soviet Congress. These policies resulted in a clear decline in production, a problem compounded by impractical experiments in collectivization. But with the party desperate for funds due to the ongoing military encirclement campaigns launched by Chiang Kai-shek and the Nationalists, the hope that wider confiscation would stream wealth to the party and its poor supporters trumped concerns over agricultural productivity. See Hsiao, *The Land Revolution in China*, chap. 3.

32. Quoted in Hsiao, *The Land Revolution in China*, 105. The two articles, "How to Analyze the Classes" and "Decisions Regarding Some Issues Arising from Agrarian Reform," were reissued during later land reform campaigns. The reprinted articles were moderated in line with later land policies.

33. Ding Shu, *Yangmou*, 9.

34. Liu Mianyu, *Tudi geming zhanzheng shi*, 191. For a recent look at the end of the Jiangxi Soviet, see Huang Daoxuan, *Zhangli yu xianjie: zhongyang suqu de geming, 1933–1934*. According to Huang, the fall of the Jiangxi Soviet cannot be solely explained by "leftist" deviations.

35. As announced in late 1935, after much of the base area had undergone agrarian reform and eliminated extreme cases of exploitation and inequality, these new policies were designed to protect prosperous farmers and ensure that dispossessed landlords were given a share of land. Further policy changes followed in 1936 with the open call for the formation of a new United Front, including more protection for landlords and rich peasants. Selden's account of the land revolution in Shaan-Gan-Ning notes the intensity of the 1935 campaign in comparison to the far more moderate 1936 campaign. This increasing moderation was tied to Mao Zedong's call for a new United Front. See Selden, *The Yenan Way in Revolutionary China*, chap. 3. Keating notes that even during the United Front, the Communists found ways to confiscate property from "spies," "traitors," or "smugglers" who ran afoul of the party. Keating, *Two Revolutions*, 69.

36. In February the Communists, still looking for a renewed United Front, publicly announced the end of the confiscation of landlord property. Japanese

advances lent an urgency to negotiations between the two sides over summer 1937, leading to a formal announcement of cooperation on September 22.

37. Selden, *The Yenan Way*, 230.

38. Keating, *Two Revolutions*, 75–77.

39. The movement did not proceed quickly. According to Pepper, it was not until after an October 1943 directive that most base areas focused on double reduction. See Pepper, *Civil War in China*, 251–252.

40. Selden, *The Yenan Way*, 232. Pepper made a similar point in her analysis of the May Fourth Directive: "The difference between rent reduction in practice, and land reform in its 1946 formulations, was more of degree than of kind." Pepper, *Civil War in China*, 249.

41. Hou, *Negotiating Socialism in Rural China*, 45.

42. The political education of base area peasants was furthered through a campaign running concurrent and in concert with double reduction, an organized attack on local power holders to "settle accounts." Pepper also notes that attacks on such men were an effective means of mass mobilization, as well as a means to transfer wealth under the context of the United Front. Pepper, *Civil War in China*, 256–258. The party also educated peasants to be on guard against landlord "tricks" to subvert double reduction. Keating, *Two Revolutions*, 167.

43. Du Runsheng, *Zhongguo de tudigaige*, 155–156.

44. Hou, *Negotiating Socialism in Rural China*, 48.

45. This is not to say, however, that 1945 represented a watershed in regard to the party's land policies. The radical experiments of the Jiangxi Soviet era, as well as the more relaxed and inclusive approach active during the war against Japan, provided the party with templates for future land policies. See Westad, *Decisive Encounters*, 129.

46. During wartime double reduction, confrontations with landlords were to be nonviolent and private. Landlords who agreed to double reduction could avoid all confrontations. If a landlord opposed the reforms, cadres would organize a "speaking-reason" meeting between the landlord and their tenants and hired hands. Only the most obstinate of landlords were to be subjected to public struggle, where peasants would confront the landlord by listing the means and extent of exploitation, as well as explaining how the landlord had defied double reduction. The Communists described this policy as "struggling one to warn one hundred." See Du Runsheng, *Zhongguo de tudigaige*, 139.

47. Gao Wangling and Liu Yang, "On a Slippery Roof," 22.

48. Hou, *Negotiating Socialism in Rural China*, 13. Hou argues that the party was not primarily concerned with production until 1949.

49. Westad, *Decisive Encounters*, 116.

50. Officially known as the Directive of the Central Committee of the Chinese Communist Party on the Land Question (Zhonggong zhongyang guanyu tudi wenti de zhishi). For an example of a call to distribute land to the tiller during this era, see "*Huazhong fenju guanyu guanche zhongyang 'wu si' guanyu tudi zhengce xin jueding de zhishi,*" *Zhongguo tudi gaige shiliao xuanbian* (May 28, 1946), 254 (hereafter ZTGSX). This collection was published in 1988

by the National Defense University of the People's Liberation Army of China. The massive collection of documents, marked for internal distribution, has no introductory essay, so it is impossible to say what motivated its publication. The editors of the collection, however, showed much forethought, including land reform documents penned by both Bo Yibo and Xi Zhongxun.

51. Thus, the May Fourth Directive did not explicitly advocate the confiscation of landlord property. Teiwes, "The Origins of Rectification," 34.

52. Quoted in Friedman, Pickowicz, and Selden, *Chinese Village, Socialist State*, 80.

53. Pepper, *Civil War in China*, 277.

54. Ma Jia, *Jiangshan cun shi ri*, 2.

55. Employing a "mobilization-transformation" narrative structure, these works provided a model for future literature claiming to represent rural realities. Cai Xiang, *Revolution and Its Narratives*, 49. For more on the production of these land reform novels, see DeMare, "The Romance and Tragedy of Rural Revolution."

56. Huaiyin Li, *Reinventing Modern China*, 8–9.

57. Shao Yanxiang, *Bie le Mao Zedong*, 157.

58. Westad, *Decisive Encounters*, 129.

59. "Dongbei ju guanyu xingshi yu renwu de jueyi," ZTGSX (July 7, 1946), 268.

60. Westad, *Decisive Encounters*, 126–127.

61. For an example of local cadres using the market, not confiscation, to redistribute land, see Thaxton, *Catastrophe and Contention in Rural China*, 70–71.

62. Du Runsheng, *Zhongguo de tudigaige*, 179.

63. "Kaizhan fanshen da jiancha, shixing 'tian ping bu qi yundong,'" ZTGSX (September 9, 1946), 310–311.

64. "Jin-Ji-Lu-Yu ju wei guanche 'wu si' zhishi chedi shexian geng zhe you qi tian de zhishi," ZTGSX (September 9, 1946), 311–312.

65. "Dongbei ju guanyu jiejue tudigaige zhong 'ban sheng bu shou' de wenti de zhishi," ZTGSX (November 21, 1946), 326–327.

66. "Zhengqu chungeng qian wancheng tudigaige," ZTGSX (December 14, 1946), 328–329.

67. Ding Shu, *Yangmou*, 11.

68. At this time due to the dangers of war, the party leadership had been divided into two; Mao remained in Shaan-Gan-Ning and did not join Liu Shaoqi in Pingshan until May 1948. Mao would later criticize this conference as "ultra-left" despite agreeing at the time with its policies. Teiwes, "The Origins of Rectification," 34.

69. Friedman, Pickowicz, and Selden, *Chinese Village, Socialist State*, 93.

70. Teiwes, "The Origins of Rectification," 39.

71. "Zhongguo tudi fa dagang," ZTGSX (September 13, 1947), 422.

72. "Xi Zhongxun guanyu tugai wenti de xin," ZTGSX (January 4, 1948), 447–448.

73. Yang Kuisong, *Zhonghua renmin gongheguo jianguo shi yanjiu 1*, 96.

74. Mao Zedong, *Report from Xunwu*, 213

75. Mao Zedong, "Report on an Investigation of the Peasant Movement in Hunan," 28.

76. Hinton, *Fanshen*, 226.

77. Ibid., 362. According to Hinton, some of the seventeen cases were clearly rape. "In regards to the others the situation was not clear, but there appeared to be at least some measure of coercion involved."

78. Du Guang, *1957 niande geming yu fan geming*, 256.

79. Gao Wangling and Liu Yang, "On a Slippery Roof," 26.

80. Liu Tong, *Dongbei jiefang zhanzheng jishi*, 419.

81. Ding Shu, *Yangmou*, 11.

82. Quoted in Luo Pinghan, *Tudi gaige yundong shi*, 273.

83. Shao Yanxiang, *Bie le Mao Zedong*, 158

84. The tiger stool was an ancient torture device that placed great pressure on the victim's joints. "Spreading phoenix wings" referred to stringing a victim up by the fingers and toes. Du Guang, *1957 niande geming yu fan geming*, 256.

85. Mao was one of the last to come to this realization and was still promoting poor peasant interests above all as late as December 1947. Friedman, Pickowicz, and Selden, *Chinese Village, Socialist State*, 100.

86. Xi Zhongzun, "Guanyu tugai zhong yixie wenti gei Mao zhuxi de baogao," ZTGSX (January 19, 1948), 450–451.

87. Westad, *Decisive Encounters*, 118.

88. Teiwes, "The Origins of Rectification," 47. Teiwes argues that Mao Zedong and Liu Shaoqi were both responsible for the escalation in violence in land reform.

89. "Zhonggong zhongyang guanyu nanfang ge youji qu zanshi bu shixing tugai de zhishi," ZTGSX (July 17, 1948), 526.

90. Friedman, Pickowicz, and Selden, *Chinese Village, Socialist State*, 101. In Wugong, villagers endured three rounds of land reform, although the first round was conducted by local cadres and not an outside work team. The party attached writers to work teams visiting model land reform villages, tightening the connections between narratives and agrarian revolution.

91. Pepper, *Civil War in China*, 309.

92. Du Runsheng, *Zhongguo de tudigaige*, 260.

93. Westad, *Decisive Encounters*, 107–108.

94. "Zhonggong zhongyang guanyu tudi fa dagang zhong ruogan wenti zhengxun ge zhongyang ju de yijian," ZTGSX (March 30, 1950), 625.

95. Mao Zedong, "Mao Zedong guanyu zanshi bu dong funong de wenti gei Deng Zihui de fushi," ZTGSX (May 1, 1950), 630.

96. "Zhonghua renmin gonggeguo tudi gaige fa," ZTGSX (June 28, 1950), 642–647.

97. Bo Yibo, *Ruogan zhongda juece*, 118–123. According to Bo Yibo's recollections, there was considerable debate in the party over the rich peasant line. The South Central Bureau, citing a higher concentration of land ownership, called for the confiscation of any lands rented out by rich peasants. In a nod to

such areas, the final draft of the land law allowed such confiscation, but only in rare cases and with high-level approval.

98. Quoted in *Women canguan tudigaige yihou*, 1–2.

99. "Zhonggong zhongyang huadongju guanyu tudigaige ruogan wenti de tongbao," ZTGSX (April, 1951), 745.

100. Quoted in *Zhongnan tudi gaige de weida shengli*, 11.

101. Ibid., 193, 12.

102. Xu Bin, *Zhang Ailing zhuan*, 311; Yang Lianfen, *Xiandai xiaoshuo daolun*, 270.

103. William Skinner happened to observe the unwelcome arrival of the grain requisition letter in one township. Skinner, *Rural China on the Eve of Revolution*, 163.

104. In Guizhou, for example, the party withdrew from twenty-eight counties in March 1950. Resisters were not suppressed until the following year. Many were drafted into the PLA and sent to the Korean front. Brown, "From Resisting Communists to Resisting America," 105–107.

105. This was the case as late as 1953, when the party brought land reform to Yunnan in Southwest China. Diamant, *Revolutionizing the Family*, 142.

106. For the role of secret societies in resisting the Communists, see Wang, *Violence and Order on the Chengdu Plain*, 149–153.

107. *Neibu cankao* (October 14, 1950), 102 (hereafter NBCK).

108. Deng Xiaoping, "Deng Xiaoping tongzhi xiang zhonggong zhongyang xinanju wenyuan hui di san ci huiyi de baogao," Chongqing Archives, East Sichuan Collection, 26-32-11, in *Zhongguo xi'nan dang'an: tudigaige ziliao, 1949–1953*, 181 (hereafter ZXD). According to the editors of *Zhongguo xi'nan dang'an*, no meaningful changes were made to the archival documents included in the collection. This included maintaining local dialects and the original archival numbering system. Mistakes in the original documents (including personal and place names) were, however, corrected.

109. This campaign still used the basic organizational methods of land reform, including locating and developing activists. For targets who had sufficiently offended their community, the result of their struggle might be execution. But even in extreme cases, a death sentence had to be approved through the proper legal channels. See Luo Pinghan, *Tudi gaige yundong shi*, 323.

110. These meetings were based on multiple administrative villages (*xiang*). Du Runsheng, *Zhongguo de tudigaige*, 391. Internal party documents show that some peasants were often confused with regard to the proper administrative unit for land reform. For example, see NBCK (November 6, 1950), 16.

111. "E'ba Chen Xiangji zuizhuang," Jiangjin County Archive, 1-1-42 (1951), 31–36 (hereafter JCA).

112. Ibid., 20–23.

113. "E'ba Liu Guoqing douzhenghui kougong," JCA, 1-1-42 (1951), 25–31.

114. These campaigns started in some areas as early as winter 1949 and ended in some regions as late as August 1951. Paying deposits was most common in Sichuan. For an example of a land reform work team that found

peasants already well mobilized by these campaigns, see "Xi'nan tudi gaige gongzuotuan di er tuan di san fentuan gongzuo baogao," Chongqing City Archives, D-65-11, ZXD (1951?), 164.

115. For two accounts of land reform toward the end of the campaign, see Potter and Potter, *China's Peasants*, chap. 2, and Ruf, *Cadres and Kin*, chap. 3.

116. Luo Pinghan, *Tudi gaige yundong shi*, 368.

117. "Record of Important All-China Events of the Chinese People's Political Consultative Conference in 1951" [1951 nian quanguo zhengxie dashi ji]. Originally published in 1952; accessed June 16, 2018. http://www.cppcc.gov.cn/zxww/2017/12/25/ARTI1514167285027512.shtml.

118. "Xi'nan tudi gaige gongzuotuan di er tuan di san fentuan gongzuo baogao," 164.

Chapter 1

1. Ding Ling, *Taiyang zhao zai sangganhe shang*, 86.

2. Zong Cheng, *Ding Ling*, 106. For more on Ding Ling's time carrying out land reform, see Yang Guixin, *Ding Ling pingzhuan*, 249–258.

3. Ding Ling, "Chongyin qianyan," 3.

4. Xiong Baishi, "Women cong 'Sangganhe shang' yu 'Baofeng zhouyu' li xuexi shenme," *Zhongguo qingnian* no. 80 (1951), 20 (hereafter ZQ).

5. This included an unintended lesson in the malleability of the Maoist class structures. In *Sanggan River*, the village villain is Qian Wengui. As Philip Huang noted, Qian "turns out to have been a middle peasant" who becomes the main target of the land reform due to "his unprincipled wheelings and dealings." P. Huang, *The Peasant Economy and Social Change in North China*, 82.

6. Ding Ling, *Taiyang zhao zai sangganhe shang*, 63–65.

7. Ibid., 100.

8. Zhang Ailing, *Chi di zhi lian*, 7.

9. Xu Bin, *Zhang Ailing zhuan*, 301–315.

10. Zhang Ailing, *Chi di zhi lian*, 1.

11. While Zhang Ailing insisted on the authenticity of her land reform narratives, she never mentioned her time on a work team. See Yang Lianfen, *Xiandai xiaoshuo daolun*, 270. Zhang's participation in land reform remains a contested issue. See "Zhang Ailing canjia guo tugai ma?" [Did Zhang Ailing participate in land reform?], http://www.guancha.cn/DongFangZao-Bao/2013_03_25_134072.shtml, accessed July 11, 2018. It seems reasonable that Zhang, like so many other intellectuals, would spend time in the countryside. If she did not, however, her novels still demonstrate a keen understanding of life in the countryside as the Communists came to power.

12. Zhang Ailing, *Chi di zhi lian*, 13.

13. Ibid., 15.

14. Ibid., 17.

15. Hinton, *Fanshen*, 12.

16. Fan Wenlan was one of the first Chinese historians to write from a Marxist perspective. A trusted friend of Mao Zedong, Fan helped popularize Mao's

unique views on the course of Chinese history. See Li, *Reinventing Modern China*, chap. 3.

17. Cohen, "Just Fifteen Books on China?" 64.

18. Hinton, *Fanshen*, 517.

19. Ibid., 266–267.

20. Ibid., 389.

21. Ibid., 366.

22. Ibid., 17–18.

23. "Taihang qu dangwei guanyu Taihang tudigaige baodao (jielu)," ZTGSX (June 15, 1947): 371.

24. The Communists created and controlled the social group they termed "intellectuals" throughout the revolutionary era. As Eddy U has argued, under CCP rule, "intellectuals" were not a natural and stable social category but instead constructed through "discursive practice (statements, assertions, utterances and their internal rules and relations) and nondiscursive practice (power relations, economic and social processes, institutional arrangements, and behavior patterns). U, "The Making of *Zhishifenzi*," 119. The role that intellectuals played in land reform, discussed throughout this book, is also explored in De-Mare, "Casting (Off) Their Stinking Airs."

25. Quoted in Pepper, *Civil War in China*, 78.

26. During the 1935 Wayaobu Conference, party leaders had decided to solve ongoing personnel shortages through the recruitment of "petit bourgeois intellectuals," setting the stage for a rapid expansion of party members. In the following years, petit bourgeois intellectuals traveled to Yan'an en masse, especially after the start of full-scale war with Japan in 1937. As dictated by party policy, they were to be welcomed into a coalition government as part of the Second United Front and even allowed considerable intellectual and creative freedom. Holm, *Art and Ideology in Revolutionary China*, 44.

27. For an overview of this process, see U, "Reification of the Chinese Intellectual."

28. Mao Zedong, *Selected Works of Mao Zedong, Vol. 1*, 297.

29. Liu Shaoqi advised all Communists to engage in self-cultivation (*xiuyang*), which meant they must "modestly learn the Marxist-Leninist stand (*lichang*), viewpoint, (*guandian*), and method (*fangfa*), learn from the noble proletarian quality of the founders of Marxism-Leninism and apply all this in our practice." Liu Shaoqi, *Selected Works of Liu Shaoqi*, 118.

30. Ibid., 121.

31. McDougall, *Mao Zedong's "Talks at the Yan'an Conference on Literature and Art,"* 61.

32. Pepper, *Civil War in China*, 221.

33. Crook and Crook, *Ten Mile Inn*, 17.

34. Ibid., 30–35, 191–194, 269.

35. Ibid., 121.

36. "Taihang qu dangwei guanyu Taihang tudigaige baodao (jielu)," 371.

37. "Dongbei ju guanyu xingshi yu renwu de jueyi," ZTGSX (July 7, 1946), 270.

38. "Dongbei ju guanyu shenru qunzhong tudi douzheng de zhishi," ZTGSX (August 29, 1946), 307.

39. "Dongbei ju guanyu xingshi yu renwu de jueyi," 270.

40. "Dongbei ju guanyu shenru qunzhong tudi douzheng de zhishi," 307.

41. Westad, *Decisive* Encounters, 127.

42. Deng Zihui, "Cong Eqian xiang douzheng lai yanjiu muqian tudigaige yundong," ZTGSX (August 1946), 293–295. Li Jianzhen, a poor peasant from Guangdong, had been introduced to rural revolution by no less of an authority than Peng Pai.

43. This meeting was for the Jin-Cha-Lu-Xiang (Shanxi-Cha'har-Shandong-Hunan) base area. Luo Pinghan, *Tudi gaige yundong shi*, 173.

44. "Zhonggong zhongyang zhengqiu guanyu jieji fenxi de yijian," ZTGSX (November 29, 1947), 438.

45. This meeting was held in the Jin-Cha-Ji base area in October 1947. Nie was the region's leading military commander. Friedman, Pickowicz, and Selden, *Chinese Village, Socialist State*, 93.

46. Bo Yibo, "Bo Yibo guanyu fucha qian buchong zhishi de baogao," ZTGSX (February 5, 1948), 460.

47. Hinton, *Fanshen*, 272.

48. Xi Zhongxun, "Guanyu xin qu gongzuo wenti de baogao (jielu)," ZTGSX (July 15, 1948), 525.

49. "Zhonggong Hebei shengwei guanyu jiancha xin qu tugai gongzuo wenti ji jinhou yijian," ZTGSX (November 11, 1949), 609–610.

50. Pepper, *Civil War in China*, 417.

51. Chen Tiqiang, "Cong tugai zhong xue maliezhuyi," 1.

52. "Guanyu nongmin xiehui zuzhi tongze de ji dian jieshi," *Renmin ribao* (July 16, 1950), 1 (hereafter RR).

53. Du Runsheng, "Zhongnan quanqu qudong jinchun tudigaige de jingguo yu zhuyao jingyan ji jinhou jihua," ZTGSX (May 9, 1951), 739–740.

54. *Zhongnan tudi gaige de weida shengli*, 12, 99.

55. Teiwes, "Establishment and Consolidation of the New Regime," 84.

56. *Zenyang zuo yi ge qingniantuan yuan*, 15. This was the journal of the New Democratic Youth League (Zhongguo xin minzhuzhuyi qingtian tuan), the party's inclusive mass student organization. In contrast to the previous Communist Youth League (Gongchanzhuyi qingnian tuan), which was now criticized as suffering from "closed-doorism," the new Youth League was open to activists of all backgrounds. Feng Wenbin, "Zhongguo xin minzhu zhuyi tuan shi shenme," 19–22.

57. "De'wei xiang di yi buzhou gongzuo" [Summary of initial work in De'wei Xiang], JCA, 95-01-03 (1951), 6.

58. "Guizhou sheng huangping xian siping zhen wuliqiao cun jieji chubu diaocha," ZXD, Chongqing City Archives, D-65-1-1 (August 24, 1950), 83.

59. Gao, "War Culture, Nationalism, and Political Campaigns, 1950–1953," 196.

60. Quoted in Bai Xi, *Kaiguo da tugai*, 355.

61. Yang Rengeng, "Gen nongmin xuexi yihou," 101.

62. "Chongqing jiaoqu dizhu ge zhong yinmou pohuai huodong qingkuang," ZXD, Chongqing City Archives, D-716-21 (1951?), 136.

63. "Sidong changshou xian nongxie gongzuo de chengji ji muqian cunzai de ji ge yanzhong wenti," ZXD, Chongqing City Archives, D-422-2 (1951?), 137.

64. Zhao Zengyi, "Cong Hechuan tudi gaige zhong suo jian dao de ji ge wenti," ZXD, Chongqing Archives, East Sichuan Collection, 46-54 10 (June 25, 1951), 151.

65. "Zhongnan tudigaige weiyuanhui guanyu zhongnan ge sheng tugai shidian gongzuo qingkuang de baogao," ZTGSX (November 26, 1950), 691–692.

66. Feng Youlan, "Canjia tugai de shouhui," 69.

67. Chen Zhenzhou, "Tugai jiaoyu le wo," 87.

68. Feng Kexi, "Canguan Chongqing shi jiaoqu tudi gaige suo jian," 68.

69. Yuan Fang, "Women de tugai gongzuo zu," 24.

70. Dang Qiaoxin, "Zai tudi gaige zhong duanlian ziji," 76.

71. Chen Tiqiang, "Cong tugai zhong xue maliezhuyi," 2.

72. Wang Xuan, "Wo zai tugai zhong de xuexi," 93.

73. Dang Qiaoxin, "Zai tudi gaige zhong duanlian ziji," 75.

74. Feng Youlan, "Canjia tugai de shouhui," 71.

75. Chen Tiqiang, "Cong tugai zhong xue maliezhuyi," 1.

76. Meng Gang, "Wo canjia le tudi gaige," ZQ No. 33 (1950), 31.

77. It is impossible to verify if Zheng Huiren was an actual student or a construct of the *China Youth* editors. This study treats him as a real student, as his concerns accurately represent the dilemmas facing students from "suspect" families. Indeed, loyalty to the state versus loyalty to the family is a problem reflecting a long philosophical debate that has its roots in the Spring and Autumn era during the first half of the Eastern Zhou period (771–476 BCE).

78. "Zai tudi gaige zhong Zheng Huiren yinggai zenyang duidai ta de dizhu jiating?" ZQ No. 77 (1951), 24.

79. Ibid.

80. "Zheng Huiren yinggai zhenyang duidai ta de dizhu jiating," ZQ No. 81 (1951), 27.

81. Lou Xianzhou, "Wo renshi le dizhu jieji the zui'e," ZQ No. 78 (1951), 72.

82. Ren Qing, "Dizhu jiating gei le wo xie shenme?" ZQ No. 80 (1951), 30.

83. Liu Zaixing, "Wo zai tudi gaige yundong zhong ganqing qile bianhua," ZQ No. 79 (1951), 22.

84. "Zhandao renmin de lichang shanglai," ZQ No. 92 (1952), 8.

85. Hou, *Negotiating Socialism in Rural China*, 12–13.

86. Shao Yanxiang, *Bie le Mao Zedong*, 160.

87. Ibid., 159.

Chapter 2

1. Ding Ling, *Taiyang zhao zai sangganhe shang*, 78–79.

2. Ibid., 167–169.

3. Ibid., 192.

4. Zhang Ailing, *Chi di zhi lian*, 17.

5. Ibid., 26.

6. Ibid., 29.

7. Ibid., 30

8. Hinton, *Fanshen*, 114.

9. Ibid., 134.

10. Ibid., 270.

11. Ibid., 324.

12. Ibid., 378, 386.

13. Hinton, *Shenfan*, 26. The question of what Hinton got right and got wrong in his account of Long Bow has long fascinated his readers. Forthcoming scholarship from Deng Hongqin and Ma Weiqiang of Shanxi University, investigating land reform in villages near Long Bow, suggests that much in Hinton's account seems atypical for the Changzhi countryside.

14. Li, *Village China Under Socialism and Reform*, 15.

15. Seybolt, "The War Within a War," 201–202. As Seybolt argues, while many Chinese collaborated with Japanese invaders, they did so for personal reasons and thus tended to be highly unreliable.

16. Dongbei ju guanyu tudi wenti ji dui ge jieceng de zhengce de yijian," ZTGSX (August 30, 1946), 309.

17. "Jinchaji ju guanyu chuanda yu jinxing zhongyang wusi zhishi de jieding (jielu)," ZTGSX (August 1946), 298.

18. Such was the case in Longkou, Shandong, where a campaign against traitors led to almost two thousand mass meetings. Lary, *China's Civil War*, 71.

19. Friedman, Pickowicz, and Selden, *Chinese Village, Socialist State*, 84–85.

20. Li Xuefeng, "Guanyu xin qu douzheng celüe ji zuzhi xingshi de baogao," ZTGSX (February 13, 1948), 471.

21. Xi Zhongxun, "Guanyu xin qu gongzuo wenti de baogao (jielu)," ZTGSX (July 15, 1948), 524.

22. Friedman, Pickowicz, and Selden, *Chinese Village, Socialist State*, 97.

23. "Huazhong fenju guanyu muqian tudigaige yundong zhong ji ge wenti de zhishi," ZTGSX (August 5, 1946), 286.

24. "Dongbei ju guanyu shenru qunzhong tudi douzheng de zhishi," 397.

25. Pan Guangdan and Quan Weitian, "Shei shuo 'jiangnan wu fengjian,'" 13.

26. While encouraging peasants to discuss their hardships under party leadership was a new practice, the term *suku* was not. See *Hanyu da cidian*, 6552.

27. PLA soldiers, however, would not later personally accuse those who had wronged them in the past. Wu, "Speaking Bitterness," 14.

28. "Zhankai fanshen da jiancha shixing tianping buqi yundong," ZTGSX (September 9, 1946), 310.

29. Westad, *Decisive Encounters*, 130.

30. "Huazhong fenju guanyu jiejue tudi wenti de buchong zhishi," ZTGSX (June 16, 1946), 263.

31. These party branches were hindrances that had to be dissolved before

land reform could proceed. "Huazhong fenju guanyu muqian tudigaige yun-dong zhong ji ge wenti de zhishi," 286.

32. Here work team members were advised to use Marxist class analysis to investigate the class background of potential activists. Deng Zihui, "Cong Eqian xiang douzheng lai yanjiu muqian tudigaige yundong," 296.

33. Xi Zhongxun, "Xi Zhongxun guanyu tugai wenti de xin," 447–448.

34. "Huazhong fenju guanyu tuanjie zhongnong de zhishi," ZTGSX (September 1, 1946), 304.

35. Xi Zhongxun, "Guanyu xin qu gongzuo wenti de baogao (jielu)," 523–524.

36. For example, in Wugong, Zhang Yukun promised a share of hidden property for those who joined picket lines in front of the houses of class enemies. Friedman, Pickowicz, and Selden, *Chinese Village, Socialist State*, 95.

37. Shao Yanxiang, *Bie le Mao Zedong*, 158.

38. Deng Zihui, "Cong Eqian xiang douzheng lai yanjiu muqian tudigaige yundong," 294.

39. Thaxton, *Catastrophe and Contention in Rural China*, 74.

40. Li, *Village China under Socialism and Reform*, 15.

41. Diamant, *Revolutionizing the Family*, 142. These predatory gangs would be a problem in 1953, long after the end of land reform.

42. Or as Aminda Smith has argued in her study of reeducation centers, "Anti-state resistance from members of the oppressed masses was essential to early-PRC rhetoric because it validated claims about the devastating effects of the old society and the transformative power of socialist 'truth.'" Smith, "Thought Reform and the Unreformable," 950–951.

43. Westad, *Decisive Encounters*, 130–131.

44. Friedman, Pickowicz, and Selden, *Chinese Village, Socialist State*, 82–83.

45. "Huazhong fenju guanyu muqian tudigaige yundong zhong ji ge wenti de zhishi," 283–284.

46. Deng Zihui, "Cong Eqian xiang douzheng lai yanjiu muqian tudigaige yundong," 294–295.

47. "Dongbei ju guanyu jiejue tudigaige zhong 'ban sheng bu shou' de wenti de zhishi," ZTGSX (November 21, 1946), 326–327.

48. "Huadong ju guanyu Jiangnan xin qu nongcun gongzuo de zhishi (jielu)," ZTGSX (April 1, 1949), 588–589.

49. Crook and Crook, *Ten Mile Inn*, 16–21.

50. Madsen, *Morality and Power in a Chinese Village*, 85–88.

51. Kipnis, *Producing Guanxi*, 161.

52. Zhao Zengyi, "Cong Hechuan tudi gaige zhong suo jian dao de ji ge wenti," ZXD, Chongqing Archives, East Sichuan Collection, 46-54 10 (June 25, 1951), 150.

53. Zhou Libo, *Baofeng zhouyu*, chap. 4.

54. "Cong Li Aijie de yisheng kan Hunan nongmin de fanshen," RR (March 30, 1951), 2.

55. "Qu dangwei xuanchuanbu guanyu zhengliang qingfei fanba jianzu tuiya

yundong zhong xuanjiao gongzuo de zhishi," ZXD, Chongqing Archives, East Sichuan Collection, 1-42-15 (September 25, 1950), 20.

56. Thaxton, *Catastrophe and Contention in Rural China*, 73.

57. "JinJiLuYu tudigaige de jiben zongjie," ZTGSX (July 1947), 392.

58. Aganost, *National Past-Times*, 29.

59. Wu, "Speaking Bitterness," 9.

60. Zhou Libo, *Baofeng zhouyu*, 37.

61. Ibid., 162–163.

62. "JinJiLuYu tudigaige de jiben zongjie," 392. As Denise Y. Ho has explained, land reform exhibits proved highly influential, providing a model that for exhibits of class enemy property during the Cultural Revolution. Ho, *Curating the Revolution*, 187–189.

63. Fang Huirong, "'Wu shijian jing' yu shenghuo shijie zhong de 'zhenshi.'"

64. By offering a direct comparison between the bitter nature of the past and the superiority of the new regime, work team members also promoted the ideal of the party and the state as the embodiment of the people. Guo Yuhua and Sun Liping, "Suku."

65. Gao Wangling and Liu Yang, "On a Slippery Roof," 21.

66. This phenomenon is investigated in *Righteous Revolutionaries: Morality, Mobilization, and Violence in the Early Years of the People's Republic of China*, Jeffery Javed's forthcoming study on collective violence, including land reform in the East China Bureau.

67. Crook and Crook, *Ten Mile Inn*, 30–35.

68. Quoted in Luo Pinghan, *Tudi gaige yundong shi*, 110.

69. Ren Qingbo, "Li Xiuyang suku," 1–5.

70. Han Jinfeng. "Wei qinniang baochou," 5–10.

71. Westad, *Decisive Encounters*, 131.

72. Hershatter, *The Gender of Memory*, 78–79.

73. Wu, "Speaking Bitterness," 12–13.

74. "JinJiLuYu tudigaige de jiben zongjie," 396.

75. "Beiyue qu tudi gaige yundong zhong fadong funü de jingyan," 50–53.

76. "Erqu funü gongzuo zongjie," JCA, 95-01-03 (1951), 128.

77. Yan, *Private Life Under Socialism*, 47–49.

78. "Guizhou sheng huangping xian siping zhen wuliqiao cun jieji chubu diaocha," ZXD, Chongqing City Archives, D-65-1-1 (August 24, 1950), 83.

79. "Hebei sheng wei guanyu dizhu he funong fangong wenti xiang huabei ju baogao," ZTGSX (November 1950), 697.

80. "De'wei xiang di yi buzhou gongzuo," JCA, 95-01-03 (1951), 3.

81. The account of team leader Li's training session is penned vertically in clear calligraphy and is most likely a product of an intellectual member of the work team. "He'ai xiang di san ci nongmin daibiao huiyi zongjie huibao," JCA, 95-01-03 (1951), 1–7.

82. "Zhonggong Hebei shengwei guanyu jiancha xin qu tugai gongzuo wenti ji jinhou yijian," 608.

83. "Beijing shi renmin zhengfu guanyu Beijing jiaoqu tudigaige de zongjie baogao," ZTGSX (November 8, 1950), 686.

84. Quoted in Dikötter, *The Tragedy of Liberation*, 76.

85. "Zhongnan tudigaige weiyuanhui guanyu zhongnan ge sheng tugai shidian gongzuo qingkuang de baogao," 691.

86. "Nanchuan xian wei jiu yue fen guanyu jizhong ganbu xuexi tugai he zongjie tugai gongzuo zonghe baogao," JCA, East Sichuan District Party Committee, 6-124 (October 20, 1951), 27.

87. "Qu dangwei guanyu Fuling Zengfu xiang tudi gaige zhong ganbu qiangpo mingling de tongbao," JCA, East Sichuan District Party Committee, 1-6-144 (November 22, 1951), 43.

88. Quoted in Wu, "Speaking Bitterness," 5.

89. "Jiangjin xian erqu Shuanglong xiang (tugai qi) di yi ci nongmindai huiyi jueyi gangyao," JCA, 95-01-03 (1951), 73.

90. Strauss, "Morality, Coercion, and State Building by Campaign in the Early PRC," 902.

91. Yan Hongyan, "Yan Hongyan weiyuan zai xinan jun zheng weiyuanhui di er ci quanti weiyuan huiyi shang de fayan," ZXD, Chongqing City Archives, D-65-10 (1950?), 11.

92. "Qu dangwei dui tudi gaige, fucha zhong ying zhuyi de ji ge wenti fu Youyang diwei," ZXD, Chongqing Archives, East Sichuan Collection, 46-54-10 (June 23, 1951), 147. The party still insisted on blaming landlords even as this investigation directly noted that local party committees were deliberately violating policies.

93. Wu, "Speaking Bitterness," 7.

94. Cheung, "Guangdong's Advantage," 95.

95. Chan, Madsen, and Unger, *Chen Village*, 20–28.

96. Potter and Potter, *China's Peasants*, 40–41.

97. Ibid., 47.

98. Siu, *Agents and Victims in South China*, 137.

99. Wu, "Speaking Bitterness," 13.

100. "De'wei xiang di yi buzhou gongzuo," 1.

101. "Jijing xiang jianzu tuiya qingfei fanba gongzuo de chubu zongjie baogao," JCA, County Party Committee Work Team, Fengjie Third District, 035-23 (January 1, 1951), 27.

102. "Yange jingyi qilai! Jieshou Fenghuang xiang heping tugai jiaoxun," JCA, East Sichuan District Party Committee, 1-32-541 (December 30, 1951), 62–65.

103. Shao Yanxiang, *Bie le Mao Zedong*, 165–166.

104. Diamant, *Revolutionizing the Family*, 143.

105. "Guanyu Guizhou sheng shaoshu minzu diqu tudigaige de ji ge wenti," ZTGSX (November 30, 1951), 787–789.

106. "Guizhou sheng huangping xian siping zhen wuliqiao cun jieji chubu diaocha," ZXD, Chongqing City Archives, D-65-1-1 (August 24, 1950), 82.

107. Diamant, *Revolutionizing the Family*, 142–143.

108. "Zai minzu zaju diqu jinxing tudigaige de ji ge jingyan: Linxia diwei tudigaige shiban gongzuo zongjie," ZTGSX (November 1951), 794.

109. "Yongchuan xian 1951 nian douzheng dizhu huiyi jilu," Yongchuan

County Archive, Yongchuan County Shijiao Village People's Government 115-
1-26 (1953), 150 (hereafter YCA).

Chapter 3

1. Ding Ling, *Taiyang zhao zai sangganhe shang,* 185.
2. Zhang Ailing, *Chi di zhi lian,* 29.
3. Ibid., 27.
4. Ibid., 54.
5. Hinton, *Fanshen,* 27.
6. A point made long ago by Philip Huang. See P. Huang, *The Peasant Economy and Social Change in North China,* 82–83.
7. Hinton, *Fanshen,* 39–41.
8. Ibid., 47.
9. Ibid., 277–286.
10. Ibid., 305.
11. Ibid., 315
12. For examples of the traditional use of *jieji,* see *Hanyu da cidian,* 9655.
13. Lippert, *Hanyu zhong de makesizhuyi shuyu de qiyuan yu zuoyong,* 170–174.
14. "Taihang qu dangwei guanyu nongcun jiejie huafen biaozhun yu juti huafen guiding (cao'an)," ZTGSX (October 12, 1946), 321.
15. Zhang Xiaojun, "Land Reform in Yang Village," 3.
16. Workers (*gongren*) labored in mines or on railways. Merchants (*shangren*), large and small, sold their wares. Vagrants (*youmin*) lived off begging, theft, gambling, banditry, or prostitution. Monks, nuns, and fortune tellers were classed as superstition professionals (*mixin zhiyezhe*), while opera singers, acrobats, and musicians were old artists (*jiu yi ren*). Doctors, teachers, and reporters were independent professionals (*ziyou zhiye zhe*). "Taihang qu dangwei guanyu nongcun jiejie huafen biaozhun yu juti huafen guiding (cao'an)," 324–325.
17. Zhang Xiaojun, "Land Reform in Yang Village," 17.
18. For classical examples see *Hanyu da cidian,* 5919.
19. Chen Yi, "Ruhe zhengque zhixing zhongyang wusi zhishi (jielu)," ZTGSX (May 1946), 260. Elsewhere, poor peasants were considered "half-proletarian" due to their farmlands. See "Huazhong fenju guanyu muqian tudigaige yundong zhong ji ge wenti de zhishi," ZTGSX (August 5, 1946), 283.
20. Mao Zedong, "Report on an Investigation of the Peasant Movement in Hunan," 32.
21. Ibid.
22. Li Zipu, "Guanyu zhongnong wenti," ZTGSX (June 18, 1946), 264–365.
23. Deng Zihui, "Cong Eqian xiang douzheng lai yanjiu muqian tudigaige yundong," 293.
24. "Taihang qu dangwei guanyu nongcun jiejie huafen biaozhun yu juti huafen guiding (cao'an)," 323.
25. Li, *Village China Under Socialism and Reform,* 16.

26. This label was in use throughout the land reform era. For an early use, see He Zhiping, "Lun zhongnong," ZTGSX (May 26, 1946), 252.

27. "Zhonggong zhongyang yijiusiqi shieryue jueyi," ZTGSX (December 1947): 443.

28. Lippert, *Hanyu zhong de makesizhuyi shuyu de qiyuan yu zuoyong*, 205–213.

29. "Huazhong fenju guanyu muqian tudigaige yundong zhong ji ge wenti de zhishi," 283–284.

30. "Taihang qu dangwei guanyu nongcun jiejie huafen biaozhun yu juti huafen guiding (cao'an)," 322.

31. Mao Zedong, "Report on an Investigation of the Peasant Movement in Hunan," 31.

32. Deng Zihui, "Cong Eqian xiang douzheng lai yanjiu muqian tudigaige yundong," 293–294.

33. According to this directive, middle peasants were not to surpass one-third of the local party branch; only true activist rich peasants and landlords might be allowed to join. "Huazhong fenju guanyu muqian tudigaige yundong zhong ji ge wenti de zhishi," 286.

34. The term, first used as early as the Eastern Zhou dynasty (771–476 BCE), meant the owner of land by the Tang dynasty (618–907 CE). The *Hanyu da cidian* defines *dizhu* in its classical use as an owner of land (*tiandi de zhuren*); in its current class meaning, the dictionary points to the writings of Mao Zedong and Zhu De as usage examples. See *Hanyu da cidian*, 1171. The use of *dizhu* to refer to a landholding social class originated in late nineteenth-century Japan and quickly spread to China, where it beat out the competing term, *tianzhu*. See Lippert, *Hanyu zhong de makesizhuyi shuyu de qiyuan yu zuoyong*, 213–216.

35. Unlike other landlords, only the agent would be given the landlord label; if the rest of his family labored, they were eligible for peasant statuses. "Taihang qu dangwei guanyu nongcun jiejie huafen biaozhun yu juti huafen guiding (cao'an)," 321–322.

36. Huang, *The Peasant Economy and Social Change in North China*, 71.

37. Ruan Zhangjing, *Chi ye he*, 10.

38. Zhou Libo, *Baofeng zhouyu*, 23.

39. The term *eba*, referring to a person who abuses authority to oppress others, was firmly rooted in the Chinese tradition. For examples, see *Hanyu da cidian*, 4305.

40. Xi Zhongxun, "Guanyu tugai zhong yixie wenti gei Mao zhuxi de baogao," 451.

41. "Zhuanfa Hechuan xian tudi gaige gongzuo zhong de di er ci baogao bing ti ge xiang wenti gong gedi zhuyi can gai," JCA, East Sichuan Party Committee, 1-88 (July 10, 1951), 1.

42. Friedman, Pickowicz, and Selden, *Chinese Village, Socialist State*, 83–84.

43. Gao Wangling and Liu Yang, "On a Slippery Roof," 23–24.

44. "Huazhong fenju guanyu guanche zhongyang wusi guanyu tudi zhengce xin jueding de zhishi," 254.

45. Li Zipu, "Guanyu zhongnong wenti," 266.

46. He Zhiping, "Lun zhongnong," 252.

47. Gao Wangling and Liu Yang, "On a Slippery Roof," 25.

48. Li Zipu, "Guanyu zhongnong wenti," 266.

49. "Huazhong fenju guanyu guanche zhongyang wusi guanyu tudi zhengce xin jueding de zhishi," 254–255.

50. "Huazhong fenju guanyu muqian tudigaige yundong zhong ji ge wenti de zhishi," 283.

51. "Zhonggong zhongyang guanyu dui funong tudi buyi tuiping gei huazhong fenju de zhishi," ZTGSX (August 8, 1947), 287–288.

52. "Beifengzhengcun ruhe shixian le gengzhe you qi tian," ZTGSX (August 24, 1946), 290.

53. "Huai'an xian gongqu Chenxuxiang jinxing tudi gaige de jingyan," ZTGSX (July 1946), 273–274.

54. Cao used the example of Chenyang village to show that leveling land-holdings did not mean widespread confiscation of peasant land. In Chenyang, of 136 households, 54 lost land, but only 2 households lost land they farmed themselves. Cao Huoqiu, "Zai tudigaige zhong laping wenti yu dui zhongfu-nong zhengce de yanjiu," ZTGSX (August 4, 1946), 276–278.

55. Deng Zihui, "Cong Eqian xiang douzheng lai yanjiu muqian tudigaige yundong," 294.

56. "Jinchaji ju guanyu chuanda yu jinxing zhongyang wusi zhishi de jieding (jielu)," 298.

57. "Huazhong fenju guanyu jiejue tudi wenti de buchong zhishi," 263.

58. "Jinchaji ju guanyu chuanda yu jinxing zhongyang wusi zhishi de jieding (jielu)," 298.

59. The Jin-Cha-Ji Bureau also demanded that commercial enterprises be-longing to landlords and rich peasants remain untouched. Ibid., 300.

60. Rich peasants were to generally keep their land, and activists were for-bidden from settling accounts with middle peasants. "Huadong ju guanyu tudi-gaige de zhishi," 301–304.

61. "Dongbei ju guanyu shenru qunzhong tudi douzheng de zhishi," 308–309. These lenient directives, however, also indicated that excess landlord land would eventually be confiscated in line with the policies of party central.

62. Deng Zihui, "Cong Eqian xiang douzheng lai yanjiu muqian tudigaige yundong," 294.

63. The directive made concessions to rich peasants: they ideally would keep all of the land farmed by their households as well as their agricultural tools. Their rented land, however, was to be confiscated and distributed to the poor alongside landlord land. But this leniency was balanced by an ominous caveat: if cadres faced difficulty satisfying the land needs of the poor, the lands person-ally farmed by rich peasants could be confiscated for redistribution. "Huazhong fenju guanyu tuanjie zhongnong de zhishi," 305–307.

64. "JinJiLuYuju wei guanche wusi zhishi chedi shixian geng zhe you qi tian de zhishi," ZTGSX (September 9, 1946), 310–312.

65. "Taihang qu dangwei guanyu Taihang tudigaige baodao (jielu)," 364–367.

66. "Huazhong fenju dui tudigaige fucha de zhishi," ZTGSX (June 20, 1947), 374.

67. According to Deng, the goal of land reform was to develop the agricultural economy, and he insisted that China would not follow the American model of capitalist managerial farming or the Soviet model of collective farming. Nor, contradicting earlier pronouncements of the some party leaders, would the future be in the "Chinese style rich peasant economy." Deng pushed for an agricultural system based on middle peasants and urged Liu Shaoqi to draft a law that would confiscate all landlord and rich peasant land, equalizing the holdings of all villagers excepting middle peasants and "new rich peasants." Deng disregarded criticism that this would depress the desire of rich peasants to produce as irrelevant: the middle peasant economy was, after all, China's future. Deng Zihui, "Gei Liu Shaoqi tongzhi zhuan zhongyang de yi feng xin," ZTGSX (July 3, 1947), 379–380.

68. Peasant associations, however, were allowed to take pity on family members of these class enemies. "Huadong ju guanyu Shandong tugai fucha de xin zhishi," ZTGSX (July 7, 1947), 382.

69. Friedman, Pickowicz, and Selden, *Chinese Village, Socialist State*, 93.

70. Pepper, *Civil War in China*, 288–289.

71. The gathered cadres immediately took up the issue of middle peasant land, and while some noted potential problems with infringing on these farmers, most praised equalization as a simple and fast method for dividing the land, with the added benefit of keeping cadres and activists from taking an unfair share of confiscated property. According to the working committee overseeing land policies, equalization would adversely affect only 20 percent of the rural population, meaning the party could expect support from 80 percent of the countryside. "Zhonggong zhongyang gongwei guanyu chedi pingfen tudi de yuanzi xiang zhongyang de qingshi," ZTGSX (September 5, 1947), 421.

72. "Zhongguo tudi fa dagang," 422–423.

73. "Zhonggong zhongyang zhengqiu guanyu jieji fenxi de yijian," 438.

74. While this document denounced basing class status on past generations, it did allow activists to check back as many as six years before the establishment of the new government in their village. "Zhonggong zhongyang gongwei guanyu jiuzheng huafen jiejie shang zuoqing cuowu de zhishi," ZTGSX (December 1947), 445. For Kang Sheng as the figure behind "checking three generations" and "shape-shifting landlords," see Luo Pinghan, *Tudi gaige yundong shi*, 123.

75. Friedman, Pickowicz, and Selden, *Chinese Village, Socialist State*, 96.

76. "Xi Zhongxun guanyu tugai wenti de xin," 447–448.

77. Xi Zhongzun, "Guanyu tugai zhong yixie wenti gei Mao zhuxi de baogao," 450–451.

78. Xi Zhongxun, "Xi Zhongxun guanyu fen san lei diqu shixing tugai de baogao," ZTGSX (February 8, 1948), 463.

79. Bo Yibo, for example, argued against equalization for taking from middle peasants and not providing enough for rich peasants and landlords. Li Xuefeng, meanwhile, advocated not even mentioning the idea of total equalization

until land reform was well underway. But Li continued to press for total equalization, with land reform run through activists in poor peasant leagues. Mao, reading Li's report, agreed that the formation of peasant associations would have to wait until poor peasant leagues had gained authority within the village. Bo Yibo, "Bo Yibo guanyu fucha qian buchong zhishi de baogao," 460. Li Xuefeng, "Guanyu xin qu dozheng celüe ji zuzhi xingshi de baogao," 471–472.

80. "Dongbei ju guanyu pingfen tudi the jiben zongjie (jielu)," ZTGSX (March 28, 1948), 489–493.

81. The lands of the well-to-do middle peasants would now be left intact, as were the commercial enterprises of village landlords and rich peasants. "Huabei ju guanyu xin qu tudigaige jueding," ZTGSX (October 10, 1949), 601–602.

82. "Huadong ju guanyu Jiangnan xin qu nongcun gongzuo de zhishi (jielu)," 588–589.

83. Zhang Xiaojun, "Land Reform in Yang Village," 17.

84. For an example, see "Chongqing shi jiaoqu tugai canguantuan di san zu gongzuo baogao," ZXD, Chongqing City Archives, D-65-19 (1951?), 188.

85. Quoted in Zhang Xiaojun, "Land Reform in Yang Village," 21.

86. Ibid., 18.

87. "Fuling diwei guanyu Fuling, Fengdu tudi gaige zhong ji ge wenti de tongbao," ZXD, Chongqing Archives, East Sichuan Collection, 1-29-8 (July 4, 1951), 142.

88. Shao Yanxiang, *Bie le Mao Zedong*, 171.

89. "Chongqing shi jiaoqu tugai canguantuan di san zu gongzuo baogao," 188.

90. The party blamed his decision on a lack of education. "Fuling diwei guanyu Fuling, Fengdu tudi gaige zhong ji ge wenti de tongbao," 141.

91. Vogel, *Canton Under Communism*, 99.

92. "Zhongnan tudigaige weiyuanhui guanyu zhongnan ge sheng tugai shidian gongzuo qingkuang de baogao," 691.

93. "Xi'nan tudi gaige gongzuotuan di er tuan chuandong fentuan chongbu cailiao," ZXD, Chongqing City Archives, D-65-11 (1950?), 169.

94. "Yong'an xiang hua jieji zongjie baogao," ZXD, Guizhou Provincial Archives, 6-1-20 (February 27, 1952), 105.

95. "Jiangjin Degan xiang shixing chatian pingchan zhong faxian ji ge wenti," ZXD, East Sichuan Collection, 1-29-8 (July 5, 1951), 143–144.

96. "Chongqing shi jiaoqu tugai canguantuan di san zu gongzuo baogao,"188.

97. "Hua jieji zhong de ji ge wenti," ZXD, Guizhou Provincial Archive, 6-1-20 (May 10, 1952), 162.

98. Strauss, "Morality, Coercion, and State Building by Campaign in the Early PRC," 902.

99. Yang Xiaojun, "Land Reform in Yang Village," 21.

100. "Zhuanfa Hechuan xian tudi gaige gongzuo zhong de di er ci baogao bing ti ge xiang wenti gong gedi zhuyi can gai," 3.

101. "Yong'an xiang hua jieji zongjie baogao," 104.

102. "Guizhou sheng huangping xian siping zhen wuliqiao cun jieji chubu diaocha," ZXD, Chongqing City Archives, D-65-1-1 (August 24, 1950), 81.

103. In Qindong district landlords even dismantled their houses. Huaiyin Li, *Village China Under Socialism and Reform*, 17.

104. "Chuanxi nongcun de fengjian tongzhi," ZXD, Chongqing City Archives, D-65-1-1 (November 21, 1951), 103.

105. "Fuling diwei guanyu Fuling, Fengdu tudi gaige zhong ji ge wenti de tongbao," 140–141.

106. "Chuanxi qu Dayi xian Tangchang xiang nongmin kongsu Liu Yuancong xuexing zuixing," ZXD, Chongqing City Archives, D-65-1-1 (April 5, 1951), 96–98.

107. Belden, *China Shakes the World*, 156.

108. "Chuanxi qu Shifang xian da eba feishou Xuan Jingxiu heng qiang hao ba shi yu xian de xuexing zuixing," ZXD, Chongqing City Archives, D-65-1-1 (December 22, 1950), 99.

109. "Chuanxi nongcun de fengjian tongzhi," 102.

110. "E'ba Wang Zixe zuizhuang," JCA, 1-1-42 (1951).

111. Tan Song, "Tugai minbing lunjian dizhu n🔲er zhisi," http://blog.sina.com.cn/s/blog_4c666f350102uvwg.html, accessed June 20, 2018.

112. Feng Youlan, "Canjia tugai de shouhui," 75.

113. Friedman, Pickowicz, and Selden, *Chinese Village, Socialist State*, 106.

114. Ibid., 105.

115. "Hua jieji zhong de ji ge wenti," 163.

116. "Xi'nan tudi gaige gongzuotuan di er tuan Chuandong fentuan buchong cailiao," ZXD, Chongqing City Archives, D-65-11, (1950?), 176–177.

Chapter 4

1. Ding Ling, *Taiyang zhao zai sangganhe shang*, 48.

2. Ibid., 193.

3. Ibid., 195.

4. Ibid., 251.

5. Ibid., 256.

6. Ibid., 257.

7. Ibid., 264–270.

8. Zhang Ailing, *Chi di zhi lian*, 58–59.

9. Ibid., 72.

10. Ibid., 84–90. In one village in Heilongjiang, a rich peasant's wife was dragged through the dirt by a draft animal after her husband fled. Gao Wangling and Liu Yang, "On a Slippery Roof," 25.

11. Hinton, *Fanshen*, 107–124.

12. Ibid., 135.

13. Ibid., 146.

14. Ibid., 202–207.

15. *Hanyu da cidian*, 7418. Like many other neologisms promoted by the Communists, *douzheng* had a basis in classical Chinese texts, but its first mod-

ern appearance was in Japanese literature. Lippert, *Hanyu zhong de make-sizhuyi shuyu de qiyuan yu zuoyong,* 174–178.

16. This is in contrast to the limited use of struggle during double reduction campaigns. In spring 1943, for example, cadres struggling recalcitrant landlords humiliated a small number of targets but used an emphasis on legality to limit beatings. There were instances of peasant violence, which were condemned in the aftermath of the campaign. Keating, *Two Revolutions,* 170–172.

17. As Vivienne Shue put it, in order to change peasant mentalities, the redistribution of land had to be preceded by the "thorough discrediting of the landlords, the exploitation, and the old social system supporting them." Shue, *Peasant China in Transition,* 82.

18. Geertz explained the connections between rituals and personal transformation in this way: "In a ritual, the world as lived and the world as imagined, fused under the agency of a single set of symbolic forms, turn out to be the same world, producing that idiosyncratic transformation in one's sense of reality." Geertz, "Religion as a Cultural System," 112.

19. For a discussion of stages in Hubei land reform, see DeMare, *Mao's Cultural Army,* 198–199.

20. "Xi'nan tudi gaige gongzuotuan di er tuan chuandong fentuan chongbu cailiao," 169.

21. Seybolt, "The War Within a War," 220.

22. Liu Tong, *Dongbei jiefang zhanzheng jishi,* 375.

23. According to Belden, this violent event took place at a "settlement meeting." This account was told to Belden by two witnesses. The struggle target was a landlord who had been accused of being a Nationalist Party member, collaborating with the Japanese, and killing many villagers. Belden, *China Shakes the World,* 31–33.

24. Hou, *Negotiating Socialism in Rural China,* 11.

25. "Taihang qu dangwei guanyu Taihang tudigaige baodao (jielu)," 371.

26. Crook and Crook, *Revolution in a Chinese Village,* 118–120.

27. Du Runsheng, *Zhongguo de tudigaige,* 179.

28. Friedman, Pickowicz, and Selden, *Chinese Village, Socialist State,* 86–87.

29. "Huazhong fenju guanyu jiejue tudi wenti de buchong zhishi," 263.

30. Chen Yi, "Ruhe zhengque zhixing zhongyang wusi zhishi (jielu)," 259.

31. "Huazhong fenju guanyu muqian tudigaige yundong zhong ji ge wenti de zhishi," 282–283.

32. Deng Zihui, "Cong Eqian xiang douzheng lai yanjiu muqian tudigaige yundong," 293.

33. This was particularly true in those areas that had already attacked local elites during previous campaigns. For more on the use of the "three generation" rule to determine class status, see Luo Pinghan, *Tudi gaige yundong shi,* 123.

34. Crook and Crook, *Revolution in a Chinese Village,* 130.

35. "Huazhong fenju guanyu guanche zhongyang wusi guanyu tudi zhengce xin jueding de zhishi," 254.

36. Belden implies that this occurred during summer 1946. Belden, *China Shakes the World,* 85.

37. Zhou Libo, *Baofeng zhouyu*, 166–168.

38. Thaxton, *Catastrophe and Contention in Rural China*, 78–79.

39. "Dongbei ju guanyu jiejue tudigaige zhong 'ban sheng bu shou' de wenti de zhishi," 326–327.

40. Crook and Crook, *Revolution in a Chinese Village*, 148.

41. Luo Pinghan, *Tudi gaige yundong shi*, 91.

42. "Taihang qu dangwei guanyu Taihang tudigaige baodao (jielu)," 369–371.

43. "Yi nian lai Dongbei tudigaige lüeshu," ZTGSX (July, 1947), 377.

44. "Zhongyang gongwei guanyu tudigaige zhong wajiao wenti de ji dian yijian," ZTGSX (July 15, 1947), 385–386.

45. Luo Pinghan, *Tudi gaige yundong shi*, 123.

46. Friedman, Pickowicz, and Selden, *Chinese Village, Socialist State*, 98.

47. Westad, *Decisive Encounters*, 133.

48. Li Changyuan, *Peng Zhen yu tugai*, 216.

49. In Da Fo, for example, all who had embraced the homecoming regiment, regardless of class background, were put to death by the village militia. Thaxton, *Catastrophe and Contention in Rural China*, 79.

50. Quoted in Luo Pinghan, *Tudi gaige yundong shi*, 92

51. "JinSui fenju guanyu chedi pingfen tudi de zhishi," ZTGSX (September 15, 1947), 424–425.

52. "Zhonggong zhongyang gongwei guanyu jiuzheng huafen jiejie shang zuoqing cuowu de zhishi," 445.

53. "Zhonggong zhongyang yijiusiqi shieryue jueyi," 444–445.

54. Luo Pinhan, *Tudi gaige yundong shi*, 199.

55. Liu Tong, *Dongbei jiefang zhanzheng jishi*, 420.

56. Ibid., 424.

57. "Dongbei ju guanyu tudi wenti ji dui ge jieceng de zhengce de yijian," 309–310.

58. Liu Tong, *Dongbei jiefang zhanzheng jishi*, 419.

59. Yang Kuisong, *Zhonghua renmin gongheguo jianguo shi yanjiu* 1, 99.

60. Xi Zhongxun, "Xi Zhongxun guanyu tugai wenti de xin," 447–448.

61. Xi Zhongzun, "Guanyu tugai zhong yixie wenti gei Mao zhuxi de baogao," 450–451.

62. Liu Tong, *Dongbei jiefang zhanzheng jishi*, 431.

63. Xi Zhongxun, "Guanyu xin qu gongzuo wenti de baogao (jielu)," 524–526.

64. Bo Yibo, *Ruogan zhongda juece yu shijian de huigu*, 116.

65. Hou, *Negotiating Socialism in Rural China*, 70.

66. Friedman, Pickowicz, and Selden, *Chinese Village, Socialist State*, 102–103.

67. "Zhonggong zhongyang guanyu jiuzheng tudigaige zhong zuoqing cuowu bu yao xianzhi nongmin biyao de douzheng gei Dongbei ju de zhishi," ZTGSX (May 10, 1948), 499–500.

68. Others simply blamed violence on the masses. "Zhonggong Hebei shengwei guanyu jiancha xin qu tugai gongzuo wenti ji jinhou yijian," 610.

69. "Huabei ju guanyu Shunyi xian ji ge tugai shixian cun zhong suo fan zuoqing wenti gei Hebei shengwei de zhishi," ZTGSX (October 1949), 606.

70. "Huabei ju guanyu xin qu tudigaige jueding," 601–602.

71. "Beijing shi renmin zhengfu guanyu Beijing jiaoqu tudigaige de zongjie baogao," 681.

72. "Zhonggong Hebei shengwei guanyu jiancha xin qu tugai gongzuo wenti ji jinhou yijian," 608.

73. "Beijing shi renmin zhengfu guanyu Beijing jiaoqu tudigaige de zongjie baogao," 684–686.

74. "Qu dangwei dui Hechuan tudi gaige wenti gei ge di de zhishi," ZXD, Chongqing City Archives, East Sichuan Collection, 1-29-8 (1951?), 14–15.

75. "Zhonggong Zhejiang shengwei guanyu tugai dianxing shiyan zongjie huiyi xiang Huadong ju de baogao (jilu)," ZTGSX (October 4, 1950), 675–676.

76. "Zhongnan tudigaige weiyuanhui guanyu zhongnan ge sheng tugai shidian gongzuo qingkuang de baogao," 691–692.

77. Du Runsheng, "Zhongnan quanqu qudong jinchun tudigaige de jingguo yu zhuyao jingyan ji jinhou jihua," 735–736.

78. "Deng Xiaoping fu zhuxi zai xi'nan junzheng weiyuanhui di yi ci quanti weiyuanhui di si dahui shang de fayan," ZXD, Chongqing City Archives, D-65-10 (1950?), 4.

79. Du Runsheng, *Zhongguo de tudigaige*, 402.

80. "Zhuanfa Hechuan xian tudi gaige gongzuo zhong de di er ci baogao bing ti ge xiang wenti gong gedi zhuyi can gai," 1.

81. Hu Yaobang, "You guan tudi gaige ji ge wenti de shuoming," ZXD, Chongqing City Archives, East Sichuan Collection, 1-31-2 (1950?), 138.

82. Shao Yanxiang, *Bie le Mao Zedong*, 160.

83. "Fuling diwei guanyu Fuling, Fengdu tudi gaige zhong ji ge wenti de tongbao," 141.

84. "Zhuanfa Hechuan xian tudi gaige gongzuo zhong de di er ci baogao bing ti ge xiang wenti gong gedi zhuyi can gai," 1.

85. Xu Yayun, "Tuanjie ziji, fenhua diren zhong de liangge juti de wenti," ZXD, Chongqing City Archives, D-65-7 (1950?), 135.

86. Hu Yaobang, "You guan tudi gaige ji ge wenti de shuoming," 138–139.

87. "Xi'nan tudi gaige gongzuotuan di er tuan Chuandong fentuan buchong cailiao," ZXD, Chongqing City Archives, D-65-11, (1951?), 179.

88. "Jiangjin xian erqu Shuanglong xiang (tugai qi) di yi ci nongmindai huiyi jueyi gangyao," JCA, 95-01-03, (1951), 73.

89. "Zhuanfa Hechuan xian tudi gaige gongzuo zhong de di er ci baogao bing ti ge xiang wenti gong gedi zhuyi can gai," 3.

90. "Qu dangwei guanyu fucha gongzuo de zhishi," ZXD, Chongqing City Archives, East Sichuan Collection, 46-54-10 (May 17, 1951), 16.

91. Siu, *Agents and Victims in South China*, 131–133.

92. "Fengjie xian zai jianzu tuiya hou jiancha chu de ji ge wenti," ZXD, Chongqing City Archives, East Sichuan Collection, 1-29-8 (July 17, 1951), 143.

93. The torture of the widow Huang was said to produce eighteen liang of gold: nearly two pounds. The numbers of deaths discussed here are estimates;

the exact figures are partly redacted in the archival documents. "Jiangjin diwei zuzhi buzhang Lin Song tongshi de jiantao," ZXD, Chongqing City Archives, East Sichuan Collection, 1-29-8 (July 18, 1951), 145.

94. "Dazu si qu quwei fushuji Duan Mingshu de jiantao," ZXD, Chongqing City Archives, East Sichuan Collection, 1-29-8 (August 10, 1951), 145.

95. "Qu dangwei jilü jiancha weiyuanhui guanyu Dazu xian weifan zhengce jiancha he chuli de tongbao," ZXD, Chongqing City Archives, East Sichuan Collection, 1-29-8 (August 8, 1951), 146.

96. Ibid.

97. Ibid., 148.

98. Ibid., 147.

99. Ibid.

100. Violence in the countryside of course existed long before the Communist revolution. As revealed in Di Wang's recent study of the "gowned brothers" secret society, centered on a father murdering his daughter, village China had witnessed shocking acts of brutality. According to Wang such tragedies occurred throughout China, and the men who committed these crimes often went unpunished. As Wang notes, "In rural areas, even those close to big cities, modern concepts of justice were far from embedded in the local society." Wang, *Violence and Order on the Chengdu Plain*, 32.

101. "Yongchuan xian 1951 nian douzheng dizhu huiyi jilu," YCA, Yongchuan County Shijiao Village People's Government, 115-1-26 (1953).

102. "Jijing xiang jianzu tuiya qingfei fanba gongzuo de chubu zongjie baogao," JCA, County Party Committee Work Team, Fengjie Third District, 035-23 (January 1, 1951).

103. "Fengjie xian di si qu tugai gongzuo jianbao," JCA, Fengjie County Fourth District Party Committee, 035-75 (December 24, 1951).

104. Xu Yayun, "Tuanjie ziji, fenhua diren zhong de liangge juti de wenti," 134.

105. "Qu dangwei dui tudi gaige, fucha zhong ying zhuyi de ji ge wenti fu Youyang diwei," ZXD, Chongqing Archives, East Sichuan Collection, 46-54-10 (June 23, 1951), 149.

106. Zhao Zengyi, "Cong Hechuan tudi gaige zhong suo jian dao de ji ge wenti," ZXD, Chongqing Archives, East Sichuan Collection, 46-54-10 (June 25, 1951), 151.

107. Siu, *Agents and Victims in South China*, 131.

108. "Zhuanfa Chuandong nongxie zhu Yu banshichu guanyu er qi tugai zhong cheng xiang jian dizhu di ge ge wenti ji yijian de baogao," JCA, 3-135 (September 14, 1951), 14–16.

109. "Fuling diwei guanyu Fuling, Fengdu tudi gaige zhong ji ge wenti de tongbao," 140–142.

110. RR (March 30, 1951), 2.

111. NBCK (December 23, 1950), 129–130.

112. Zhao Zengyi, "Cong Hechuan tudi gaige zhong suo jian dao de ji ge wenti," 151.

113. Huang was also asked to turn over some grain, although he was not

expected to comply. "Xi'nan tudi gaige gongzuotuan di er tuan Chuandong fentuan buchong cailiao," 177.

114. Xi Zhongxun, "Muqian Xibei diqu de tudigaige gongzuo he jianzu gongzuo," ZTGSX (November 22, 1951), 785–786.

115. Xi Zhognxun, "Xi Zhongxun tongzhi gei Mao zhuxi di er ci zonghe baogao (jielu)," ZTGSX (May 4, 1952), 814.

116. The attack would have to wait until the party trained enough ethnic minority cadres. "Xi Zhongxun tongzhi gei Mao zhuxi he zhongyang de baogao (jielu)," ZTGSX (April 10, 1951), 742–743.

117. "Zai minzu zaju diqu jinxing tudigaige de ji ge jingyan: Linxia diwei tudigaige shiban gongzuo zongjie," 794–795.

118. Hu Shihua, "Renmin minzhu zhuanzheng zai nongcun zhong sheng le gen," 64.

119. Ibid., 67–68.

120. Li Junlong, "Douzheng zhong de Hunan nongmin," 50.

121. Zheng Linzhuang, "Douzheng dizhu shi you ganbu tiaobo qilai de ma," 75–76.

122. Cheng Houzhi, "Canjia jingjiao tugai gongzuo de jingyan jiaoxun," 101.

Chapter 5

1. Ding Ling, *Taiyang zhao zai sangganhe shang*, 298.

2. Ibid., 292–293.

3. Yang Guixin, *Ding Ling pingzhuan*, 258.

4. Ibid., 248.

5. Ibid., 253.

6. Ding Ling, "Ding Ling jiu ronghuo Sidalin jiangji fabiao tanhua," RR (March 18, 1952), 4.

7. Ding Ling, *Taiyang zhao zai sangganhe shang*, 3.

8. Zhang Ailing, *Chi di zhi lian*, 74–75.

9. Hsia, *A History of Modern Chinese Fiction: Second Edition*, 427.

10. Zhang Ailing, *Chi di zhi lian*, 202.

11. For a recent reevaluation of the English-language version of the novel, see Link, "Introduction." For an overview of the many changes between the Chinese and English versions of the novel, see Yu-Yun Hsieh, "Eileen Chang's Changes: From *Love in Redland* to *Naked Earth*," *Open Letters Monthly: An Arts and Literature Review*, August 1, 2015, https://www.openlettersmonthly.com/eileen-changs-changes-from-love-in-redland-to-naked-earth/.

12. Hinton, *Fanshen*, vii.

13. Luo Pinghan, *Tudi gaige yundong shi*, 59.

14. Hinton, *Fanshen*, 363.

15. Ibid., 441.

16. Ibid., 609.

17. Ibid., 613.

18. Zhou Libo, *Baofeng zhouyu*, 12.

19. *Hanyu da cidian*, 5593.

20. Thaxton, *Catastrophe and Contention in Rural China*, 73.

21. "Taihang qu dangwei guanyu Taihang tudigaige baodao (jielu)," 365.

22. "Dongbei ju guanyu pingfen tudi the jiben zongjie (jielu)," 488.

23. Mao Zedong, "Report on an Investigation of the Peasant Movement in Hunan," 53.

24. *Guizhou shengzhi: wenhua zhi*, 61.

25. Yang Rengeng, "Gen nongmin xuexi yihou," 101.

26. Quoted in Luo Pinghan, *Tudi gaige yundong shi*, 45.

27. Li Guangtian, "Weishenme bu neng 'heping fentian?'" 38–39.

28. "Zhengqu chungeng qian wancheng tudigaige," ZTGSX (December 14, 1946), 329.

29. "Taihang qu dangwei guanyu Taihang tudigaige baodao (jielu)," 368.

30. Cheng Houzhi, "Canjia jingjiao tugai gongzuo de jingyan jiaoxun," 99–107.

31. Tian Liu, "Tugai sannian hou de beiman nongcun," RR (July 18, 1950), 2.

32. Li Junlong, "Douzheng zhong de Hunan nongmin," 48–49.

33. "Chongqing shi jiaoqu tugai canguantuan di san zu gongzuo baogao," ZXD, Chongqing City Archives, D-65-19 (1951?), 189.

34. Sun Qingju and Wu Shaoqi, "Nongcun jishi," 27–28.

35. Yi Su, "Tai xian fanshencun xin jingxiang," 62.

36. Ibid., 64.

37. Ibid.

38. "Chongqing shi jiaoqu tugai canguantuan di si zu gongzuo baogao," 193.

39. *Guo Shuzhen*, 1.

40. For one example of the party promoting free marriage, see Chen Bozhong and Wang Dahai, "Tudi gaige hou de nongcun funü," 70.

41. Feng Ming, "Dongbei nongcun yi yue jianwen," 28–31.

42. Liu Mianzhi, "Bu yong jinqian ziyou hun, ge ren ai shangle xinshang de ren," 35–37.

43. Chen Bozhong and Wang Dahai, "Tudi gaige hou de nongcun funü," 65.

44. Ibid., 69.

45. "Zai minzu zaju diqu jinxing tudigaige de ji ge jingyan: Linxia diwei tudigaige shiban gongzuo zongjie," 795.

46. This includes memberships in poor peasant leagues. Liu Zhi, "Ding xian funü da fanshen," 17–18.

47. "Tudi gaige yundong zhong chuxian le xinxing de funü zuzhi xingshi," 43.

48. Stacey, *Patriarchy and Socialist Revolution in China*, 116–117.

49. Ibid., 130–135.

50. Stranahan, *Yan'an Women and the Communist Party*, 109.

51. Ibid., 95.

52. Quoted in Diamant, *Revolutionizing the Family*, 144.

53. "Huadong ju guanyu Shandong tugai fucha de xin zhishi," 383.

54. "Zhonggong zhongyang huadongju guanyu tudigaige ruogan wenti de tongbao," 745.

55. Chen Zhenzhou, "Tugai jiaoyu le wo," 88–92.

56. Feng Youlan, ""Canjia tugai de shouhui," 70.

57. Dang Qiaoxin, "Zai tudi gaige zhong duanlian ziji," 76.

58. Wu Xinxiang and Zhao Zuwang, "Canjia tugai de ji dian tiyan," 86.

59. Yuan Fang, "Women de tugai gongzuo zu," 20–24.

60. "Chongqing shi jiaoqu tugai canguantuan di san zu gongzuo baogao," 191.

61. Hu Du, "Wo zai nongmin de jiaoyu xia jianding le yizhi," ZQ No. 47 (1950), 21.

62. Ibid., 22.

63. Li Hua, "Tugai jiejue le wo de sixiang wenti," ZQ No. 36 (1950), 38.

64. Esherick, *Ancestral Leaves*, 242.

65. "Xi'nan tudi gaige gongzuotuan di er tuan di san fentuan gongzuo baogao," ZXD, Chongqing City Archives, D-65-11 (1951?), 166.

66. NBCK (August 28, 1950), 88–89.

67. Ibid. (December 21, 1951), 91–92.

68. See, for example: Zhao Zengyi, "Cong Hechuan tudi gaige zhong suo jian dao de ji ge wenti," ZXD, Chongqing Archives, East Sichuan Collection, 46-54-10 (June 25, 1951), 151.

69. Tian Liu, "Tugai sannian hou de beiman nongcun," 4.

70. Deng Zihui, "Cong Eqian xiang douzheng lai yanjiu muqian tudigaige yundong," 293.

71. "Zhonggong zhongyang guanyu tudigaige zhong yingai zhuyi de ji ge wenti gei JinChaJi ju, ReLiao jude zhishi," ZTGSZ (June 12, 1946), 262.

72. Hou, *Negotiating Socialism in Rural China*, 11.

73. "JinJiLuYuju wei guanche wusi zhishi chedi shixian geng zhe you qi tian de zhishi," 311.

74. "Dongbei ju guanyu shenru qunzhong tudi douzheng de zhishi," 307.

75. Gao Wangling and Liu Yang, "On a Slippery Roof," 29.

76. In response, party leaders suggested joining these villages into administrative units so that they could share their fruits of struggle or negotiating for a transfer of property between villages. "JinJiLuYuju wei guanche wusi zhishi chedi shixian geng zhe you qi tian de zhishi," 313.

77. "Taihang qu dangwei guanyu Taihang tudigaige baodao (jielu)," 364–370.

78. Friedman, Pickowicz, and Selden, *Chinese Village, Socialist State*, 97.

79. Ibid., 104.

80. Xi Zhongxun, "Xi Zhongxun guanyu fen san lei diqu shixing tugai de baogao," 463.

81. "Zhonggong Hebei shengwei guanyu jiancha xin qu tugai gongzuo wenti ji jinhou yijian," 609–610.

82. According to the report, before land reform many farmlands were owned by Manchu nobles, eunuchs, warlords, traitors, and bureaucrats. Nobles also had "tomb slaves" who rented fields and also took care of Manchu tombs. "Beijing shi renmin zhengfu guanyu Beijing jiaoqu tudigaige de zongjie baogao," 681–682.

83. Ibid., 682–683.

84. "Xi'nan ju guanyu zai jianzu tuiya yundong zhong bixu jianjue baohu zhongnong liyi de yijian," ZXD, Chongqing City Archives, D-699-25 (February 28, 1950), 87.

85. "Fengjie xian zai jianzu tuiya hou jiancha chu de ji ge wenti," ZXD, Chongqing City Archives, East Sichuan Collection, 1-29-8 (July 17, 1951), 142.

86. The work team blamed this shortage on landlord sabotage. "Chongqing shi jiaoqu tugai canguantuan di san zu gongzuo baogao," 189.

87. NBCK (March 7, 1951), 55–56.

88. "Xi'nan nongcun qunyun zhong guanyu yikao pingu gong tuanjie zhongnong de cailiao" ZXD, Chongqing City Archives, D-700–33 (March 1, 1951), 90.

89. Ibid., 91.

90. The directive demanded that cadres follow Liu Shaoqi and the land law by giving the unemployed a share of land and housing as needed. "Qu dangwei dui tudi gaige zhong chuli youguan gongren nongmin gongtong liyi shang mou xie juti wenti gonggu gongnong lianmeng de zhishi," ZXD, Chongqing City Archives, East Sichuan Collection, 46-54-10 (July 2, 1951), 18.

91. "Zhuanfa Chuandong nongxie zhu Yu banshichu guanyu er qi tugai zhong cheng xiang jian dizhu di ge ge wenti ji yijian de baogao," JCA, East Sichuan Party Committee, 3-135 (September 14, 1951), 8–11.

92. Ibid., 12–13.

93. Ibid., 14–16.

94. NBCK (June 25, 1951), 89–90.

95. Hou, *Negotiating Socialism in Rural China*, 94–97.

96. NBCK (October 21, 1952), 263–266.

97. Quoted in Cai Xiang, *Revolution and Its Narratives*, 52.

98. Deng Zihui, "Cong Eqian xiang douzheng lai yanjiu muqian tudigaige yundong," 294.

99. NBCK (August, 14, 1951), 29.

100. "Di er ci daibiaohui qian de qingkuang," JCA, 95-1-3 (1951?), 95–102.

101. Hou, *Negotiating Socialism in Rural China*, 93.

102. NBCK (August 27, 1951), 85–88.

103. Ibid. (November 19, 1951), 41–43.

104. Friedman, Pickowicz, and Selden, *Chinese Village, Socialist State*, 95.

105. For example, see Thaxton, *Catastrophe and Contention in Rural China*, 71–73.

106. "Huazhong fenju guanyu jiejue tudi wenti de buchong zhishi," 263.

107. "JinJiLuYuju wei guanche wusi zhishi chedi shixian geng zhe you qi tian de zhishi," 311.

108. "Huazhong fenju dui tudigaige fucha de zhishi," 374.

109. "Huadong ju guanyu Shandong tugai fucha de xin zhishi," 383.

110. Unfortunately, the party mistook corruption as a symptom of continuing feudal power. Friedman, Pickowicz, and Selden, *Chinese Village, Socialist State*, 94.

111. "Jiangjin xian erqu Shuanglong xiang (tugai qi) di yi ci nongmindai huiyi jueyi gangyao," JCA, 95-01-03 (1951), 73.

112. "Fuling diwei guanyu Fuling, Fengdu tudi gaige zhong ji ge wenti de tongbao," ZXD, Chongqing Archives, East Sichuan Collection, 1-29-8 (July 4, 1951), 141.

113. By overvaluing the fruits they gave to Li and other peasants, activists were able to keep more for themselves and their late night feasts. "Fengjie xian zai jianzu tuiya hou jiancha chu de ji ge wenti," 142.

114. Li, *Village China Under Socialism and Reform*, 17.

115. "Nanchuan xian wei jiu yue fen guanyu jizhong ganbu xuexi tugai he zongjie tugai gongzuo zonghe baogao," JCA, East Sichuan District Party Committee, 6-124 (October 20, 1951), 28–29.

116. Zhao Zengyi, "Cong Hechuan tudi gaige zhong suo jian dao de ji ge wenti," 150.

117. "Guanyu muqian nongcun gongzuo zhong de ruogan xin qingkuang," ZXD, Sichuan Provincial Archive, Rural Work Department 1-12 (1952?), 152.

118. Hou, *Negotiating Socialism in Rural China*, 115.

119. "Taihang qu dangwei guanyu nongcun jiejie huafen biaozhun yu juti huafen guiding (cao'an)," 322.

120. Wenjing was an administrative village in Fushun County. "Guanyu muqian nongcun gongzuo zhong de ruogan xin qingkuang," 152–153.

121. Shao Yanxiang, *Bie le Mao Zedong*, 167–168.

122. NBCK (December 16, 1950), 86–87.

123. Westad, *Decisive Encounters*, 113–114. By 1948, almost half of the PLA was composed of soldiers from Nationalist forces.

124. NBCK (September 24, 1951), 112–113.

125. Ibid. (March 14, 1952), 117–118.

126. Ibid. (November 19, 1951), 41–43.

127. Ibid. (December 24, 1951), 111–112.

128. Ibid. (July 28, 1951), 156.

129. Ibid. (August 13, 1951), 25–26.

130. Ibid. (July 30, 1951), 158–159.

131. Ibid. (July 28, 1951), 156.

132. Ibid. (December 24, 1951), 111–112.

133. "Taihang qu dangwei guanyu nongcun jiejie huafen biaozhun yu juti huafen guiding (cao'an)," 322–323.

134. "Zhonggong zhongyang yijiusiqi shieryue jueyi," 444.

135. Zenyang quanmian jieshu tudigaige yundong, 32–35.

136. Friedman, Pickowicz, and Selden, *Chinese Village, Socialist State*, 101.

137. Xi Zhongxun, "Guanyu tugai zhong yixie wenti gei Mao zhuxi de baogao," 451.

138. Du Runsheng, "Zhongnan quanqu qudong jinchun tudigaige de jingguo yu zhuyao jingyan ji jinhou jihua," 736.

139. Zhang Xiaojun, "Land Reform in Yang Village," 17.

Conclusion

1. The Han and Roman empires, which simultaneously dominated oppo-

site sides of the globe, were quickly framed as the forces of civilization fighting against barbarian hordes, be they Xiongnu or Hun. Writers of antiquity, straddling the line between prose and history, reduced vast military clashes to the personal heroics of the great emperors and soldiers—that of Liu Bei and Guan Yu, Caesar and Agrippa. Stories of individual genius and determination formed the basis for tales of Zhu Yuanzhang and Napoleon, the "great men" of obscure origin who forged empires in their own images. And the revolutions that wrested power from rulers into the hands of citizens were similarly told as stories of liberty and reaction, good versus evil, of Sun Yat-sen and Yuan Shikai, Lafayette and Robespierre.

2. Here, historians in China and the West went in vastly different directions. During the Enlightenment, the West embraced a grand tale of modernization and progress, unjustly recasting the Middle Ages as little more than a dark and gloomy shadow to be cast off in favor of ever-greater freedom and knowledge. In China, meanwhile, historians had long relied on the concept of the Mandate of Heaven to explain the passing of one dynasty to the next, each era rising and falling in an endless cycle.

3. Li, *Reinventing Modern China*, 6–15.

4. Shao Yanxiang, *Bie le Mao Zedong*, 177

5. Ibid., 178.

6. Liao Luyan, "San nian lai tudigaige yundong de weida shengli," 841–843.

7. For an overview of the economic changes wrought by land reform, see Wong, *Land Reform in the People's Republic of China*, chap. 6.

8. Dikötter, *The Tragedy of Liberation*, 83.

9. In this study, Zhou Zhiqiang posits that the particular form of feudalism that appeared in China stunted economic growth, and once coupled with Western imperialism, blocked modernization. Zhou argues because the Nationalist Party relied on capitalist and feudal power, only the Communists could have destroyed feudalism and set the stage for later economic transformation. Zhou Zhiqiang, *Zhongguo gongchandang yu zhongguo nongye fazhan daolu*, 69–84.

10. Du Runsheng, *Zhongguo de tudigaige*, 2.

11. Ibid., 4.

12. Strauss, "Rethinking Land Reform and Regime Consolidation in the People's Republic of China," 24.

13. For Tan Song, see Luo Siling, "Chongqing Teacher Spends Years Investigating the Truth About Land Reform, Suddenly Fired Before Big Nineteen" [Chongqing jiaoshi duo nian diaocha tugai zhenxiang, shijiuda qian tu zao kaichu], *Niuyue shibao zhongwen wang* (September 29, 1017), https://cn.nytimes.com/china/20170929/cc29-tansong/, accessed June 21, 2018. For Liu Xiaofei, see Vanessa Piao, "Grandson of China's Most-Hated Landlord Challenges Communist Lore," *New York Times* (July 26, 2016), https://www.nytimes.com/2016/07/27/world/asia/china-landlord-liu-wencai.html, accessed May 22, 2018.

14. Oiwan Lam, "China Bans 'Soft Burial,' An Award Winning Novel About the Deadly Consequences of Land Reform," *Hong Kong Free Press* (June 12, 2017), https://www.hongkongfp.com/2017/06/12/china-bans-soft-burial-

award-winning-novel-deadly-consequences-land-reform/, accessed May 22, 2018.

15. NBCK (February 5, 1952), 31.

16. Madsen, *Morality and Power in a Chinese Village*, 81–82.

17. Gao, *Born Red*, 50.

18. Ibid., 75.

19. "Resolution on Certain Questions in the History of Our Party Since the Founding of the People's Republic of China," adopted on June 27, 1981, https://www.marxists.org/subject/china/documents/cpc/history/01.htm, accessed June 20, 2018.

20. Madsen, *Morality and Power in a Chinese Village*, 87.

21. Li, *Village China under Socialism and Reform*, 26.

22. Madsen, *Morality and Power in a Chinese Village*, 42–44.

23. Chan, Madsen, and Unger, *Chen Village*, 21.

24. In Jiangsu's Qindong district, for example, landlords were left with about two mu of land per person, while poor peasants were given just under three mu of land per person. (One mu is roughly equivalent to 797 square yards.) Li, *Village China under Socialism and Reform*, 18.

25. Chan, Madsen, and Unger, *Chen Village*, 282.

26. Day, *The Peasant in Postsocialist China*, 37–38.

27. Shao Yanxiang, *Bie le Mao Zedong*, 170.

BIBLIOGRAPHY

Abbreviations for Archives, Collections, and Serials

JCA   Jiangjin County Archive. Sichuan, China.

NBCK   *Neibu cankao* [Internal reference materials]. Beijing: Xinhua chubanshe.

RR   *Renmin ribao* [The People's Daily]. Beijing: Renmin ribao she.

YCA   Yongchuan County Archive. Chongqing, China.

ZQ   *Zhongguo Qingnian* [China Youth]. Beijing: Zhongguo qingnian chubanshe.

ZTGSX   *Zhongguo tudi gaige shiliao xuanbian* [Selected historical materials from China's land reform]. For internal distribution. Beijing: Guofang daxue chubanshe, 1988.

ZXD   *Zhongguo xi'nan dang'an: tudigaige ziliao, 1949–1953* [Southwest China archives: The documents of land reform, 1949–1953]. Edited by Zhang Peitian and Zhang Hua. Kingsford: International Culture Press, 2009.

Aganost, Ann. *National Past-Times: Narrative, Representation, and Power in Modern China*. Durham, NC: Duke University Press, 1997.

Averill, Steven C. "Party, Society, and Local Elite in the Jiangxi Communist Movement." *Journal of Asian Studies* 46, no. 2 (May 1987): 279–303.

Bai Xi. *Kaiguo da tugai* [The great state founding land reform]. Beijing: Zhonggong dangshi chubanshe, 2009.

"Beiyue qu tudi gaige yundong zhong fadong funü de jingyan" [Experiences of mobilizing women in the Beiyue land reform movement]. In *Zhongguo jiefangqu nongcun funü fanshen yundong sumiao* [A sketch of rural women fanshen in China's liberated areas]. Tangshan: Jindong xinhua shudian, 1949.

Belden, Jack. *China Shakes the World*. New York: Monthly Review Press, 1970.

Bo Yibo. *Ruogan zhongda juece yu shijian de huigu* [Recollections on some major policy decisions and events]. Beijing: Zhonggong zhongyang dang xiao chubanshi, 1991.

Brown, Jeremy. "From Resisting Communists to Resisting America: Civil War and Korean War in Southwest China, 1950–1951." In *Dilemmas of Victory: The Early Years of the People's Republic of China*. Edited by Jeremy Brown and Paul G. Pickowicz. Cambridge, MA: Harvard University Press, 2007.

Buck, John L. *Land Utilization in China*. Shanghai: Commercial Press, 1937.

Cai Xiang. *Revolution and Its Narratives: China's Socialist Literary and Cultural Imaginaries, 1949–1966*. Edited and translated by Rebecca E. Karl and Xueping Zhong. Durham, NC: Duke University Press, 2016.

Chan, Anita, Richard Madsen, and Jonathan Unger. *Chen Village: From Revolution to Globalization*, 3rd ed. Berkeley: University of California Press, 2009.

Chen Bozhong, and Wang Dahai. "Tudi gaige hou de nongcun funü" [Rural women after land reform]. In *New Scenes in the Post-Land Reform Countryside* [Tugaihou nongcun xin jingxiang]. Shanghai: Xinhua shudian huadong zongfendian, 1950.

Chen Tiqiang. "Cong tugai zhong xue maliezhuyi" [Learning Marxism-Leninism from land reform]. In *Cong tugai zhong xuexi* [Learning from land reform]. Beijing: Xinjianshe zazhi chubanshe, 1950.

Chen Zhenzhou, "Tugai jiaoyu le wo" [Land reform educated me]. In *Tugai xuexi shouce: Hanjia jiaoshi jiangxihui yong* [Land reform studies handbook: For the Winter Break Teachers' Lecture and Study Meeting]. Luzhou: Chuannan renmin xingzhenggongshu wenjiao ting, 1951.

Cheng Houzhi. "Canjia jingjiao tugai gongzuo de jingyan jiaoxun" [Experiences and lessons from participating in land reform near Beijing]. In *Tugai xuexi shouce: Hanjia jiaoshi jiangxihui yong* [Land reform studies handbook: For the Winter Break Teachers' Lecture and Study Meeting]. Luzhou: Chuannan renmin xingzhenggongshu wenjiao ting, 1951.

Cheung, Peter T. Y. "Guangdong's Advantage: Provincial Leadership and Strategy Toward Resource Allocation Since 1979." In *Provincial Strategies of Economic Reform in Post-Mao China: Leadership, Politics, and Implementation*. Edited by Peter T. Y. Cheung, Jae Ho Chung, and Zimin Lin. New York: Routledge, 2015.

Cohen, Jerome Alan. "Just Fifteen Books on China?" *Harvard Magazine* (October 1975): 62–66.

Crook, David, and Isabel Crook. *Revolution in a Chinese Village: Ten Mile Inn*. London: Routledge and Kegan Paul, 1959.

———. *Ten Mile Inn: Mass Movement in a Chinese Village*. New York, Pantheon Books, 1979.

Dang Qiaoxin. "Zai tudi gaige zhong duanlian ziji" [Steeling myself in land reform]. In *Chongqingshi ge minzhupai canjia jianzu tuiya fanba ji tugai gongzuo baogao* [Work reports of Chongqing City's democratic elements' participation in rent reduction, returning deposits, opposing tyrants, and land reform]. Chongqing: Zhongguo gongchandang Chongqing shi weiyuanhui, 1951.

Day, Alexander F. *The Peasant in Postsocialist China: History, Politics, and Capitalism*. Cambridge: Cambridge University Press, 2013.

DeMare, Brian. "Casting (Off) Their Stinking Airs: Chinese Intellectuals and Land Reform, 1946–52." *China Journal* no. 67 (January 2012): 108–129.

———. "The Romance and Tragedy of Rural Revolution: Narratives and Novels of Land Reform in Mao's China." *Clio: A Journal of Literature History and the Philosophy of History* 43, no. 3 (2014): 341–365.

———. *Mao's Cultural Army: Drama Troupes in China's Rural Revolution.* Cambridge: Cambridge University Press, 2015.

Diamant, Neil. *Revolutionizing the Family: Politics, Love, and Divorce in Urban and Rural China, 1949–1968.* Berkeley: University of California Press, 2000.

Dikötter, Frank. *The Tragedy of Liberation: A History of the Chinese Revolution, 1945–1957.* New York: Bloomsbury Press, 2013.

Ding Ling. *Taiyang zhao zai sangganhe shang* [The sun shines over the Sangguan River]. Beijing: Renmin wenxue chubanshe, 2001.

Ding Shu. *Yangmou: fan youpai yundong shimo* [Open conspiracy: The complete story of Chinese Communist Party's anti-rightist campaign]. Hong Kong: Kaifang chubanshe, 2007.

Du Guang. *1957 niande geming yu fan geming* [Revolution and counterrevolution of 1957]. Hong Kong: Wuqixue chubanshe, 2014.

Du Runsheng. *Zhongguo de tudigaige* [China's land reform]. Beijing: Dangdai zhongguo chubanshe, 1996.

Esherick, Joseph. "Number Games: A Note on Land Distribution in Prerevolutionary China." *Modern China* 7, no. 4 (October 1981): 387–411.

———. *Ancestral Leaves: A Family Journey Through Chinese History.* Berkeley: University of California Press, 2011.

Fang Huirong, "'Wu shijian jing' yu shenghuo shijie zhong de 'zhenshi': Xicun nongmin tudi gaige shiqi shehui shenghuo de jiyi" ["Non-event state" and "truth" in the life world: The memories on social life of Xicun peasants during the period of land reform]. In *Kongjian, jiyi, shehui zhuanxing* [Spaces, memories, and social transitions]. Edited by Yang Nianqun. Shanghai: Shanghai renmin chubanshe, 2001.

Feng Kexi. "Canguan Chongqing shi jiaoqu tudi gaige suo jian" [Seen while observing land reform in the suburbs of Chongqing City]. In *Chongqingshi ge minzhupai canjia jianzu tuiya fanba ji tugai gongzuo baogao* [Work reports of Chongqing City's democratic elements' participation in rent reduction, returning deposits, opposing tyrants, and land reform]. Chongqing: Zhongguo gongchandang Chongqing shi weuyuanhui, 1951.

Feng Ming. "Dongbei nongcun yi yue jianwen" [Seen and heard during one month in the Northeast countryside]. In *New Scenes in the Post-Land Reform Countryside* [Tugaihou nongcun xin jingxiang]. Shanghai: Xinhua shudian huadong zongfendian, 1950.

Feng Wenbin. "Zhongguo xin minzhu zhuyi tuan shi shenme?" [What is the Chinese New Democratic Youth League?]. In *Zenyang jianli xin minzhu qingniantuan* [How to establish the New Democratic Youth League]. Beijing: Zhongguo qingnian she, 1949.

Feng Youlan. "Canjia tugai de shouhui" [My harvest from participating in land reform]. In *Tugai xuexi shouce: hanjia jiaoshi jiangxihui yong* [Land reform studies handbook: For the Winter Break Teachers' Lecture and Study Meeting]. Luzhou: Chuannan renmin xingzhenggongshu wenjiao ting, 1951.

Friedman, Edward, Paul G. Pickowicz, and Mark Selden. *Chinese Village, Socialist State*. New Haven, CT: Yale University Press, 1993.

Galbiati, Fernando. *Peng Pai and the Hai-Lu-Feng Soviet*. Stanford, CA: Stanford University Press, 1985.

Gao, James Z. "War Culture, Nationalism, and Political Campaigns, 1950–1953." In *Chinese Nationalism in Perspective: Historical and Recent Cases*. Edited by C. X. George Wei and Xiaoyuan Liu. Westport, CT: Greenwood Press, 2001.

Gao Wangling, and Liu Yang. "On a Slippery Roof: Chinese Farmers and the Complex Agenda of Land Reform." *Études rurales* no. 179 (2007): 19–34.

Gao Yuan. *Born Red: A Chronicle of the Cultural Revolution*. Stanford, CA: Stanford University Press, 1987.

Geertz, Clifford. *The Interpretation of Cultures*. New York: Basic Books, 1973.

Guizhou shengzhi: Wenhua zhi [Guizhou provincial gazetteer: Culture gazetteer]. Guiyang: Guizhou renmin chubanshe: 1999

Guo Shuzhen: Chuchu dialing yangyang zuo mofan de nu laofang [Guo Shuzhen: Female model worker, everywhere a leader and in everything a model]. Beijing: Quanguo gongnongbing laodong mofan daibiao huiyi mishuchu, 1950.

Guo Yuhua and Sun Liping. "Suku: yi zhong nongmin guojia guannian xingcheng de zhongjie jizhi" [Speaking bitterness: A mediated mechanism for the shaping of the peasants' idea of the state]. In *Xin shi xue: duoxueke de tujing* [New historical studies: scenes of interdisciplinary dialogue]. Edited by Yang Nianqun, Huang Xingtao, and Mao Dan. Beijing: Zhongguo renmin daxue chubanshe, 2003.

Han Jinfeng. "Wei qinniang baochou: Lei Yuzhi suku" [Getting revenge for her mother: Lei Yuzhi speaks bitterness]. In *Zhongguo jiefangqu nongcun funü fanshen yundong sumiao* [A sketch of rural women fanshen in China's liberated areas]. Tangshan: Jindong xinhua shudian, 1949.

Hanyu da cidian. Edited by Luo Zhufeng. Shanghai: Hanyu da cidian chubanshe, 1997.

Harrison, James Pinckney. *The Long March to Power: A History of the Chinese Communist Party, 1921–72*. New York: Praeger, 1972.

Hershatter, Gail. *The Gender of Memory: Rural Women and China's Collective Past*. Berkeley: University of California Press, 2011.

Hinton, William. *Shenfan: The Continuing Revolution in a Chinese Village*. New York: Random House, 1983.

———. *Fanshen: A Documentary of Revolution in a Chinese Village*. Berkeley: University of California Press, 1997.

Ho, Denise Y. *Curating the Revolution: Politics on Display in Mao's China*. Cambridge: Cambridge University Press, 2018.

Hofheinz, Roy Jr. *The Broken Wave: The Chinese Communist Peasant Movement: 1922–1928*. Cambridge, MA: Harvard University Press, 1977.

Holm, David. *Art and Ideology in Revolutionary China.* New York: Oxford University Press, 1991.

Hou, Xiaojia. *Negotiating Socialism in Rural China: Mao, Peasants, and Local Cadres in Shanxi, 1949–1953.* Ithaca, NY: Cornell University East Asia Program, 2016.

Hsia, C. T. *A History of Modern Chinese Fiction,* 2nd ed. New Haven, CT: Yale University Press, 1962.

Hsiao, Tso-liang. *The Land Revolution in China, 1930–1934.* Seattle: University of Washington Press, 1969.

Hu Shihua. "Renmin minzhu zhuanzheng zai nongcun zhong sheng le gen" [The people's democratic dictatorship takes root in the countryside]. In *Women canguan tudigaige yihou* [After we observed land reform]. Beijing: Wushi niandai chubanshe, 1951.

Huang Daoxuan. *Zhangli yu xianjie: zhongyang suqu de geming, 1933–1934* [Tensions and limits: Revolution of the Central Soviet Area, 1933–1934]. Beijing: Shehui kexue wenxian chubanshe, 2011.

Huang, Philip C. C. "The Jiangxi Period: A Comment on the Western Literature." In *Chinese Communists and Rural Society: 1927–1934.* By Philip C.C. Huang, Lynda Schaefer Bell, and Kathy Lemons Walker. Berkeley: Center for Chinese Studies, 1978.

———. *The Peasant Economy and Social Change in North China.* Stanford: Stanford University Press, 1985.

———. "Rural Class Struggle in the Chinese Revolution," *Modern China* 21, no. 1 (January 1995): 105–143.

Hunt, Lynn. *Politics, Culture, and Class in the French Revolution.* Berkeley: University of California Press, 1984.

Keating, Pauline B. *Two Revolutions: Village Reconstruction and the Cooperative Movement in Northern Shaanxi, 1934–1945.* Stanford: Stanford University Press, 1997.

Kipnis, Andrew. *Producing Guanxi: Sentiment, Self, and Subculture in a North China Village.* Durham,NC: Duke University Press, 1997.

Lary, Diana. *China's Civil War: A Social History, 1945–1949.* Cambridge: Cambridge University Press, 2015.

Li Changyuan. *Peng Zhen yu tugai* [Peng Zhen and land reform]. Beijing: Renmin chuban she, 2002.

Li Guangtian. "Weishenme bu neng 'heping fentian'?" [Why can't we have 'peaceful land reform'?]. In *Women canguan tudigaige yihou* [After we observed land reform]. Beijing: Wushi niandai chubanshe, 1951.

Li, Huaiyin. *Village China Under Socialism and Reform: A Micro-History, 1948–2008.* Stanford: Stanford University Press, 2009.

———. *Reinventing Modern China: Imagination and Authenticity in Chinese Historical Writing.* Honolulu: University of Hawaii Press, 2013.

Li Junlong, "Douzheng zhong de Hunan nongmin" [Hunan peasants in struggle]. In *Women canguan tudigaige yihou* [After we observed land reform]. Beijing: Wushi niandai chubanshe, 1951.

Ling Buji and Shu Long, eds. *Zhonghua suweiai gongheguo shi* [A history of the Chinese Soviet Republic]. Nanjing: Jiangsu Renmin Chubanshe, 1999.

Link, Perry. "Introduction." In *Naked Earth*, by Eileen Chang. New York: New York Review of Books, 2015.

Lippert, Wolfgang. *Hanyu zhong de makesizhuyi shuyu de qiyuan yu zuoyong* [The origin and function of Marxist terminology in Chinese]. Translated by Zhao Qing, Wang Cao, and Zhu Pingzhu. Beijing: Zhongguo shehui kexue chubanshe, 2003.

Liu Mianyu. *Tudi geming zhanzheng shi* [A history of the land revolution war: 1927–1937]. Nanchang: Jiangxi jiaoyu chubanshe, 2001.

Liu Mianzhi. "Bu yong jinqian ziyou hun, ge ren ai shangle xinshang de ren" [Free marriage without purchase, everyone loves who they want]. In *Zhongguo jiefangqu nongcun funü fanshen yundong sumiao* [A sketch of rural women fanshen in China's liberated areas]. Tangshan: Jindong xinhua shudian, 1949.

Liu Shaoqi. *Selected Works of Liu Shaoqi*. Beijing: Foreign Languages Press, 1984

Liu Tong, *Dongbei jiefang zhanzheng jishi* [Record of the Northeastern War of Liberation]. Beijing: Renmin chubanshe, 2004.

Liu Zhi. "Ding xian funü da fanshen" [The great fanshen of Ding County Women]. In *Zhongguo jiefangqu nongcun funü fanshen yundong sumiao* [A sketch of rural women fanshen in China's liberated areas]. Tangshan: Jindong xinhua shudian, 1949.

Luo Pinghan, *Tudi gaige yundong shi* [A history of the land reform movement]. Fuzhou: Fujian renmin chubanshe, 2005.

Ma Jia, *Jiangshan cun shi ri* [Ten days in Jiangshan village]. Shenyang: Cunfeng wenyi chubanshe, 1979.

Madsen, Richard. *Morality and Power in a Chinese Village*. Berkeley: University of California Press, 1984.

Mao Zedong. "Report on an Investigation of the Peasant Movement in Hunan." In *Selected Works of Mao Tse-tung*, vol. 1. Beijing: Foreign Language Press, 1965.

———. *Report from Xunwu*. Translated by Roger R. Thompson. Stanford: Stanford University Press, 1990.

Marks, Robert B. *Rural Revolution in South China: Peasants and the Making of History in Haifeng County, 1570–1930*. Madison: University of Wisconsin Press, 1984.

McDonald, Angus W., Jr. *The Urban Origins of Rural Revolution: Elites and the Masses in Hunan Province, China, 1911–1927*. Berkeley: University of California Press, 1981.

McDougall, Bonnie S. *Mao Zedong's "Talks at the Yan'an Conference on Literature and Art": A Translation of the 1943 Text with Commentary*. Ann Arbor: Center for Chinese Studies University of Michigan, 1980.

Merkel-Hess, Kate. *The Rural Modern: Reconstructing the Self and State in Republican China*. Chicago: University of Chicago Press, 2016.

Neibu cankao [Internal reference materials]. Beijing: Xinhua chubanshe.

Pan Guangdan and Quan Weitian. "Who Says 'Jiangnan Is Not Feudal'?" [Shei shuo "Jiangnan wu fengjian]. In *Women canguan tudigaige yihou* [After we observed land reform]. Beijing: Wushi niandai chubanshe, 1951.

Pantsov, Alexander V., with Steven I. Levine. *Mao: The Real Story.* New York: Simon and Schuster, 2007.

Pepper, Suzanne. *Civil War in China: The Political Struggle, 1945–1949*, 2nd ed. Lanham, MD: Rowman and Littlefield, 1999.

Perry, Elizabeth. "Reclaiming the Chinese Revolution," *Journal of Asian Studies* 67, no. 4 (2008): 1147–1164.

Potter, Sulamith, and Jack M. Potter. *China's Peasants: The Anthropology of a Revolution.* Cambridge: Cambridge University Press, 1990.

Ren Qingbo. "Li Xiuyang suku" [Li Xiuyang speaks bitterness]. In *Zhongguo jiefangqu nongcun funü fanshen yundong sumiao* [A sketch of rural women fanshen in China's liberated areas]. Tangshan: Jindong xinhua shudian, 1949.

Renmin ribao [People's daily]. Beijing: Renmin ribao she.

Ruan Zhangjing. *Chi ye he* [Red-Leaf River]. Beijing: Xinhua Shudian, 1950.

Ruf, Gregory A. *Cadres and Kin: Making a Socialist Village in West China, 1921–1991.* Stanford: Stanford University Press, 1991.

Selden, Mark. *The Yenan Way in Revolutionary China.* Cambridge, MA: Harvard University Press, 1971.

Seybolt, Peter J. "The War Within a War: A Case Study of a County on the North China Plain." In *Chinese Collaboration with Japan, 1932–1945: The Limits of Accommodation.* Edited by David P. Barrett and Larry N. Shyu. Stanford: Stanford University Press, 2001.

Shao Yanxiang. *Bie le Mao Zedong: huiyi yu sikao, 1945–1958* [Farewell Mao Zedong: Recollections and reflections, 1945–1958]. Hong Kong: Oxford University Press, China, 2007.

Shue, Vivienne. *Peasant China in Transition: The Dynamics of Development Toward Socialism, 1949–1956.* Berkeley: University of California Press, 1980.

Siu, Helen F. *Agents and Victims in South China: Accomplices in Rural Revolution.* New Haven, CT: Yale University Press, 1989.

Skinner, William. *Rural China on the Eve of Revolution: Sichuan Fieldnotes, 1949–1950.* Seattle: University of Washington Press, 2016

Smith, Aminda M. "Thought Reform and the Unreformable: Reeducation Centers and the Rhetoric of Opposition in the Early People's Republic of China." *Journal of Asian Studies* 72, no. 4 (November 2013): 937–958.

Stacey, Judith. *Patriarchy and Socialist Revolution in China.* Berkeley: University of California Press, 1983.

Stranahan, Patricia. *Yan'an Women and the Communist Party.* Berkeley: University of California Press, 1983.

Strauss, Julia C. "Morality, Coercion, and State Building by Campaign in the Early PRC: Regime Consolidation and After, 1949–1956." *China Quarterly* 188, no. 1 (2006): 891–912.

———. "Regimes and Repertoires of State Building: The Two Chinas and

Regime Consolidation in the Early 1950s." In *State Formations: Global Histories and Cultures of Statehood.* Edited by John L. Brooke, Julia C. Strauss, and Greg Anderson. Cambridge: Cambridge University Press, 2006.

———. "Rethinking Land Reform and Regime Consolidation in the People's Republic of China: The Case of Jiangnan, 1950–1952." In *Rethinking China in the 1950s.* Edited by Mechthild Leutner. Berlin: Lit Verlag, 2007.

Sun Qingju and Wu Shaoqi. "Nongcun jishi" [On-the-spot rural report]. In *Tugaihou nongcun xin jingxiang* [New scenes in the post–land reform countryside]. Shanghai: Xinhua shudian huadong zongfendian, 1950.

Tawney, R. H., ed. *Agrarian China: Selected Source Materials from Chinese Authors.* London: George Allen and Unwin, 1939.

Teiwes, Frederick C. "The Origins of Rectification: Inner-Party Purges and Education Before Liberation." *China Quarterly* no. 65 (March 1976): 15–53.

———. "Establishment and Consolidation of the New Regime." In *The Cambridge History of China, Vol. 14: The People's Republic Part I, The Emergence of Revolutionary China, 1949–1965.* Cambridge: Cambridge University Press, 1987.

Thaxton, Ralph A. Jr. *Catastrophe and Contention in Rural China: Mao's Great Leap Forward Famine and the Origins of Righteous Resistance in Da Fo Village.* Cambridge: Cambridge University Press, 2008.

"Tudi gaige yundong zhong chuxian le xinxing de funü zuzhi xingshi" [New types of women's organization emerge in the land reform movement]. In *Zhongguo jiefangqu nongcun funü fanshen yundong sumiao* [A sketch of rural women fanshen in China's liberated areas]. Tangshan: Jindong xinhua shudian, 1949.

U, Eddy. "The Making of *Zhishifenzi*: The Critical Impact of the Registration of Unemployed Intellectuals in the Early PRC." *China Quarterly* no. 173 (2003): 100–121.

———. "Reification of the Chinese Intellectual: On the CCP Concept of Zhishifenzi." *Modern China* 35, no. 6. (2009): 604–631.

Vogel, Ezra F. *Canton under Communism: Programs and Politics in a Provincial Capital, 1949–1968.* Cambridge, MA: Harvard University Press, 1969.

Wang, Di. *Violence and Order on the Chengdu Plain: The Story of a Secret Brotherhood in Rural China, 1939–1949.* Stanford, CA: Stanford University Press, 2018.

Wang Xuan, "Wo zai tugai zhong de xuexi" [My studies during land reform]. In *Tugai xuexi shouce: Hanjia jiaoshi jiangxihui yong* [Land reform studies handbook: For the Winter Break Teachers' Lecture and Study Meeting]. Luzhou: Chuannan renmin xingzhenggongshu wenjiao ting, 1951.

Westad, Odd Arne. *Decisive Encounters: The Chinese Civil War, 1946–1950.* Stanford, CA: Stanford University Press, 2003.

Women canguan tudigaige yihou [After we observed land reform]. Beijing: Wushi niandai chubanshe, 1951.

Wong, John. *Land Reform in the People's Republic of China: Institutional Transformation in Agriculture.* New York: Praeger, 1973

Wu, Guo. "Speaking Bitterness: Political Education in Land Reform and Military Training Under the CCP, 1947–1951." *Chinese Historical Review* 21, no. 1 (Spring 2014): 3–23.

Wu Xinxiang, and Zhao Zuwang, "Canjia tugai de ji dian tiyan" [Some points on learning through practice in participating in land reform]. In *Tugai xuexi shouce: Hanjia jiaoshi jiangxihui yong* [Land reform studies handbook: For the Winter Break Teachers' Lecture and Study Meeting]. Luzhou: Chuannan renmin xingzhenggongshu wenjiao ting, 1951.

Xu Bin. *Zhang Ailing zhuan* [A biography of Zhang Ailing]. Guangxi: Guangxi shifan daxue chubanshe, 2001.

Yan Yunxiang. *Private Life Under Socialism: Love, Intimacy, and Family Change in a Chinese Village*. Stanford, CA: Stanford University Press, 2003.

Yang Guixin. *Ding Ling pingzhuan* [A critical biography of Ding Ling]. Chongqing: Chongqing chubanshe, 2001.

Yang Kuisong. *Zhonghua renmin gongheguo jianguo shi yanjiu 1* [Research on the founding of the PRC, vol. 1]. Nanchang: Jiangxi renmin chubanshe, 2009.

Yang Lianfen. *Xiandai xiaoshuo daolun* [Introduction to modern novels]. Sichuan: Sichuan Daxue Chubanshe, 2004.

Yang Rengeng. "Gen nongmin xuexi yihou" [After studying with the peasantry]. In *Women canguan tudigaige yihou* [After we observed land reform]. Beijing: Wushi niandai chubanshe, 1951.

Yi Su. "Tai xian fanshencun xin jingxiang" [New scenes in Tai County Fanshen Village]. In *Tugaihou nongcun xin jingxiang* [New scenes in the post–land reform Countryside]. Shanghai: Xinhua shudian huadong zongfendian, 1950.

Yuan Fang, "Women de tugai gongzuo zu" [Our land reform work team]. In *Cong tugai zhong xuexi* [Learning from land reform]. Xinjianshe zazhi chubanshe, 1950.

Zenyang zuo yi ge qingniantuan yuan [How to be a Youth League member]. Wuhan: Zhongnan qingnian chubanshe, 1952.

Zenyang quanmian jieshu tudigaige yundong [How to bring the land reform campaign to a complete close]. Shanghai: Beixin shuju, 1952.

Zhang Ailing. *Chi di zhi lian* [Love in Redland]. Taibei: Huangguan wenhua chubanshe, 2003.

Zhang Xiaojun. "Land Reform in Yang Village: Symbolic Capital and the Determination of Class Status." *Modern China* 30, no. 1 (January 2004): 3–45.

Zheng Linzhuang. "Douzheng dizhu shi you ganbu tiaobo qilai de ma" [Do cadres incite the struggling of landlords?]. In *Women canguan tudigaige yihou* [After we observed land reform]. Beijing: Wushi niandai chubanshe, 1951.

Zhongguo qingnian [China youth]. Beijing: Zhongguo qingnian chubanshe.

Zhongguo tudi gaige shiliao xuanbian [Selected historical materials from China's land reform]. Marked for internal distribution. Beijing: Guofang daxue chubanshe, 1988. *Zhongguo xi'nan dang'an: tudigaige ziliao, 1949–1953* [Southwest China Archives: The documents of land reform, 1949–1953].

Edited by Zhang Peitian and Zhang Hua. Kingsford: International Culture Press, 2009.

Zhongnan tudi gaige de weida shengli [The great victory of South Central land reform]. Wuhan: Zhongnan renmin wenxue yishu chubanshe, 1953.

Zhou Libo. *Baofeng zhouyu* [The hurricane]. Beijing: Renmin wenxue chubanshe, 2001.

Zhou Zhiqiang. *Zhongguo gongchandang yu zhongguo nongye fazhan daolu* [The Chinese Communist Party and the path of Chinese agricultural development]. Beijing: Zhonggongdang shi chubanshe, 2003.

Zong Cheng. *Ding Ling*. Beijing: Zhongguo huaqiao chubanshe, 1999.

INDEX

CPSIA information can be obtained
at www.ICGtesting.com
Printed in the USA
JSHW022035281022
32237JS00002B/5